MORE PRAISE FOR
KNIGHTS OF THE SEA

"Much more than a book about a battle, *Knights of the Sea* is a fine meditation on the culture, politics, and several key charismatic individuals who shaped the Early Republic."

—Christopher Pastore, author of *Temple to the Wind*

"David Hanna's *Knights of the Sea* is the finest kind of narrative history—thoroughly researched, informative, and a plain good read. Hanna takes a dramatic but little-known incident, the battle between the small men-of-war *Boxer* and *Enterprise*, and uses that event to explore the lives of two men, the captains of the ships, and two navies, the British navy at the peak of its power and domination and the nascent navy of the United States, just feeling its oats. *Knights of the Sea* will not disappoint any who love a good rousing history, or any who are drawn to the fascinating world of combat under sail."

—James L. Nelson, author of *George Washington's Great Gamble*

"Through the prism of a single battle between two sailing ships, David Hanna focuses on the stories of the opposing commanders and unearths their opinions, principles, and motives—the very essence of their lives. Woven into this narrative is a skillful exploration of the politics and events behind the War of 1812, alongside a vivid portrait of wartime experiences on land and sea."

—Roy Adkins, author of *Nelson's Trafalgar* and
The War for All the Oceans

"David Hanna establishes his credibility both as a writer and with the quality and depth of his historical research in *Knights of the Sea*. His capturing of a little-known maritime battle during the War of 1812 is surprisingly relevant in modern-day exploration of military strategy."

—Captain Philip Kasky, USN (Ret.),
former commander, USS *Suribachi*

continued . . .

"A fascinating look at a pivot point in naval warfare." —*Time.com*

"*Knights of the Sea* is the stirring tale of two warships, one American and one British, that clashed in a legendary battle during the War of 1812. It is also the highly engaging story of the two gallant captains of those ships, both of whom were as intrepid as C. S. Forester's fictional creation Horatio Hornblower. The book provides a wonderful blend of fascinating historical detail about the maritime war and the men who fought it. Meticulously researched and thoroughly enjoyable."
—Robert J. Mrazek, author of *A Dawn Like Thunder*

"Highly readable, this book will appeal to those interested in naval warfare and the War of 1812 as well as those with any interest in early U.S. history. Strongly recommended." —*Library Journal*

"Great characters, great research, and a great premise make this a must-have for anyone who wants to know more about American history."
—*San Francisco Book Review*

"When wars two hundred years in the past sound eerily like today's contemporary events, it's time to sit up and take notice. And even when that history is about a relatively obscure naval engagement off the coast of Maine, the lessons it offers about individual sacrifice can be far-reaching, compelling—and also a bit unsettling." —*Down East*

"In a compact, well-organized, and carefully illustrated book, Hanna propels the reader both general and scholarly with sure, swift, and colorful prose." —*Portland Press Herald*

"This book is academically rigorous, yet the narrative is engaging and thrilling to read." —*History in Review*

"In Hanna's skilled storytelling, heroic seamen and stout ships come alive in this rousing tale and converge on the Maine coast for a short, bloody sea battle. . . . The well-illustrated *Knights of the Sea* is a great read for folks interested in Maine or maritime history."
—*Bangor Daily News*

KNIGHTS OF THE SEA

THE TRUE STORY OF THE *BOXER* AND THE *ENTERPRISE* AND THE WAR OF 1812

DAVID HANNA

NAL
CALIBER

NAL CALIBER
Published by New American Library, a division of
Penguin Group (USA) Inc., 375 Hudson Street,
New York, New York 10014, USA
Penguin Group (Canada), 90 Eglinton Avenue East, Suite 700, Toronto,
Ontario M4P 2Y3, Canada (a division of Pearson Penguin Canada Inc.)
Penguin Books Ltd., 80 Strand, London WC2R 0RL, England
Penguin Ireland, 25 St. Stephen's Green, Dublin 2,
Ireland (a division of Penguin Books Ltd.)
Penguin Group (Australia), 250 Camberwell Road, Camberwell, Victoria 3124,
Australia (a division of Pearson Australia Group Pty. Ltd.)
Penguin Books India Pvt. Ltd., 11 Community Centre, Panchsheel Park,
New Delhi - 110 017, India
Penguin Group (NZ), 67 Apollo Drive, Rosedale, Auckland 0632,
New Zealand (a division of Pearson New Zealand Ltd.)
Penguin Books (South Africa) (Pty.) Ltd., 24 Sturdee Avenue,
Rosebank, Johannesburg 2196, South Africa

Penguin Books Ltd., Registered Offices:
80 Strand, London WC2R 0RL, England

Published by NAL Caliber, a division of Penguin Group (USA) Inc. Previously published in an NAL Caliber hardcover edition.

First NAL Caliber Trade Paperback Printing, February 2013
10 9 8 7 6 5 4 3 2 1

NAL Caliber Trade Paperback ISBN: 978-0-451-23920-4

The Library of Congress has catalogued the hardcover edition of this title as follows:

Hanna, David, 1967–
    Knights of the sea: the true story of the Boxer and the Enterprise and the War of 1812/David Hanna.
        p. cm.
    Includes bibliographical references and index.
    ISBN 978-0-451-23562-6
    1. Boxer (Brig: 1813). 2. Enterprise (Brig: 1812–1823). 3. United States—History—War of 1812—Naval operations.
4. Blyth, Samuel, 1783–1813. 5. Burrows, William, 1785–1813. 6. Great Britain. Royal Navy—Officers—Biography.
7. United States, Navy—Officers—Biography. 8. United States—History—War of 1812—Biography. 9. Atlantic
Coast (Me.)—History, Naval—19th century. 10. Pemaquid Region (Me.)—History, Naval—19th century. I. Title.
E360.H36 2012
973.5'245—dc23 2011031879

Set in MT Std
Designed by Ginger Legato

Printed in the United States of America

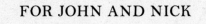

FOR JOHN AND NICK

Acknowledgments

It has been a real joy completing this project. One of the reasons it has been so is that I was never alone in the process. There are many people I would like to thank, but none more so than my wife, Katie. She always believed I could do this, and she always cheerfully put up with my moods and late nights. I would also like to thank Dr. Joyce Bibber of the University of Southern Maine History Department (ret.), who provided oversight for the entire project, as well as many useful materials. Thanks also to Chris Pastore, John Steele Gordon, Rosa Baylor Hall, Ken Milano, and Captain Phil Kasky, USN (ret.), for their advice and encouragement at key stages in the research, writing, and publishing process.

In addition I would like to thank my brother Josh for proofreading the manuscript and providing sound advice; my sisters Meagan and Tammy for spending time in libraries I was unable to get to and for being so meticulous; my sister Cory and her partner, Nancy Adams, for useful materials and advice; and my mother, Carolyn Hanna, for her encouragement and support. I would also like to thank those friends and colleagues of mine who took the time to read through parts of my manuscript and offer valuable insights and further encouragement, in particular Rick Detwiler.

Acknowledgments

My agent, John Ware, pushed me to become a better writer, while never flagging in his belief that we would see this through. The same can be said of Mark Chait and Talia Platz at NAL/Penguin. Their enthusiasm for this project provided a tremendous boost to my confidence, and their suggestions on how to improve the manuscript were invaluable. I have been very fortunate to have John, Mark, and Talia in my corner.

Last, I would like to recognize the following for their efforts on my behalf during the research process, some of whom I have not had the pleasure to meet face-to-face (a wonder and a symptom of the age of the Internet): Jamie Kingman-Rice at the Maine Historical Society; Liza Verity at the National Maritime Museum in Greenwich, England (ret.); Scott Wixon and Eleanor Gillers at the New-York Historical Society; Jack Gumbrecht at the Historical Society of Pennsylvania in Philadelphia; Bruno Pappalardo at the National Archives in Kew, England; Mimi Aldridge at the Bristol Area Library (Maine); Craig Bruns at the Independence Seaport Museum (Philadelphia); Roy Goodman at the American Philosophical Society (Philadelphia); Pete Lesher at the Chesapeake Bay Maritime Museum; Alan King at the Portsmouth (England) Central Library; Dick Doyle of Portland, Maine; Geoffrey Blyth of Billericay, Essex, England; Dr. Christine Holden of the University of Southern Maine History Department; David Bair of New Wilmington, Pennsylvania, and São Paulo, Brazil; Dr. Roger C. Richardson of Winchester University; Bill Hershey of the *Dayton Daily News*; Patrick Runyon of the Swift Boat Sailors Association; and Senator Doug White of the Ohio State Senate (ret.) and Vietnam Veterans of America.

Contents

To the crew of the Boxer; *enemies by law, but by gallantry brothers.*

—Toast made at naval dinner in honor of
the crew of the USS *Enterprise*,
Portland, Maine, 1813

KNIGHTS
OF THE SEA

September 5, 1813

Early September is a delicious time of year along the Maine coast. Lingering golden summer is mixed with hints of autumn's brisk, invigorating bite. It is a melancholy time as well. Hard to let go of a summer so hard-earned the previous winter.

No place along the Maine coast embodies its rugged beauty like Pemaquid Point. It juts like some rocky reckoning toward the vast Atlantic beyond. The name itself, in fact, is from the ancient Abenaki tongue, meaning "long finger of land." It is aptly named. In nearly a direct line to its southeast lies the island of Monhegan. On a warm afternoon in September 1813, four British officers on a shooting party were waiting on Monhegan for their vessel to retrieve them, according to a prearranged schedule. They had enjoyed an afternoon shooting plentiful game birds and exploring the island's majestic cliffs. Their reception by the local islanders had been cordial. It was easy for them to forget that these same islanders and their nation were at war with the British Empire. This isolated truce was jarringly broken when His Britannic Majesty's brig *Boxer* failed to make its rendezvous; the casualness of their excursion, then, would stand in stark contrast to the life-and-death struggle of sea combat that would occur before their eyes.

1

The *Boxer's* youthful commander, Samuel Blyth, had defiantly, and somewhat provocatively, ordered the British colors nailed to its mast. Then in the *Boxer's* very first exchange of broadsides* with the USS *Enterprise*, he was nearly cut in half by a cannonball. His opposite number, the younger still American commander William Burrows, struck in the groin by a musket ball fired by a British marine marksman, lay dying on the deck of the *Enterprise*. The people of the island and the peninsula strained their necks to see which way the two ships would sail as the firing stopped and the smoke cleared: east to the British base at Halifax with the *Enterprise* taken as a prize, or west to Portland Harbor with the *Boxer* taken prize?

The only major sea engagement of the War of 1812 witnessed by landsmen ended in only forty minutes. But the brutality of those minutes and the men who lived them, most particularly the men who commanded, can serve as a window into an era and way of life that seem as alien to us in the present as they seemed to the great majority of their contemporaries. What drove young men to risk drowning, burns, dismemberment, and death in exchanges of broadsides or hand-to-hand combat? A war's just cause? A flag? A monarch? A constitution? And if not these, then what did drive them? Samuel Blyth and William Burrows almost certainly weren't looking for death that golden September afternoon off Pemaquid Point. But they were almost certainly, eagerly seeking a situation in which this was possible and even likely—why?

I AM FRANKLY NOT CERTAIN when I first became aware of this story. The first five years of my life I lived within sight of the waters where the battle took place. My father, a painter, had moved our family to the

---

* "Broadside" was the term used to describe bringing all of one side of a vessel's guns to bear at the same time, or in a rolling barrage.

old lighthouse keeper's cottage at Pemaquid Point to be near the sea. He would regularly walk the rocks of the Point with me during the five years we lived there. I can recall the beacon light throwing shadows across my room as a small boy, the sounds of foghorns and the marker buoy's bell, and the salty freshening carried up on the breeze over the rocks. Our neighbor—my father's good friend and fellow painter, Alex Breede—would share stories of his time as a young seaman aboard one of the last of the great merchant schooners. These elicited a respect for the sea's terrible majesty that has never left me. I can still recall the octogenarian with his massive, gnarled hands, telling my father how in a gale it was "one hand for the ship and one hand for yourself."

The site was rich in history long before the lighthouse had been constructed in 1826. A plaque affixed to a stone there commemorates the wreck of the *Angel Gabriel* in 1635. The survivors, Puritan colonists, planted deep roots in New England soil. At some point I must have seen a map depicting historical sites in the area, or overheard a conversation about the battle that took place during the War of 1812 in the waters off the Point. The echoes of that war, though faint, could still be heard if one listened. One could feel it there, buried deep in the collective folk memory of the community. Whatever the case, the *Boxer* and the *Enterprise* stuck in my head. To my boyhood sensibilities there was something lyrical about the juxtaposition of the two ships' names. They conjured up a world that, though it had passed, seemed strangely near—the Age of Fighting Sail, as C. S. Forester had called it. This was a time when maritime warriors considered it the highest honor to represent their countries, and harnessed the wind to meet their foes. Or so my imagination led me to believe.

Only later, as a student of history, did I learn of the joint funeral for the two vessels' commanders—the Englishman, Blyth, and the American, Burrows—both immortalized in Henry Wadsworth Longfellow's poem "My Lost Youth." This touching gesture of burial by the citizens of Longfellow's hometown struck a deep chord in me, and his words also brought me back to my own boyhood on the rocks of Pemaquid Point:

> *I remember the sea-fight far away*
> *How it thundered o'er the tide!*
> *And the dead sea-captains as they lay*
> *In the graves o'erlooking the tranquil bay*
> *Where they in battle died.*
> *And the sound of that mournful song*
> *Goes through me with a thrill:*
> *"A boy's will is the wind's will,*
> *And the thoughts of youth are long, long thoughts."*

This is the first time the full story of the *Boxer* and the *Enterprise* has been told (Sherwood Picking's 1941 *Sea Fight off Monhegan* is a highly regarded account of the battle itself, though it unfortunately was published in a largely unedited form, following Picking's untimely death). This book is an attempt to place all of the events, rich in pathos, in a larger transatlantic sociopolitical context. This story is in part a story of the hometowns that shaped each of the vessels' commanders: Portsmouth, England, and Philadelphia, respectively. It is also a story of a proud, apparently omnipotent navy and of an equally proud upstart navy. Finally, it is the story of a war whose convoluted causes I believe have too often been overlooked or oversimplified by historians.

The September 5, 1813, battle took place roughly midway through the oddly named War of 1812. This war, which in fact lasted until 1815, has been portrayed as America's second war of independence by many historians. The issue these historians stress is the newly minted republic's need to force her former sovereign to respect American rights, particularly at sea.

The Royal Navy routinely forced American seamen into serving aboard His Majesty's men-of-war. This process, somewhat innocuously called "impressment," took place both ashore, where "press gangs" swept the streets of port towns, and on the high seas, where the Royal Navy stopped and searched merchant vessels. Many of the Yankee "jack-tars,"* who had become ubiquitous in the port towns of the Atlantic and Mediterranean worlds, felt the heavy hand of the British press gang fall on their backs. Wives, mothers, children, sweethearts could only guess where their loved one and provider was and if and when they would ever see him again. The anxiety and resentment the Royal Navy's callousness bred is difficult to calculate, but can well be imagined.

Because the United States had quickly become a major maritime power economically, it was also inevitable that many of its other citizens would be affected by Britain's policies. American-owned vessels carried American-owned cargoes that represented the investments of tens of thousands of American merchants and sea captains, to destinations all over the world. These cargoes were, in turn, subject to seizure by the Royal Navy if they did not originate in, or were not bound for, British ports. Investors as well as seamen's families and employers turned to the government in Washington for redress. The cavalier manner in which British naval officers, and to a certain degree the British government, dismissed or diminished official American grievances added further to strained American feelings. For their part, the British never doubted that their actions were justified because they served the greater good.

The greater good was doing whatever was necessary to defeat, or at least contain, the threat posed by Napoleon Bonaparte. British ships needed full crews if they were to keep him bottled up on the European

---

*Nickname of the era's seamen, derived from the black tar that was applied to the circular hats they wore ashore.

continent, and American complaints indeed seemed trivial when compared to this imperative. Besides, from Britain's perspective, the Americans' insistence on the right to trade with both sides meant they had to accept the associated risks of such a policy.

Britain's feelings toward her former colonies were essentially those of a frustrated parent whose children had struck out on their own. These children could be willful, wrongheaded, and hypocritical, as well as infuriatingly self-righteous—but they were nonetheless seen as family. Ties of blood, language, law, religion, and literature bound the two peoples on either side of the Atlantic, whether they liked it or not. What this meant in practical terms was that the battle in which Samuel Blyth and William Burrows lost their lives took place in what was essentially a quasi–civil war.

No region in the United States was more sensitive to this state of affairs than New England. Its representatives had voted convincingly against President James Madison's request for a declaration of war. Their opposition, it should be noted, was specifically to war against Britain; if Madison had requested a declaration of war against France, he likely would have found significant support among New Englanders. Maine, then part of Massachusetts, largely shared these views. There was certainly pride there in the victories won in the early part of the war by the U.S. Navy. There was also increasing anxiety about the presence of the Royal Navy in Maine waters, and, as well, about the increasing predations there of British and Canadian privateers. However, overall there was little enthusiasm for the war often derisively referred to as "Mr. Madison's war." Thus, the residents of Pemaquid and Portland were caught up in a war they did not want, against a people they felt were not an enemy.

The joint funeral staged by Portland's residents for Blyth and Burrows allowed them to express their shared sense of sorrow and frustration about the war, as well as their solidarity with the surviving crews of both the *Boxer* and the *Enterprise*. It also allowed them to reciprocate the honor earlier shown a fallen American commander by the citizens of Halifax, Nova Scotia, who had buried him with full naval honors. This was made all the more poignant by the fact that Samuel Blyth had volunteered to help carry the fallen American commander's coffin. Blyth was a man whose quality was known not only to his friends in Halifax, but to strangers in Portland.

The man whose coffin Samuel Blyth helped to carry to the grave in Halifax had been one of the U.S. Navy's most popular officers. James Lawrence had risen to command of the light frigate *Chesapeake* in May 1813 and soon after had brought her out of Boston Harbor looking for a fight. The result was a gruesome encounter with HBMS *Shannon*, in which the *Chesapeake*'s largely untried crew faltered at the critical moment after their commander had suffered what would prove to be a fatal wound. Lawrence's death, and his famous admonition to his crew, "Don't give up the ship," had deeply moved Americans, regardless of how they felt about the war itself. William Burrows and his fellow junior officers were particularly affected. The small but capable U.S. Navy had inflicted some very bloody noses on their British counterparts in the first year of the war. The *Chesapeake*'s defeat at the hands of the *Shannon* in the summer of 1813, however, shook the confidence these victories had raised. Burrows's *Enterprise* had the opportunity to avenge this defeat and restore this lost confidence with a victory over Blyth's *Boxer*. Therefore, the stakes involved in this engagement were far higher than they appeared at first glance. For Mainers, of course, the outcome of the battle was not just a matter of morale. They may not have wanted or supported war with Britain, but they could not escape its impact. Mainers understood that the battle had commercial and security implications that were immediate. If Canadian privateers and the Royal Navy were permitted to run amok in Maine's coastal waters, trade would be paralyzed and raids would become a distinct possibility. It was no wonder the residents of Pemaquid "strained their necks" to determine who the victor was.

In the final analysis, I believe it is clear that both Blyth and Burrows achieved what they wanted. Neither was suicidal or fanatical in an ideological sense, but throughout their entire careers they had demonstrated a single-minded commitment to their craft that made life and death less important than honor. They had conducted themselves according to an unwritten code by which naval officers of the era lived, fought, and died. This code owed more to the Middle Ages than to the industrial revolution of their own era. Whether they represented an empire or a republic, they were truly "knights of the sea."

The war in which Blyth and Burrows sacrificed their lives was shunted to the margins of history on both sides of the Atlantic soon after its termination. The historians who have since shaped its larger meaning as an assertion of American national sovereignty deemphasize the degree to which it was also a war of national expansion (only partially successful), fought largely at the expense of Native American tribes. Young "war hawks" (as they were dubbed by the press), such as Henry Clay and John Calhoun, had looked greedily at Native American lands in the old Northwest, as well as in the Southeast and in Canada. The resulting land grab had little or nothing to do with the war's stated aims of protecting seamen's rights and upholding America's national sovereignty. And it is doubtful whether Samuel Blyth or William Burrows were aware (or cared much if they were aware) whether the United States was going to absorb Canada, or if the Creek Indians would be forced off their ancestral lands, or the Spanish elbowed out of Florida. The moral clarity that the war at sea provided was muddied ashore. Thus, there is good reason to view both commanders' sacrifices as a waste. But this would be false.

Samuel Blyth and William Burrows were not motivated by murky political aims. Their lives epitomized the best of what would soon be a vanished breed. The Age of Sail was on the verge of being replaced at sea by the age of steam. The engagement between the *Boxer* and the *Enterprise* would prove to be one of the last fought between sailing vessels representing Western powers. In addition, the fact that it played itself out in front of large numbers of spectators made it unique in the annals of the War of 1812, and established a connection between the combatants and ordinary people that existed on no other occasion. Longfellow's poem merely placed an exclamation point on the people's possession of this battle and these men. The battle was emblematic of an era and of a cherished, if often violent, way of life that provokes awe and commands respect.

CHAPTER 1

Portsmouth, England

The Greeks called it Albion. Later, the Romans would call it Britannia, though it was the invading Germanic tribe known as the Angles who gave the island nation its modern appellation: "Angle-Land," England. William Shakespeare perhaps best captured what his countrymen—renowned for their understatement—quietly felt in their heart of hearts about their island home:

> *This royal throne of kings, this scepter'd isle,*
> *This earth of majesty, this seat of Mars,*
> *This other Eden, demi-paradise,*
> *This fortress built by Nature for herself*
> *Against infection and the hand of war,*
> *This happy breed of men, this little world,*
> *This precious stone set in the silver sea,*
> *Which serves it in the office of a wall,*
> *Or as a moat defensive to a house,*
> *Against the envy of less happier lands;*
> *This blessed plot, this earth, this realm, this England*
> —from *Richard II*, act 2, scene 1 (Shakespeare)[1]

Samuel Blyth was born on this "blessed plot" on February 23, 1783. He would never know his father and mother. Both died within weeks of his birth. The most likely cause was disease. Epidemics routinely swept the densely packed port town in which they lived. The swiftness with which those in the prime of life could be cut down is startling for those accustomed to modern sanitation and medicine. It was not startling for those living at the time, though the loss was no less painful to bear. Thus, it would be Samuel's paternal grandparents who would nurse the baby and raise the boy, and in turn shape the man.

His first sensations would have included the sounds of hustle and bustle in the cobblestoned streets of Portsea, the cry of the ever-present seagulls, and the smell of the sea: everywhere the smell of the sea. Portsea at that time was a relatively new neighborhood adjacent to the expanded royal dockyard north of the old city of Portsmouth. It was a busy place—busier in time of war—full of seamen, riggers, victualers, and brewers:

> *Queen Street (twice the length of most streets) had 94 businesses and inns; The Hard had 35 of which 13 were inns, including many familiar establishments like the Keppel's Head. St. George's Square housed three attorneys, a surgeon, and a navy-agent . . . The Old Rope-walk, and Butcher, Hanover, Union, Havant, and Cross Streets each had between eleven and seventeen shops and inns listed . . . 27 butchers and 25 bakers, and 63 [that] sold clothing and textiles, primarily boots and shoes but everything else also from hats to hose . . .[2]*

The bustle of Portsea and its older sister town would have been tempered, however, in 1783. England had just lost a war. The thirteen American colonies with the assistance of France had humbled the world's greatest maritime empire. What would have especially stung was that it was the French West Indies squadron under Admiral de

Grasse that had sealed the British army's fate off Yorktown. Britain had prided itself on dominating the seas, and controlling the sea-lanes at the crucial moment in the crucial place. But this time the French beat them to it, thus ensuring that the besieged General Cornwallis and his troops would have to capitulate to the upstart colonials. Portmuthians saw the British (Royal) Navy's successes as their successes, and its defeats as their own. It would have smarted. The unsuspecting babe in the cradle would have had no way of knowing that he would meet his destiny in combat with this same country, whose independence his king grudgingly recognized in that year of his birth.

PORTSMOUTH, OF WHICH PORTSEA WAS an integral part, was the Royal Navy's largest base. Founded in 1180 by a Norman merchant named John de Gisors, whose ancestors had arrived in England with William the Conqueror, Portsmouth was centuries old by the time of Samuel's birth. England's kings had used the site intermittently throughout the Middle Ages to launch military operations against France. The French, in turn, raided and burned the town on at least three separate occasions.[3] It was not until the Tudor period (1485–1603) that Portsmouth finally began to realize its potential as a base where lay a "haven notable great and standing by Nature easy to be fortified."[4] Throughout the Stuart period (1603–1649 and 1660–1714), and on into the eighteenth century, the base and its adjacent dockyard experienced alternating periods of expansion and stagnation, followed by even greater expansion. This accelerated when the perceived threat to, or target of, Britain was France. The reason was simple geography—Portsmouth was the largest harbor in close proximity to the French coast.

Today, the city's martial past is evident, but it is largely in the past, as the Royal Navy has shuttered much of its once sprawling establishment. However, in the period of Samuel Blyth's childhood and right on through the Victorian high noon of empire, Portsmouth stood unrivaled. The novelist C. S. Forester described what it was like for the generations of seamen and their officers entering the harbor, coming home:

> *And there was England, dimly seen but well remembered, the vague outline to be gazed at with a catch of the breath. The Start, and at last St. Catherine's, and the hour of uncertainty as to whether they could get in to the lee of the Isle of Wight or would have to submit to being blown all the way up-Channel. A fortunate slant of wind gave them their opportunity, and they attained the more sheltered waters of the Solent, with the unbelievable green of the Isle of Wight on their left hand, and so they attained Portsmouth, to drop anchor where the quiet and calm made it seem as if all the turmoil outside had been merely imagined.[5]*

The city itself is located on an island (also known as Portsea) separated from the mainland by a narrow tidal backwater known as Port Creek. The creek connects Langstone Harbor to the east with Portsmouth Harbor in the west. Behind the island, guarding the passage to the north into the interior, lies Portsdown Hill. Brooding like a silent sentinel, the hill commands the island and its harbors, and provides a glimpse of the fair Isle of Wight on the southern horizon. At the head of Portsmouth Harbor is the ancient town of Portchester, home to one of the finest remaining forts of the Roman era—Portchester Castle.

The Romans arrived in the region in A.D. 43, when the II Augusta Legion under the command of the future emperor Vespasian established a supply base and occupied the surrounding territory.[6] Portsmouth Harbor sheltered Roman galleys, whose primary purpose in later centuries was to hunt down barbarian pirates marauding along the English Channel coastline.[7] In the end the barbarians prevailed and descended on Portsea Island and its hinterland. In this region, the

Portchester Castle

Germanic tribe known as the Jutes were the dominant migrant-conquerors. However, on Portsea Island itself their cousins, the Saxons, held sway. Whether Samuel Blyth was of Saxon ancestry is not known. Likely his ancestry was an amalgamation of Romano-Briton, Anglo-Saxon, Viking, and Norman blood. All had left their genetic footprint on his native land. That said, Portsmouth also hosted a disproportionate number of England's foreign guests and migrants, and it is certainly within the realm of possibility that Samuel Blyth could count one of these among his ancestors as well. At the very least the young boy growing up in the port city would have become accustomed to a mix of ethnicities and tongues alien to the great majority of his fellow Englishmen. As James H. Thomas explained:

> *If there was one characteristic which predominated, it was the cosmopolitan nature of the area. Any visitor to the region after 1650 was likely to rub shoulders with Swedish or Russian sailors*

or with crews of Dutch, Spanish or Portuguese merchantmen. Lebanese princes visited Portsmouth, as did traders from Danzig and representatives of the North African regencies. This social richness was further accentuated by the presence of Cherokee chiefs in 1762 and by that of Omai the Tahitian, returned to the Sandwich Islands [Hawaii] by Captain Cook in 1777.[8]

Only the great metropolis of London could claim such a diverse population.

Two days' journey to the north-northeast by stagecoach, London made the decisions that determined the daily existence of the majority of Portsmouth's residents—indeed, matters of life and death. A great naval expedition planned and ordered by the reigning monarch, or in later years by 10 Downing Street,* meant jobs and prosperity but also risked catastrophe. None of these catastrophes was more famous than the fate of the mighty *Mary Rose*. Built in Portsmouth in 1509, the *Mary Rose* was one of the largest naval vessels of her era. She had an unusually high center of gravity, though, due to her fortresslike fo'c'sle and poop deck. Henry VIII had prioritized the port as his primary base for war against France; and on July 19, 1545, while moving to engage the French fleet, Henry's pride and joy capsized, taking her officers and crew with her. The reason for the disaster remains uncertain, though it was likely a combination of her design, being temporarily overburdened with seven hundred men when her crew normally numbered but four hundred, and a failure by that same crew to close her gun ports as she made a sudden turn, allowing the sea to rush in belowdecks.

This type of devastating turn of fortune had a ripple effect in the streets and alleys of Portsmouth and Portsea. As would occur later following the sinking of the *Royal George* in an accident just off Portsmouth at Spithead in 1782—or in 1916 following the Battle of Jutland

---

* The official residence of Britain's prime ministers.

PUBLIC DOMAIN

HMS *Mary Rose*, from the Anthony Roll

against the German High Seas Fleet—the wives, children, and sweethearts of crews saw their worlds turned horribly upside down. As John Webb explained:

> *The large proportion of seafarers among local families meant that in the event of a naval disaster whole districts were not only plunged into mourning, but also suffered severe economic distress, since a sailor's pay stopped immediately he was reported dead . . . in 1916 following the Battle of Jutland, when a large number of local sailors were among the six thousand who died, "Scarcely a family was to be found in which there was not one dead . . . In one street alone 40 women became widows overnight."*[9]

Fortunately, however, the catastrophes were few and the successes were many. Portmuthians held far more celebrations than wakes. The vessels they outfitted for sea, and the men they sent to command and man them, returned home victorious far more often than not. And in some cases they returned enriched with booty seized from the enemy. The fine line between making war and piracy was one that was often blurred. Admiral "Black Dick" Howe's haul in 1794, when he arrived amid a carnival atmosphere in the harbor with six French "prizes," signified an important military success, yet also meant money in the pockets of officers and crew.[10] Patrick O'Brian closed a slim volume he wrote explaining the Royal Navy of the era with these lines from a tune sung by the era's seafaring sons of Albion:

> *Her colors struck, my boys, she then became our prize,*
> *And our young ship's company subdued our enemies*
> *Altho' they were superior in metal and in men.*
> *Of such engagements you may seldom hear again.*
> *And now in Portsmouth Harbour our prize is safely moor'd.*
> *Success to all brave sailors that enter now on board;*
> *A health to Captain Pellew, and all his sailors bold,*
> *Who value more their honor than misers do their gold.*[11]

The Blyths were seafaring sons of Albion, and they would have fully understood the sentiments expressed in the above song: the satisfaction of the successful pirate, yet the ennobling sense of a higher purpose that separated them from common thugs. Samuel Blyth heard songs such as these as a boy from his grandfather's lips, and from his grandfather's fellow navy men. For a group of men that knew far more privation than comfort, they were a mirthful lot. By all accounts Samuel was a light-hearted lad in the spirit of these men. Nobility, a hint of mischief, and a sense of humor marked Samuel's people, and he was one of them.

Samuel Blyth's grandfather was the kind of man that made the Royal Navy such a formidable institution. He had enlisted as a young man, and had risen in the service through his demonstrated capacity to handle both vessels and their crews. The elder Samuel Blyth attained the rank of sailing master. As such, he was responsible for the navigation of the vessels he served aboard: a crucial role, but a somewhat undervalued one in the Royal Navy of that era. As Patrick O'Brian explained:

> *The master was a relic from the times when sailors sailed the ships and soldiers did the fighting . . . he usually began as a midshipman, became a master's mate, and then, having few social advantages and no influence, gave up all hope of a commission, accepted a warrant and so reached the highest rank that he was ever likely to attain.*[12]

What this meant was that the elder Samuel Blyth was an officer, but not a gentleman. Social rank in eighteenth-century Britain was rigidly stratified. Trying to cross the chasm from commoner to gentleman status was daunting. In the end, the elder Samuel Blyth resigned himself to serving his country as a noncommissioned officer. His ambitions and aspirations would instead be delayed, and transferred to his grandson. And what was their relationship like? By all accounts it was warm and loving. The elder Samuel was described as "kind and indulgent."[13] It is certain that young Samuel would have grown up being fed a steady diet of maritime adventure stories. His grandfather would have had a deep well of experiences and anecdotes to draw from, none more so than his central role aboard Sir Samuel Hood's flagship HMS *Barfleur* in the victory of April 12, 1782.

Hood, a crusty veteran of the service, was acting as second in command of the British fleet sent to protect Jamaica from an impending Franco-Spanish invasion. Admiral de Grasse, flush with his success in the Chesapeake, which had sealed Cornwallis's fate, looked to capitalize on perceived British weakness in the Caribbean. On April 12, near the chain of islands known as the Saintes, located between Dominica and Guadeloupe, Jamaica's defenders confronted the invasion force. The result was a devastating reversal of fortune in which the Franco-Spanish fleet lost six battleships of the line, and by some reports upwards of eight thousand men. The war in America had been lost, but a satisfying revenge had been wrought on de Grasse as he was brought back to Britain a prisoner of His Majesty's Navy. Hood's *Barfleur*, with the elder Samuel Blyth acting as sailing master, was dispatched five days later to find and harass the retreating enemy. They captured a further two prizes. Hood was a fighter. His example made a lasting impression on those who served with him. It was in the Caribbean at this time that a young frigate captain became Hood's protégé. His name was Horatio Nelson.

Sir Samuel Hood. Nelson called him "the greatest sea officer I ever knew."

The Royal Navy that Hood, Nelson, and the elder Blyth served in had its roots centuries earlier in the Saxon era. Alfred the Great is credited with being the father of the Royal Navy for building a fleet to fight the Danes in A.D. 897. The two fleets met at the mouth of an estuary after the Danes had sacked the Isle of Wight. The Saxons captured two vessels and forced the remainder of the raiding force to flee. In the end, only one of the Danes' longboats made it home. Young Samuel Blyth may have heard stories of this ancient victory from his grandfather. He probably heard as well of the defeat of the mighty Spanish Armada in 1588; the victories over England's North Sea rival, Holland, in the seventeenth century; and the string of victories over France in the eighteenth century. This unbroken legacy of maritime success was his patrimony. His own family had played a role in forging it—not only his grandfather, but the father he never knew, who was also a noncommissioned officer. His uncle, Thomas Blyth, also served the navy as a paymaster. There probably was little doubt about what young Samuel's career path would be. In essence, the Royal Navy *was* his family.

This family was both blessed and cursed to a certain extent by the success it had enjoyed against its opponents over time. The blessings came in the form of the esteem in which naval officers were held by the public at large. They also came in the form of the gratitude of Parliament and the nation for allowing Britain to punch far above its weight economically, by securing a far-flung empire.

In the year of Samuel Blyth's birth, Britain ruled an overseas empire stretching from neighboring Ireland across the Atlantic, to balmy Jamaica and Barbados, north to Hudson Bay's frozen fur-trapping paradise, and clear across the globe to Bengal and Malaya. The wealth generated by the acquisition of foreign resources and markets fed Britain's industrial growth. This would have been impossible without the exertions of the navy. The Royal Navy also played the older role for which it had originally been formed all those centuries ago—to defend the island of Britain. What was often overlooked, however, and increasingly taken for granted over time, was how much hard work all of this took. Samuel Blyth's grandfather clearly would have understood this. But over time, younger officers began to see the Royal Navy's dominance as their due, believing that simply by showing up and being aggressive, victory would follow. As C. S. Forester explained:

> *The British public, and even the navy, could be excused for forming the belief that there was something intrinsically superior in British seamanship and perhaps British material. Ships commanded by British officers could expect victory over ships of comparable force of any other nation. A British captain who avoided action against anything less than a force obviously and overwhelmingly superior did so at his peril; nor did it often happen, for British officers were sublimely confident of victory and went into action with the assurance to be expected of men who seriously believed they represented a chosen race destined to pre-eminence.*[14]

This was the curse of centuries of hard-earned success. The Royal Navy's dominance at sea was seen as a result of a cultural, even racial, superiority, not of what in fact it was the result of: hard work, capable leadership, and a little luck. In addition, if nothing else, the Royal Navy simply outlasted its opponents by staying at sea longer. As Patrick O'Brian succinctly pointed out, "you can only learn to be a sailor at sea, and the English Navy was at sea all the year round, whatever the weather, whereas the French and Spaniards were shut up in their harbours."[15] This side of the Royal Navy was decidedly unglamorous, but again, it had much to do with its success. But whatever the real or perceived reasons for this success, that it would continue was not seriously questioned by anyone in or out of the service. Samuel Blyth grew up in a confident nation in a confident time.

———

At some point in the late 1700s, Samuel Blyth's hometown took on a new moniker—Pompey. The origins of this name are inconclusive, but the story that drunken seamen slurred the name Portsmouth rings true. Today, the city's professional soccer club, Portsmouth F.C., is known affectionately as "Pompey" by its die-hard supporters. For Royal Navy seamen of an earlier era the name possessed an even more nostalgic significance: "Pompey was home, where wives and families awaited their return and pubs and prostitutes provided rowdy relief from monotony."[16] The last were a common sight in the old town of Portsmouth throughout this period: "during wartime hordes of women and girls roamed the streets or operated from well-established brothels."[17] The names of the Green Rails, the Spring Clock, the Hole in the Wall, and the Brass Knocker[18] were widely known among seamen who called Portsmouth home, and among those who were simply making a port call. The neighborhood just outside the main gate of the naval base was ground zero for illicit behavior. It was known as the Devil's Acre, and an unwary jack-tar could be fleeced of all of his earnings in an extremely short space of time there. As Dr. George Pinckard remarked disapprovingly in 1795:

> . . . hordes of profligate females are seen reeling in drunkenness, or plying upon the Streets in open day . . . poor Jack, with pockets full of prize money, or rich with the wages of a long and dangerous cruise, is, instantly, dragged . . . to a bagnio, or some filthy pot-house, where he is kept drinking, smoking, singing, dancing, swearing and rioting, amidst one continual scene of debauchery . . . until his every farthing is gone.[19]

One could be excused for wondering if "Jack," in fact, loved every minute of it. In later decades, Protestant missionaries set up seamen's recreation centers to provide an alternative to sin. But these did not exist in Samuel Blyth's lifetime. Sin had little competition.

One diversion, however, that did begin to make inroads among the island's young men at this time was cricket. Both soccer and rugby had yet to be developed in any organized manner, but "By the 18th century cricket was well established in Portsmouth."[20] It would have been unusual if Samuel Blyth had not picked up a cricket bat as a boy. However, the green lawns often associated with the sport would have been few and far between. The local paper referred to Portsea boys playing the game in the streets, much to the chagrin of passersby, as one might imagine.[21] Cobblestones and ship's bells; creaking doors and nagging wives; crying babies and a tune, lubricated with a spot of rum—all these sounds would have made up Samuel's world. In the end, though, it was the doings at the navy yard and those just off the harbor's mouth at the anchorage called Spithead that excited the most interest.

One of the city's landmarks in this era was the so-called platform. The platform was, in essence, a promenade and an observation deck of sorts. It commanded a view out to the anchorage, where the vessels of the Royal Navy were on a more or less continuous revolving display as they came in from duty at sea to refit and provision. Beyond the vessels could be seen the Isle of Wight on the southern horizon. The isle was a mere five-mile ferry ride's distance at its closest point. In later decades, the isle became renowned as the home of Queen Victoria's seaside palace and the Royal Yacht Club at Cowes—but in the late 1700s it was noted more for its shipyards.

On the platform, young Samuel would have learned from his grandfather to observe the various comings and goings of His Majesty's Navy. In *Mansfield Park*, the novelist Jane Austen described the excitement that naval maneuvers in the yard, harbor, and anchorage generated. Her novel's heroine, Fanny Price, hears her father's recounting of a morning's activities:

By God, you lost a fine sight by not being there in the morning to see the Thrush go out of the harbor. I would not have been out of the way for a thousand pounds. Old Scholey ran in at breakfast time, to say she had slipped her moorings and was coming out. I jumped up, and made but two steps to the platform. If ever there was a perfect beauty afloat, she is one; and there she lays at Spithead . . .[22]

Austen was quite familiar with navy life, as two of her brothers were officers in the Royal Navy. One of them, Francis, made the city his home. Therefore, her portrayal is a valuable window on Portsmouth in that era—albeit a narrow one, as her heroine, Fanny, though Portsmouth-born, lives with her relatives on a distant estate, and only returns to live with her family temporarily when she frustrates her uncle's efforts to marry her off to a wealthy man. Her father, an ex-marine, can be seen as typical of the majority of the island's permanent male population:

He did not want [for] abilities; but he had no curiosity, and no information beyond his profession; he read only the newspaper and the navy-list; he talked only of the dock-yard, the harbor, Spithead, and the Motherbank; he swore and he drank . . . There . . . remained only a general impression of roughness and loudness . . .[23]*

Portsmouth was a navy town. It did not suffer from a total lack of genteel diversions, but the thrust of the place was unmistakable: "Everything looks, breathes and smells of soldiers, sailors, and dockmen, the three classes who rule the state of society here."[24] That said, naval officers did hold an elite status in the town. As the brother of

---

* A shallow sandbar off the northeast coast of the Isle of Wight.

Austen's Fanny remarks, "The Portsmouth girls turn up their noses at anybody who has not a commission."[25]* It would have been the fondest hope of Samuel Blyth the elder and his wife to raise their grandson to one day receive one of these coveted commissions.

Over the course of his life, Samuel Blyth's grandmother would prove to be his greatest supporter. Noted for her "kindness,"[26] Mrs. Blyth doted on the boy who had entered her life under such tragic circumstances. Perhaps he reminded her of his father. It is clear they enjoyed a close and loving relationship. It was later said that he "dwelt with an affectionate remembrance that does honour to his heart,"[27] when asked about her. It is very likely she took him for walks along the ramparts in the Southsea neighborhood of the town. This was one of the few entertainments female Portmuthians could enjoy. It was a nice spot. Later generations would make a vacation destination of it once hotels were built. In that time, however, strollers had the sea largely to themselves. Austen's Fanny Price describes an "uncommonly lovely" day there in *Mansfield Park*:

> *It was really March; but it was April in its mild air, brisk soft wind, and bright sun, occasionally clouded for a minute; and everything looked so beautiful under the influence of such a sky, the effects of the shadows pursuing each other, on the ships at Spithead and the island beyond, with ever-varying hues of the sea now at high water, dancing in its glee and dashing against the ramparts with so fine a sound.*[28]

Southsea was also a popular bathing area for the young men and boys of the town. Baring all, they took the plunge off the gravelly shingle of Southsea beach into the sea. But as John Webb explained, "Nude bathing by the poorer inhabitants along the more remote

---

*These girls most likely did not work in the Devil's Acre.

Spithead, with the exact situation and appearance of the "Royal George", wrecked with dour 600 people on board - 29 August 1782.

The masts of the submerged *Royal George*

stretches of the beach was socially acceptable. . . ."[29] There were risks, however, more dangerous than losing social approbation. The local *Hampshire Telegraph* noted, "As there are a number of persons bathing at this season of the year in this neighborhood, it may be well to apprise them that it is not always safe to swim far from shore."[30] This was a restrained way of saying that "a large shark had been seen" near the beach.[31] If young Samuel Blyth had joined the throng and been looking out to sea, out of the corner of his eye to the southwest he would have seen an eerie reminder of the perils of the life he was being groomed for. Like three giant grave markers, could be spied the tops of the masts of the submerged *Royal George*.

In the year before Samuel Blyth's birth, Portsmouth suffered arguably its greatest tragedy. HMS *Royal George* was a vessel with a long and proud history dating back to its launch in 1756. Its home port in 1782 was Portsmouth. At that time, the practice of permitting family and friends to visit their loved ones aboard ship when at anchor at Spithead was the norm. On August 29, hundreds of women and children were on the ship. Thus, the tragedy that occurred off Southsea beach was even greater than it otherwise would have been. In the process of heeling the ship over to conduct maintenance just below the waterline, the larboard (port)-side gun ports took in too much water and upset the ship's precarious equilibrium. She capsized, taking over

900 souls with her, nearly 360 of whom were women and children. That was how it was at sea—disaster could happen in an instant, even within sight of home. The three grim markers were a powerful testimony to that.

It is easy to picture young Samuel Blyth forming his vision of what the world was, and what his place in it would be. He had "salt" in his blood. His destiny was "out there," somewhere beyond the Solent and the fair Isle of Wight. But what "out there" would hold for him he could only have guessed. His imagination must have run rampant with a future filled with ferocious gales, swaying palms, savage encounters with enemies who deserved their grisly fate, grateful golden-curled ladies and almond-eyed beauties, and two proud grandparents, who in fact were the only parents he had ever known. Boys' fantasies are limitless, as they should be . . . "A boy's will is the wind's will, and the thoughts of youth are long, long thoughts."

EIGHT-YEAR-OLD SAMUEL BLYTH LEFT PORTSMOUTH IN 1791, leaving behind one navy town and moving to his new home in another. His grandfather, now retired from duty at sea, was granted a position as master attendant at the Royal Navy's yard in Sheerness, Kent. In this, "he was more fortunate than most of his brethren."[32] The Royal Navy could be notoriously ungrateful toward those who had given the better part of their lives to its service. The elder Samuel Blyth could count on a steady source of employment and income as he entered late middle age. His duties would have been to oversee the movement of both Royal Navy vessels in and out of the yard, and the smaller craft that were necessary to move people and provisions about. To a certain extent, however, the job was a sinecure: a reward from the navy for a lifetime of jobs well done.

Samuel would have found much of his new surroundings very familiar. Sheerness is located on the River Medway, which flows from the south into the Thames River estuary near its mouth at the English Channel. Today it is a quaint seaside village with reminders of its naval past not difficult to find. In Samuel Blyth's time as well, it was a smaller town than Portsmouth. Much as Portsmouth had been vulnerable to French raids through the years, Sheerness had in its time been subject to raids by the Dutch. The oldest part of town was known as Blue Town, and it is likely here that the Blyths would have lived during their time in Sheerness. The neighborhood gained this name from the blue-gray naval paint that shipyard workers brought back from the nearby yard to paint their houses. Like Portsmouth, Sheerness was essentially a creation, an extension, of the navy. It was as if Samuel Blyth was already part of its rhythms long before he ever was entered onto the muster rolls of any Royal Navy vessel.

By the time Samuel Blyth looked forward to his eleventh birthday, he had grown impatient to embark on a life at sea. In later years his biographer explained that Blyth

> . . . *was educated with a view to his serving in the navy; in favor of which, from his earliest days, he displayed the strongest inclination: this feeling, however, was perfectly natural, when his descent, place of birth and residence, and the objects by which he was surrounded, are considered.*[33]

He was clearly a product of his environment. The question was whether Samuel would have the opportunity to enter the service as a midshipman, with a patron prominent enough to give him a fighting chance at eventually attaining a lieutenant's commission, or whether he would follow in the footsteps of his father and grandfather, and hope to rise no further than a noncommissioned officer. Besides his palpable impatience at donning midshipmen's blues, "His natural disposition was peculiarly playful, generous, and bold."[34] It is doubtful that such a good-natured and fearless boy would have realized what he was up against. His grandfather did. As "a seaman of the old school, who was highly esteemed for qualities that, under a more wise and liberal system, would have carried him far towards the top of his profession," Samuel Blyth the elder had been "Restrained by a regulation, alike impolitic and illiberal, to the humble rank of master."[35] Sentiments like those expressed by Horatio Nelson that "Aft the more honour, forward the better man"[36]* would have been cold comfort for a man who was not seen as such by society at large. His wish for his grandson to break out of the social straitjacket in which he had been confined would have consumed his efforts. His long service paid dividends when Admiral Sir Thomas Pasley consented to take the boy on as "Mid" in 1794.

Preparations for young Samuel's entry into the service as a midshipman aboard HBMS *Bellerophon* would have been frantic and costly. He was only just turning eleven years old, which might seem to modern sensibilities an outrageously tender age to be entering hard military service, but according to regulations it met the minimum requirement. Pasley's decision to take Samuel aboard would have come with no frills and the expectation that Samuel's family would provide him "an allowance of as much as £50 a year. . . ."[37] In addition his sea chest would have contained items as diverse as eating utensils, logbooks, pens, stockings, coats, tooth powder, a quadrant, and a copy of Robinson's *Elements of Navigation*.[38] All these cost money, and the Blyths were a family of modest means. This was partly why young men from working-class families were excluded from the officer corps. They simply could not afford the start-up costs.

The Blyths gathered in excited anticipation as the day neared for Samuel to go to sea. In those moments before sleep when his thoughts turned to the future, he likely saw himself "dressed in the uniform of a Mid, with his little dirk by his side, parading the quarter-deck . . .

---

* "Aft" in reference to the officers' quarters, "forward" in reference to the crew's quarters.

Delighted beyond expression with the actual attainment of the great-est object of his desire."[39] Samuel Blyth was about to embark on a career that would have fulfilled all of his youthful fantasies, and more. He was about to seize his patrimony and stamp his name on it. It could not be any other way. After all, all of the streets in Portsea and Blue Town led down to the sea.

CHAPTER 2

Philadelphia

On October 6, 1785, William Burrows was born into a nation that had itself only recently been born. Named for his father, a South Carolina gentleman and Revolutionary War officer of distinction, the younger William would know a life of privilege from his earliest days. His father's adopted city of Philadelphia was the most populous and important on the continent. As befitted a Southern gentleman of means, William Ward Burrows chose to make his home not in the city, but just outside its limits, in the Northern Liberties.* His estate, Kinderton Farm, had been purchased by his wife's grandfather earlier in the decade as a replacement for a smaller country seat he had owned. Late-eighteenth-century Philadelphia County would have presented a green panorama fronting on the blue Schuylkill River to the west and the blue Delaware River to the east, which in those days were filled with shad.† So much so, in fact, that the district to the northeast of the city center along the Delaware came to be known as Fishtown.

---

*At that time, the neighborhood included present-day upper and lower North Philadelphia.

†A type of herring that spawns in freshwater.

A member of the Pennsylvania Council named Anthony Palmer had purchased the land on which Fishtown was later located in 1735. Palmer was a large-scale slave owner who had migrated to the Delaware Valley from Barbados. He named his domain Kensington after the royal family's estate near London. This land was already mythologized by Philadelphians as the site of the famous first meeting between their city's founder, William Penn, and the local Lenape Indians in 1682. The resulting Shackamaxon Treaty, agreed to under a famous elm tree, gave rise to an enlightened version of the past that young William Burrows would certainly have been aware of growing up in Philadelphia. William Penn's pronouncements to the local Indians that "the great God . . . hath made us not to devoure and destroy one another but live Soberly and kindly together in the world"[1] stood in stark contrast to the predatory history of most of Pennsylvania's sister colonies in their relations with the original inhabitants of North America. By the time of Burrows's birth Penn's colony was a state—no longer part of an empire, but instead part of a republic. Philadelphia's role in the American Revolution that had formed the republic was unrivaled in its depth and centrality. The city had known combat on its outskirts and occupation in its center. Many of the city's most prominent families had opposed independence, while on the other hand the most radical of the Revolutionaries had taken control of the city and state and pushed through a state constitution that was the most democratic the continent had yet seen. This was frightening for many people, not all of them Tories. The decade of Burrows's birth saw the repeal of the radical state constitution of 1776, and its replacement with a more moderate and hierarchical document. The heady days of Thomas Paine, or to use Paine's own turn of phrase, "the times that try men's souls," had passed, leaving much in their wake—but they had passed.

Twenty-five-year-old William Ward Burrows and his teen bride, Mary Bond, were married in Philadelphia on October 16, 1783. Mary

was the daughter of the Continental Army's chief surgeon and pur-
veyor. It was said of her that "she sang sweetly and danced delight-
fully."[2] Her husband was the scion of an old Charleston family—the
heir to vast estates in the subtropical sun. William Ward Burrows had
been shaped by the great events of his generation, and now he looked
to play a role in shaping the country he'd fought to create. Though
Philadelphia undermined its claim to being named the permanent
national capital when rioting veterans staged a protest on the steps of
the Pennsylvania State House in the year of Mary and William's mar-
riage, it still held its own as the political center of gravity in the United
States. After embarking on a grand honeymoon tour of South Carolina, the couple returned to Philadelphia to carve out a life for themselves among the ambitious, the powerful, the principled, and the
glittering. Their son, William, grew up in a world in which his father
was on a friendly, if not intimate, basis with financiers such as Robert
Morris and political leaders such as John Adams, Alexander Hamilton,
and Charles Cotesworth Pinckney. The author Washington Irving later
referred to him as "A gentleman of accomplished mind and polished
manners."[3] In another time, in another place, young William could
have hoped to inherit a coat of arms and a title from his father. But this
was republican America, and though privileged, the Burrows family
had to accept a new relationship between socioeconomic classes. As
one European visitor to Philadelphia remarked in 1783, "People think,
act, and speak here as it prompts them; the poorest day-laborer on the
bank of the Delaware holds it his right to advance his opinion, in religious as well as political matters, with as much freedom as a gentleman."[4]

Apparently, William Ward Burrows did not transfer the institution of African-American slavery to his new estate at Kinderton.
According to the 1790 census, no blacks occupied a place in the Burrows household.[5] Whether Burrows was a progressive man or merely
abiding by social convention is unclear. Certainly, the climate

for owning slaves in Pennsylvania had become increasingly hostile, culminating in an act establishing the gradual abolition of the practice entirely in the state from 1780 on.[6] Between 1790 and 1800, in fact, the number of slaves decreased from 3,737 to 1,706, and by 1810 to 795.[7] Thus, young William from his earliest days would have breathed not only the clear air of Kinderton but the free air of a freshly minted republic.

No CITY IN THE NEW REPUBLIC could lay claim to a more cosmopolitan or more culturally and politically sophisticated social elite than Philadelphia. Young William's roots in this great city ran deep on his mother's side. Mary Bond's grandfather, Dr. Thomas Bond Sr., had been one of the city's most prominent figures, as well as its leading physician, for nearly half a century. An intimate of Benjamin Franklin, Bond collaborated with him in the founding of the Pennsylvania Hospital, the American Philosophical Society, and the College of Philadelphia (the forerunner of the University of Pennsylvania). Dr. Bond's skill as a surgeon and as a lecturer led to his reputation reaching far outside the city's confines.

Bond had arrived in Philadelphia from Maryland with his half brother in 1730. The city at that time had begun to take shape as something more than a colonial outpost. Franklin himself had arrived only seven years before, looking to make his fortune after reneging on his apprenticeship at his brother's Boston print shop. Philadelphia was originally founded in 1682 as a haven for persecuted Quakers, and its founder and proprietor, William Penn, had early on made a concerted effort to attract as many skilled laborers as he could to his new "holy experiment," regardless of their religious beliefs or nationality—even going so far as to print circulars praising the wonders and opportunities of the new colony in multiple languages and have them distributed throughout Europe. Due to this initial investment in "human capital,"

Philadelphia

Penn's colony largely avoided the grim early periods of other colonies, such as those at Jamestown and Plymouth. To be fair, Pennsylvania also was founded considerably later in the seventeenth century than those other colonies, and had behind it not only Penn's vast personal fortune but those of the other "first-purchasers." Built on a high and firm piece of land between the Delaware River and its main tributary, the Schuylkill, Philadelphia had been the site of a mixed forest of pine and hardwoods. Penn, who as a youth had been jolted by the Great London Fire of 1666, determined that his new city would be a healthful, "greene Country Towne" with straight, wide streets intersecting at right angles. His desire for the colony to become populous, economically profitable, and industrious on the one hand, and his wish to maintain Philadelphia as a green New World antidote to the cramped firetrap that he'd known in London, were somewhat at variance with one another. Very quickly, the Delaware riverfront became a congested warren of wharves, chandleries, breweries, shipyards, and taverns. Though upstream some 120 miles from the Atlantic Ocean, Philadelphia afforded mariners a "deep and commodious harbor."[8] More important, opportunities for maritime trade grew exponentially. As Mary Maples Dunn and Richard S. Dunn explained of Philadelphia's advantageous geography:

> *It lay at the center of a circle of splendid farm country which reached fifty miles in every direction, drawing New Jersey as well as Pennsylvania and Delaware into its orbit. And the new settlers who poured into this region and cleared its forests in the late seventeenth and early eighteenth centuries not only produced commodities for Philadelphia merchants to export but also created a market for Philadelphia imports.*[9]

A little over a century after its founding, Philadelphia was exporting over 400,000 barrels of flour every year.[10] The youthful Thomas

Bond apparently recognized a growing concern when he saw one and decided to open an apothecary and begin seeing patients. A number of years later, like Franklin, he journeyed to Europe to study his profession for a time. He returned to carve out a place of prominence for himself in the town a British visitor would soon refer to perhaps a bit prematurely as "a great and noble city" and as "one of the wonders of the world."[11]

Though Dr. Bond was born and raised a Quaker, he did not pass on his religion to his descendants. Adopting the Anglican Church of his second wife, Bond was very much a man of the world—and a slaveholder as well, owning at least two slaves at the time of the drafting of his will.[12] Bond was also a Freemason, like so many prominent men in the colonies during the era of the Enlightenment. Today he is best remembered as the father of bedside medical instruction, in which internists learn by diagnosing and healing patients alongside their instructors.[13] E. H. Thomson, in her biography of the doctor, commented on his distinctly progressive views:

The Southeast Prospect of Philadelphia, Peter Cooper, circa 1720

In an age of drastic medical treatment, he counseled moderation and common sense. He was not content to be a skillful surgeon, a successful physician, but was untiring in his efforts to advance medicine and the conditions under which it was practiced. He urged "diligent investigation" of the causes of the disease and the effect of climate on its manifestations. He advocated consideration of the environment of sick people and emphasized the preventive aspects of medicine.[14]

William Burrows's maternal great-grandfather was clearly a remarkable man. To be born and raised Dr. Thomas Bond Sr.'s great-grandson in Philadelphia carried with it a certain degree of social clout, gravity, and responsibility. Thomas died the year before William's birth, but his shadow must have been long. After all, he had purchased the house the Burrows family lived in.

His son, Dr. Thomas Bond Jr., followed in his father's weighty footsteps, and, like so many sons of great men, was not quite the man his

father had been. The younger Dr. Bond had served the revolutionary cause with some distinction as surgeon and purveyor-general to the Continental Army, most notably in his untiring efforts on behalf of wounded veterans. Yet he seemed to be temperamentally more inclined to pursue the good life. In addition to his practice he owned an unsuccessful stocking company, speculated in land, and, according to John Adams, was a "Lover of pleasure" who used wine and women "very freely" and kept a mistress in a room opposite his lodgings in town."[15] His daughter Mary was only a teenager when she first met her future husband, William Ward Burrows. Judging from his portrait, Burrows cut a dashing figure.

William Ward Burrows, father of William Burrows

William Ward Burrows was born in 1758 in Charleston, South Carolina. His father "was wealthy and respected and gave his son all the advantages that wealth and influence could buy."[16] The Burrows family kept both an elegant town house in Charleston as well as nearly three hundred acres of land outside the city along the west bank of the Cooper River. A European education was de rigueur for a South Carolina planter's son in the eighteenth century; William Ward Burrows was no exception in this regard. At the age of fourteen he traveled to London to study law at the Inner Temple at the Inns of Court. But events began to upset the established order of things—William returned home without completing his studies, and was soon swept up in the heady, sublime, and terrible days of the American Revolution.

Burrows served officially in a capacity as an officer of South Carolina marines, but he may also have been involved in intelligence work. His son, William Jr., would, in turn, almost certainly have imbibed the recollections of his father's wartime experiences from earliest childhood. Like so many officers, William Ward Burrows became an ardent nationalist, identifying with his country's interests foremost. For a South Carolinian this was no small ideological leap. He was a well-connected man. His membership in the Society of the Cincinnati was certainly proof of this. The organization was composed of the Continental Army's officer corps and was created to foster an aristocratic, selfless elite that would form a governing class for the new nation. Named for the Roman farmer-citizen-soldier who saved Rome from her enemies and wanted no reward but to return to his fields, the society quickly gained critics for its pretensions to becoming a hereditary nobility. Chief among these critics were Thomas Jefferson and Benjamin Franklin.

The nation itself was in a fluid state in those years. The 1783 Paris Treaty, which officially ended the war and granted British diplomatic recognition to the United States, had been very generous in its terms to the young country. However, that country was more a country in name than in actual practice. The Articles of Confederation adopted in 1781 provided for a weak central government. Individual states were basically sovereign in matters of taxation, conscription, and trade. In addition, collectively the infant united states were saddled with a massive debt accumulated in the course of fighting and winning the Revolutionary War. This, in turn, placed a considerable strain on the economy. The 1780s were a difficult time for many, including many veterans. These men who had fought to create the United States must have seen the promise of the new country they had fought for slipping away from them. The Constitutional Convention called for the summer of 1787 in Philadelphia looked to salvage the situation. Two-year-old William Burrows knew nothing of the import of these meetings taking place just to the south of Kinderton Farm in the city's center. He would have known, however, that it was hot that summer, but not nearly as hot as within the shuttered Pennsylvania State House, where the delegates, pledged to secrecy, debated and negotiated the final document. The United States Constitution that resulted proved to be in the short term the very thing the country needed, and in the long term one of the most admired, copied, and flexible political documents ever produced. The selection of New York as the country's new capital would have come as a disappointment to many Philadelphians, who had hoped their city would garner that honor. But only three years later the federal government moved its headquarters from Manhattan to William Penn's "greene Country Towne."

The nation's first treasury secretary, Alexander Hamilton, had made a deal with his political and ideological rival, Thomas Jefferson, to have the capital moved to a location in the near South along the Potomac River. This was in exchange for the Southerner, Jefferson, dropping his resistance to a plan to have the federal government assume responsibility for paying off all of the individual states' debts from the Revolutionary War. The site chosen was a swampy lowland around a small hillock. It would take ten years to ready the site for habitation. In the meantime it was agreed that Philadelphia would temporarily host the capital. This period, the period of William Burrows's boyhood (1790–1800), was in many respects Philadelphia's golden age. National in the reach of its responsibilities, cosmopolitan in its composition, the city of Burrows's youth would know grandeur in a very real sense, but also tragedy of the darkest nature.

IN YOUNG WILLIAM BURROWS'S FIFTH YEAR the first United States census was taken. Its purpose was to provide the newly strengthened federal government with a portrait of just who exactly inhabited the different states, counties, and towns of the sprawling nation. Philadelphia was listed as having a population of 42,520 souls. This represented an increase of approximately 10 percent in the city's population since the end of the Revolutionary War eight years before.[17] Economic recovery had been a companion to this population growth. The markets, wharves, manufactories, and shops of the city were making up for ground lost during the Revolution. Philadelphia's leading merchant families, the Mifflins, Walns, Morrises, Drinkers, Hazelhursts, and others, had begun even before 1790 to penetrate the markets of Asia that had previously been the preserve of the British East India Company. In fact, the first American merchantman to initiate direct trade with China, the *Empress of China*, was a joint venture of New York's Daniel Parker and Philadelphia's own Robert Morris. The *Empress* sailed from New York Harbor; that same year the merchantman *United States*, sailing from Philadelphia, became the first U.S. vessel to trade directly with India. Two years later, the Philadelphia-based captain Thomas Truxton* sailed his merchantman *Canton* to its namesake port and opened direct trade between China and Philadelphia. Because the Chinese were mostly uninterested in American products,

---

*Truxton would later command an American naval squadron in the West Indies.

Philadelphia merchants and captains were forced to become adept at triangular trading to turn the handsome profits they desired. As Edgar P. Richardson explained:

> *Their ships collected cargoes for Canton in Amsterdam, Antwerp, and Gibraltar; they stopped at Valparaiso for hides, Smyrna for opium, in Batavia or Malacca for tin, and on the Malabar coast for sandalwood and pepper . . . In return they brought home from Canton chiefly tea, and also silks, nankeens, porcelains, and camphor.*[18]

Great fortunes were being made. Wealth rippled into the city and out from it. Where once settlers struggled to carve out a life for themselves from the riverbank and the forest, now their descendants could choose from a variety of shops dealing in imported luxury goods from Europe. The expectations of the city's self-styled elite began to evolve from merely aping European high culture (and that poorly) to matching or exceeding it in quality. The merchant and Federalist politician William Bingham's town house, constructed during this era, was a fine example of this new confidence. Modeled "on the London showplace of the Duke of Manchester," it featured marble stairs, a formal garden, French wallpaper, large parlor mirrors, and expensive patterned carpets.[19] The residence also occupied the better part of an entire city block. To preside over his showpiece home, Bingham relied on his wife, Anne. Described as "Rich, attractive, shrewd, witty, and elegantly dressed,"[20] Anne Bingham possessed pretensions to presiding over her own French Enlightenment–style "salon." She certainly kept entertaining company, and as the upheavals of the latest waves of revolution crashed over France and its colony in Saint-Domingue,* Philadelphia and Mrs. Bingham found themselves playing host to large numbers of

---

* Present-day Haiti.

French émigrés and intriguers. Anne Bingham's guests included "the duc d'Orleans (later King Louis Philippe) and the duc de la Rochefoucald-Liancourt," as well as "such visiting English worthies as Alexander and Henry Baring, of the great financial house, who married two of her daughters."[21] The Binghams and the Burrowses inhabited the same social circles. And though young William and his family lived just outside the city, the Binghams' world was his world—privileged, cosmopolitan, genteel.

The new president, George Washington, austere yet highly conscious of maintaining both his personal dignity and the dignity of his new office, added his own luster to the city by traveling its streets in a coach and six with "the handsome horses carefully matched, the coach freshly and elaborately repainted and reupholstered by the brothers David and Francis Clark of Chestnut Street."[22] And the city's streets themselves had taken on a characteristic look that would define the city for many of its visitors, a city that, as Edgar P. Richardson remarked, was "urban but preindustrial, a tree-lined checkerboard of red-brick houses trimmed in white."[23] William Penn's utopian vision for Philadelphia still carried considerable meaning for the city's leaders and well-to-do citizens. The desire to show Philadelphia's best face, and thus raise the tone of the city as a whole, was very prevalent. As Peter Thompson pointed out:

> *The idea that a man's mood and behavior could be altered or determined by his surroundings had a peculiar resonance among Philadelphians. The city's grid of streets and squares was laid out in the belief that it would promote health and sobriety among the city's population.*[24]

But in the side streets and markets, on the wharves, and in the taverns and coffeehouses, life took on a direction of its own.

Philadelphia's burgeoning merchant and maritime classes inter-mingled with a frequency that defied rigid socioeconomic distinctions. The closer one got to the Delaware, the more democratic the atmosphere. As Thompson went on to explain:

> Over the course of the eighteenth century numerous taverns were established along the Delaware riverfront. Their keepers hoped to profit from the thirst of the city's stevedores, shipwrights, and sailors. Sailors gravitated toward taverns to celebrate the completion of a voyage or to sign up for their next job. Newspaper advertisements called upon sailors to sign up for voyages in waterfront taverns, some with names like the Ship-A-Ground or the Boatswain and Call, that advertised their association with the sea. But these waterfront taverns, intimately connected with the city's maritime trade, also drew visits from ships' captains, merchants, supercargoes, clerks, and travelers with the money to take passage to far away places . . . Conversely, the owner of a vessel might sit in a coffeehouse, thus drawing to him, and into the coffeehouse, sailors, clerks, and laborers charged with delivering cargo.[25]

The degree to which young William Burrows would have been exposed to this side of Philadelphia's economy and society is likely very little. His father, returning to law as a profession, took on a number of clients and perhaps conducted some business in the setting of a coffeehouse or tavern. However, these were the domain of men, not boys. Functioning almost as social clubs would a few generations later, William Bradford's Old London Coffeehouse on the corner of High and Front streets and the City Tavern on Second and Walnut were examples of ostensibly public establishments founded by private subscription. Well-to-do merchants, politicians, and their various hangers-on

Arch Street Ferry, Philadelphia, William Birch, 1800

considered these "their" bars, which, in fact, they were. This was, in turn, reciprocated by the regular patrons of the various lower-end taverns and "dram shops," both licensed and unlicensed, in the city. A gentleman could expect a rough familiarity in these environs whether he desired it or not. Thus, one could see in Philadelphia a society emerging that was both elitist and at the same time (though not among the same segment of the citizenry) more democratic. Business tied the two together. And where it was conducted, especially as regarded maritime trade, tended to be a point of convergence. And business was thriving.

The nascent industrial revolution was only just beginning to make its impact felt in 1790s America. Manufacturing had yet to take on many of the characteristics of the high industrial age. That said,

Philadelphia was already producing manufactured goods and employing significant numbers of laborers at an impressive rate by century's end, particularly in processing commodities. For instance, by 1794, "twenty-seven snuff and tobacco factories in Philadelphia employed over 400 workers." In addition, Philadelphia "refined about 35,000 pounds of sugar that year."[26] To feed the desire of Philadelphia's great merchant families to build and outfit merchantmen involved in the export-import trade, shipyards, ropewalks, and sail lofts also were expanding their efforts. Shipbuilders, such as Charles West in Kensington and Joshua Humphreys in the Southwark district, established the city as a leader in maritime industry. Humphreys would, in fact, become the nation's preeminent naval architect, designing some of the youthful U.S. Navy's first vessels. James Forten, an African-American who had escaped a British prison hulk during the Revolutionary War and then walked barefoot from New York back to his hometown of Philadelphia to become a sailmaker, eventually bought out his employer in 1798, and then "turned it into one of Philadelphia's premier maritime enterprises. By 1807 he had amassed a personal fortune of $100,000. His racially mixed crew of thirty workmen produced the precisely fabricated sails for many of the city's largest merchant ships."[27] Thus, even in a state where slavery was still technically legal,* the city's prosperity was reaching at least some in the most marginalized segments of Philadelphia society.

African-Americans, by the time of William Burrows's birth in 1785, had established themselves as a distinct cultural group in the city. No longer forced laborers arriving in Philadelphia without personal autonomy over even their own bodies, by the late eighteenth century blacks were asserting their individual and collective autonomy as never before. Central to this was their church. Two figures in particular within the African-American church became the founding

---

*Due to the gradual abolition of the practice provided for in the 1780 law.

fathers of the city's black community: Absalom Jones, the minister of St. Thomas's African Episcopal Church, and Richard Allen, the minister of Mother Bethel Church. Unlike the entrepreneur James Forten, who had been born free, as had his father before him, both Jones and Allen had been born slaves, but had since gained their freedom. Though one was an Episcopalian and the other Methodist, they joined their efforts and in 1787 created the Free African Society. The society functioned as a mutual aid organization, "devoted to helping widowed, ill, or out-of-work African-Americans."[28] It also provided African-Americans with a vehicle for becoming involved in the city's civic life in ways intended to promote an improved impression of blacks among the broader city population as a whole. This goes some way toward explaining why the Reverend Richard Allen was so emphatic in exhorting the society's members to become deeply involved during the city's darkest hour. Even at the peril of risking their own lives.

THE YELLOW FEVER EPIDEMIC OF 1793 was, arguably, the defining event in Philadelphia history. Much as, for instance, the 1863 Draft Riots were arguably the defining event in New York City history, or the 1906 earthquake the defining event in San Francisco history, the epidemic forced the city to look into the mirror at its soul. And what it saw was both deeply troubling and reassuringly affirming.

The epidemic started in the port district near the Delaware River wharves. One physician, a Dr. Foulke, attributed it according to one account to "a pungent odor in the air," the source of which was "the sloop *Amelia* out of Santo Domingo," which had "dumped a cargo of damaged coffee on Bell's Arch Street wharf on July 24, and the coffee had putrified."[29] No less a worthy than the eminent physician and statesman Benjamin Rush concurred. That the source lay in or near the port district appears to have been accurate; but rotting coffee was not the cause. Almost certainly it was a recent boatload of refugees, fleeing the black slave uprising on Santo Domingo, that carried the plague of yellow fever from the Caribbean with them. In addition, the *Aedes aegypti* mosquito, a carrier and transmitter of yellow fever, was indigenous to the lower Delaware Valley and had bred proficiently that year due to an unusually dry summer following an unusually wet spring. As August 1793 arrived, so too did the first reports of the tell-tale symptoms of yellow fever, followed by painful, and often shockingly rapid, deaths. The fever was accompanied by "nausea, eruptions of the skin, a black vomit, and eventually deep lethargy, rapid feeble pulse, incontinence, and a morbid yellow coloring of the skin."[30] It was a horrible way to die. There was no dignity, no peace; and the most distressing thing of all for many was the fact that it seemed to strike the young and healthy as swiftly and powerfully as the elderly or infants. Social bonds were strained to the breaking point. And then things got worse.

When news of the fever deaths began to spread throughout the city, many of those who could leave did. The exodus of the city's well-to-do residents to their country estates, or even farther afield, led to divisions in the city that would outlast the epidemic itself. Who had fled, who had stayed? That there was a socioeconomic aspect to the answer to this question was lost on few at the time. The poor, stuck in their situation, often could not leave. This immobility could mean the difference between living and dying. To be fair, not all of the fever's victims were poor, and not all of the city's wealthier residents fled the city. The mayor, Matthew Clarkson, chose to stay and organize relief as best he could. During this hour of peril Richard Allen offered the city the services of his Free African Society. The work that he and his fellow society members performed during this terrible civic ordeal was arguably one of the greatest single acts of courage and humanity ever exhibited in the United States of America. At great risk to themselves, the members of the Free African Society nursed the sick and dying, collected and buried the dead, and tended the orphaned, both white and black.* The pain (both physical and emotional) that was being experienced must have tested the resolve of the best of both men and women. Physicians, approximately eighty in number at the epidemic's start, were divided in opinion about how best to treat the fever. Rush, a progressive man in most other respects, championed an almost medieval purgative of bloodletting that likely hastened many of his patients' ends. The French émigré physician Jean Devèze and his colleagues, on the other hand, argued for "rest, fresh air, and lots of fluids."[31] This so-called West Indies treatment certainly produced far better results for recovery. Treasury Secretary Alexander Hamilton, for instance, and his wife were both struck by the epidemic, but after subscribing to the latter treatment made full recoveries.

Hamilton was unusual in having stayed on, as much of the government had chosen to leave the city. When he and his wife finally did leave the city for her home in upstate New York, they were "shunned like lepers" along the way.[32] For his part, President Washington stayed true to his usual routine and returned, as usual at that time of year, to his home at Mount Vernon, Virginia, leaving the city on September 10. Without his presence, however, the city seemed to come unglued. As Thomas Jefferson, Washington's secretary of state, explained in a letter to James Madison at the time, "Everybody who can is flying from the city," adding darkly, "The panic of the country people is likely to add famine to the disease."[33] In this, Jefferson wasn't far off. Country folk were extremely reluctant to risk their own lives to bring their produce to market. Prices soared. That there was profiteering there is little doubt. Public order began to break down as death carts plied the city piled with corpses, shops and private homes were looted, and the church bells stopped pealing for the dead. August, September, and into October the plague raged unabated. The city's first attempts

---

*Curiously, many white Philadelphians believed blacks enjoyed immunity from yellow fever.

to quarantine and nurse the sick had proved to be disastrous. A temporarily abandoned circus was first used but proved to be too near the city center for an adequate quarantine. This was followed by the transformation of an aging country estate in the Northern Liberties, Bush Hill, into the city's primary quarantine and hospital. Described by the historian Richard G. Miller as a "hell-hole of neglected, stinking, filthy victims of the fever wallowing in their own vomit and excrement, occasionally visited by physicians,"[34] Bush Hill was a house of horrors during the early period of the epidemic. How much seven-year-old William Burrows was aware of this tragedy unfolding nearby can only be guessed at. But that he must have been, at least partially, conscious of disaster lurking seems very likely. Bush Hill was not far from Kinderton Farm, and the epidemic itself was spreading out of the city center. In an alarming letter, Dr. Rush reported:

> This fever was confined for a while to Water Street, between Race and Arch-streets; but I have lately met with it in Second-street, and in Kensington; but whether propagated by contagion, or by the original exhalation, I cannot tell.[35]

The paralysis that gripped the city and its environs at this time was palpable. Fear, cold and stark, exposed the fragility of not only social convention but family ties. Charles Brockden Brown commented on how "Wives were deserted by husbands, and children by parents. The chambers of diseases were deserted, and the sick left to die of negligence."[36] In the end, it was ironically the house of horrors at Bush Hill, restaffed and reprovisioned through the efforts of another remarkable French émigré, Stephen Girard, that started to stem the tide of suffering that had been compounded by ignorance. The first autumn frosts achieved what the limited medicine of the day could not, ending the mosquito-borne contagion. Against the counsel of his advisers, President Washington reentered the city on November 10, a

Sunday. His return marked an end to the most painful epoch in the city's annals, and Philadelphians got on with the business of living.

In the end, approximately five thousand people died of yellow fever during the epidemic. Many more were incapacitated temporarily, or weakened permanently. The total of deaths during those three months in 1793 represented 10 percent of the city's pre-epidemic population.[37]

KINDERTON FARM, located on the city's outskirts, would have provided William Burrows and his family with a refuge in a time of great uncertainty. The sense of security that young William must have felt would have been tempered, however, by the tragedy lapping like a tide at the edges of a rocky isle. Of the thousands that perished, 543 were residents of the Northern Liberties.[38] On October 6, as the epidemic still raged, William turned eight years old. Did his family celebrate the occasion? Or would this have tempted fate too much?

During the darkest days of the plague all of the city's newspapers but one, Andrew Brown's *Federal Gazette*, suspended operations. That a city of Philadelphia's stature could come so close to being without printed news was further testament to the depth of the calamity. In the 1790s Philadelphia could boast at least two dozen newspapers.[39] These papers, often heavily partisan politically and devoting significant space to advertising, helped Philadelphians navigate their world in a way that was previously unavailable. What the Internet would one day do for the dissemination of information (both accurate and scurrilous) for a later generation, newspaper publishers did for William Burrows's generation. Benjamin Franklin's own grandson, in fact, Benjamin Franklin Bache, was one of the city's most prominent newspaper publishers at this time. His *Aurora* adopted a combatively pro-Jefferson position in the city's editorial wars. Franklin likely would have approved—if not necessarily of his grandson's politics, at least of his participation in the city's publishing business, which Franklin had done so much to create. Publishing at that time, in fact, was not limited to broadsheets, but included books, plays, and sheet music. As Gary Nash emphasized, "By 1795 Philadelphia boasted forty-three printers, evidence of a print explosion. . . ."[40] Where once the youthful Franklin and Thomas Bond would have found it necessary to purchase books in London to add to their common stock of knowledge, by the time William Burrows was learning to read this was happily no longer the case. Furthermore, the city was not simply a large-scale processor of knowledge; it had become a major contributor to it.

Benjamin Franklin's experiments with electricity had made him a household name on both sides of the Atlantic. As a result, his adopted city was able to bask to a certain degree in the reflected radiance of his achievement. But by the time of William Burrows's birth, Philadelphia had proven itself to be more than simply the home city of the great man. It could boast of a scientific elite with a diverse list of accomplishments: men such as the inventor and astronomer David Rittenhouse, the botanist William Bartram, and the painter and naturalist Charles Willson Peale. Though Rittenhouse's observation of the transit of Venus from a specially constructed platform behind the State House had made him a popular figure in the city, it was Peale's museum that attracted the widest popular acclaim. Charles Willson Peale had played an important role as a younger man in the more radical period of Revolutionary Philadelphia, but after the Revolution he had devoted himself to mythologizing its great names in portraits, eventually exhibiting them in a building with a special skylight that he had constructed next to his home on Third and Lombard streets.[41] In 1784, apparently quite randomly, a collection of mastodon bones belonging to Dr. John Morgan was added to the display. After a time, Peale couldn't help but realize that the bones were what were drawing the most visitors and refashioned his museum into a "Repository for Natural Curiosities."[42] Over the next four decades Peale built a collection that would serve as an archetype for such later institutions as the Field

Charles Willson Peale, *The Artist in His Museum*

Museum of Natural History in Chicago and the American Museum of Natural History in New York.

As Richard G. Miller explained:

> *He arranged specimens of living creatures according to the Lin-*
> *naean classification and inanimate materials in a similar orderly*
> *fashion based on their place of origin . . . He employed his artistic*
> *skills to paint backgrounds which along with rocks and foliage*

*created habitat arrangements, an idea he originated. His scope
was to teach the public as well as to enlarge the knowledge of
scholars.*[43]

That the public Peale wished to instruct could have included a
young William Burrows appears likely. What a treat that must have
been. Young William's ticket would have read, "NATURE. The Birds
and Beasts will teach thee."[44] At twenty-five cents, admission wasn't
cheap, though it was certainly within the means of a wealthy family,
such as the Burrowses. Inside he would have seen "golden pheasants
from Mount Vernon, enormous rattlesnakes, an anteater measuring
more than seven feet from snout to tail, a jackal, swordfish, East Indian
insects, birds by the hundreds, a Damascus sword, skulls of the royal
tiger, an African bow brought to South Carolina by a slave, and wax
models from humans from afar."[45] For a young boy it must have been
a wonder to see the exhibits. In fact, it must have been wonderful in
general to have been a boy in Philadelphia in those days. Fishing and
swimming in the Schuylkill or the Delaware in the summers; ice-
skating on the Schuylkill in the winters; perhaps taking a hand at an
oar or a sail line; early, luxuriant springs and crisp, golden autumns
with the smell of hot scrapple in the nose. And the people . . . Indians
still occasionally visited the city on tribal business to treat with the
federal government. The salty "Jack Tars' with their earrings and
deeply tanned faces branded by some far-off tropical sun. The French-
men on the make, carrying themselves with a sense of style mixed
with a hint of desperation. The Pennsylvania "Deutsch," or Germans,
to the north of the city in Germantown and in Kensington with their
newspapers, their church, and their traditions. And of course, always
near at hand, the reminders of the great events of their fathers' age.
The Revolution, the battle sites to the south of the city along Brandy-
wine Creek and to the north at Germantown. One could go see the
bullet holes in the houses still and perhaps find a lead ball in the earth

that had been discharged by a musket in the heat of battle. The market, the shops, the wharves collectively would have presented a mix of vibrant colors, smells, textures, tastes, and sounds. For a boy with even average levels of energy and curiosity, Philadelphia and its environs would have provided an extremely rich tableau of opportunities. William Burrows was indeed very fortunate to be young in that country, in that city, in that age, and to have been born into that family. But who was he?

Certain characteristics of the boy's personality began to manifest themselves from a relatively early age. An early biographer wrote of him possessing "a warm and benevolent heart . . . concealed behind a cold and repulsive exterior, and a cautious guardedness of reserve."[46] He continued, "On the subject of his own merits he maintained a severe and inflexible silence, while he conversed freely and fluently on the merits of his youthful comrades and associates."[47] The latter passage establishes two facts: William was humble and he had friends. Any parent would have been reassured by this combination. However, it is worth noting that William had, if not a dark streak, at least an inclination to be morose and particularly hard on himself. All throughout his life William would be his own most severe critic. William's father had high expectations for his boy. He personally supervised his education— hiring tutors instead of sending him to local schools. In the genteel Philadelphia society of that era a young man would have to be accomplished in any number of areas. Gary Nash wrote how even a generation earlier, "It was not enough to dress well or live well; one had to walk with grace, appreciate music, dance and ride skillfully, and know classical literature and languages."[48] How William danced is not known, but his ability in languages was noted on a number of occasions. French, the language then currently in vogue among wealthy Philadelphians, seemed to hold little interest for William. His tutors were frustrated by his indifference, the more so because he demonstrated early on an easy aptitude in language . . . in German. Whether because of boyhood contact with the city's German population or simply because of an attraction to its structure and cadence, William mastered the tongue of Goethe and Kant. In fact, "at the age of thirteen he would converse in that language as fluently as in his native tongue."[49] This obstinate demonstration of his ability to learn a language that *he* chose to learn provides further insight into William's character. However, whether he was speaking in English or French or German, as he grew William spoke less and less. His friends and tutors could not help noticing how he increasingly "appeared to retire in himself; to cherish a solitary independence of mind, and to rely as much as possible on his own resources."[50] These attributes would serve him well as a future naval commander, but at that time no one suspected a naval career was in the stars for him, least of all his father.

By the 1790s, William Ward Burrows occupied his own lofty crag on Olympus. And what a view: a beautiful young wife, two lovely daughters, and a son who carried his name filling a home that an English squire would admire full of life. He enjoyed connections in the highest circles, in particular after the election of his friend and fellow Federalist John Adams to the presidency in 1796, and received invitations to all of the smartest parties. He enjoyed status, stature, respect. Described as "short, stocky, and popular,"[51] and further as "polished, accomplished, a brilliant conversationalist and an indefatigable worker,"[52] William Ward Burrows had it all, and wanted the same for his son. But his son wanted something different. This first became apparent in a rather roundabout way when young William's drawing master noticed how his pupil returned again and again to the same theme in his drawings and paintings. He would "sometimes surprise him neglecting the allotted task, to paint the object of his silent adoration—*a gallant ship of war*."[53]

Where this interest with the sea and the U.S. Navy had its origin is unclear, but clearly William's doodling fed his daydreams, and vice versa. The U.S. Navy of William's youth was a phantom of what it had once been during the American Revolution. But the boy clearly was aware of his country's once proud naval traditions. These had been built during the thirteen colonies' struggle to free themselves from British rule in the late 1770s and early 1780s. The exploits of such heroes as Esek Hopkins, John Barry, and, above all, John Paul Jones made for thrilling storytelling. Jones's famous fight in the *Bonhomme Richard** against His Majesty's frigate *Serapis* off Flamborough Head, England, on September 23, 1779, was the stuff of legend. Outgunned and outclassed, Jones used a ruse of appearing to flee and then intentionally crashed his vessel into *Serapis*, forcing hand-to-hand combat in which he and his crew outfought their opponents and made a prize of their vessel. Those days, however, had long since passed, as the old Continental Navy had been either sold off or allowed to rot at the wharves before William was even born. By William's ninth year, though, the new federal government under President Washington had authorized the construction of a fleet of six frigates that would form the nucleus of a new navy. One of these, the *Philadelphia*, could be seen under construction at Joshua Humphreys's yard in Southwark. It was an impressive sight.

William's father was also swept up in the drive to build a new U.S. Navy when President John Adams asked the elder Burrows to form and lead a United States Marine Corps to serve aboard the vessels being launched. That Adams would call on his friend, the ex-officer of South Carolina marines, to serve in this capacity demonstrated the esteem in which he was held and the confidence Adams possessed in Burrows's patriotism. Why else would an independently wealthy member of the gentry relinquish a life of ease for "$50 per month and four rations per day"?[54] On August 23, 1798, Burrows established his permanent headquarters at Philadelphia. He was a vigorous commander who strove to place this new arm of the American maritime forces on

---

*Named for his friend Benjamin Franklin, the author of *Poor Richard's Almanack*.

a firm foundation. By all accounts he succeeded. As Fletcher Pratt explained, the Royal Marines provided a model for Adams and Burrows in their creation of the corps:

> *They were to operate according to British precedent, a seagoing police force to keep unruly sailors in order, to lead shore expeditions and boarding parties, and in battle to act as small-arms men. As it was anticipated that they would identify themselves with the service in general rather than with a particular ship (which sailors follow), their term of enlistment was fixed at one year, or until ten days after reaching port if the year had expired while they were at sea.*[55]

Burrows made "his Philadelphia headquarters a model camp, staged parades, and moved his camp outside the city during the summer to escape the fevers."[56] The Marine Corps of today owes no small measure of its famous esprit de corps to Burrows's exertions in its infancy. One aspect of boosting morale and popularizing the corps was his creation of the United States Marine Corps Band. Its first concert was, in fact, given in Philadelphia's own City Tavern. Young William must have been proud of his father's service. The connection to the sea was there as well, further reinforcing William's deeply felt ambitions. His family at this time noted, "Even among the gentle pursuits of a polite education . . . the rugged symptoms of the sailor continually breaking forth."[57] William wanted to be a naval officer. As a former marine William's father understood all too well what that life would mean. One could easily imagine him doing what he could to dissuade his willful young son from pursuing a life that would be dangerous, ill-paid, uncomfortable, and one that would take him far from his loved ones. In the end, he relented, arranging for instruction in naval science and procuring a warrant in November 1799 for his son to serve aboard a man-of-war.

William was his own man, or as much his own man as a fourteen-year-old can be. If he had not been he never would have gone to sea. As William Ward Burrows's son, and more important as Thomas Bond Sr.'s great-grandson, the natural path for William to follow would have been to study either medicine or law and establish himself in the city of his birth. Philadelphia was familiar and filled with interesting and able people. Doors would be open to William simply because he was a Burrows and a Bond. Perhaps this was what led him to reject a life of genteel ease and to embrace its polar opposite at sea. Life in his city would not have been a challenge. And besides, his city was changing.

The year 1800 would be the end of an era in Philadelphia, and in the life of the Burrows family. After ten years in William Penn's "greene Country Towne," the federal government began moving its various arms south to the Potomac and the new capital. Still half finished, and like the country as a whole, a bit raw, Washington was a muddy, malarial work in progress. Along with the government, the military relocated as well. As Marine Corps commandant, William Ward Burrows brought his wife and two daughters to Foggy Bottom, near the capital's Georgetown neighborhood, and established himself in the new city. The golden years of raising a family and making a life together in the most exciting city on the continent were coming to an end. For Mary Bond Burrows, the third generation of her family to have lived in Philadelphia, this meant leaving the only home she had ever known. For Philadelphia the government's move meant no longer being the center of things in the republic. First Washington would eclipse it politically; then, within a generation, New York would eclipse it financially. Ever since, it has occupied a place as the other great city of the Eastern Seaboard, located somewhat awkwardly between its two ancient rivals.

For the Burrows family, 1800 would also be the year that they would say good-bye to William. Their quiet, resourceful daydreamer of all things to do with the sea was going to sea: to France on the far side of the stormy Atlantic Ocean on a winter voyage. How does one say good-bye to one's fourteen-year-old son, knowing he is putting himself in harm's way? It must have broken his mother's heart, but William was determined to become the man he had dreamed of becoming, not what someone else had dreamed for him.

CHAPTER 3

The *Boxer*

"boxer"—"One who fights with the fists"

His Britannic Majesty's ship *Bellerophon* would have risen like a floating castle above eleven-year-old Samuel Blyth's eyes as he came aboard his first man-of-war. All of his young life he had dreamed of this day: donning midshipman's blues and looking ahead to a life full of perils he would conquer, adventures he would seize, and battles from which he would emerge blooded but not bloodied. What else could reasonably be expected to go through an eleven-year-old boy's mind at such a moment? And Samuel Blyth was very much a boy when he entered the man's world of the Royal Navy. But although he was still a boy, there can be little doubt his grandfather would have made certain he understood that his one route to a commission and promotion would be in combat. He could not afford to enter the ring tentatively. He would need to enter it throwing punches, and continue to throw punches until he got his name in the newspapers; and then he would need to keep his name in the newspapers. Poor boys weren't given command of His Majesty's vessels, but a poor boy that ate fire, and then ate it again, and again, might just. The hopes of the seafaring Blyths were pinned on his youthful frame.

When Samuel Blyth arrived on the deck of the *Bellerophon* on May 7, 1794, he was boarding a line-of-battle ship, one of 153 in His Majesty

King George III's Navy. A line-of-battle ship was the most intimidating class of vessel afloat in that era. Rated as carrying seventy-four guns, the *Bellerophon* fell under the most common classification of these "battleships." Overall, the vessel "weighed about 1,700 tons and she needed some 2,000 oak trees to build her"—in total, "57 acres of forest."[1] With three decks full of guns, the damage that could be inflicted by one of these giants could be truly awe-inspiring. Samuel Blyth's first cruise was aboard a vessel named for the ancient Greek hero who rode Pegasus, the winged horse, to victory over the monster Chimera. In 1794, the monster the latter-day *Bellerophon* was fighting was revolutionary France. France at that time was enduring the convulsions of the Reign of Terror at its most ghoulish. The thought of the guillotine being erected on English soil was generally sufficient motivation for Royal Navy officers to fight with determination against republican France.

One of the most important duties of Britain's navy at this time was to enforce a blockade of the French coast. Midshipman Samuel Blyth spent his first few months at sea on just such duty. It could be dull, monotonous work—broken only by violent gales and the occasional French sortie or bold blockade-running merchantman. Understanding only too well how food shortages had triggered the storming of the Bastille in 1789, the new French government led by Maximilien Robespierre and his fellow radicals, the Jacobins, realized it must feed its people or risk its own violent overthrow. To this end, the new government had purchased large quantities of American grain. Crossing the Atlantic under convoy protection from the French fleet, the grain ships encountered the British blockade approximately four hundred miles west of the island of Ushant. The result of this encounter—"The Glorious First of June," as it came to be called in Royal Navy annals—was the largest sea fight up to that time between Britain and republican France.

The enormity and terrifying majesty of fifty-one battleships of the line colliding on the high seas was undoubtedly a wonder to young Samuel. Here was fantasy made reality, but reality was not as clean and glossy. Not just the enemies' blood would be spilled this day.

The *Bellerophon* took its place "in the line" of the mighty Channel fleet under Lord Howe. Howe's plan called for an unconventional and bold move in which the ships under his command would turn directly into the French line forming only a few miles away, breach them, rake them, then come about and cut off any means of escape with additional broadsides. This would expose the British to a potentially terrific concentration of fire being brought to bear from French broadsides on their bows as they closed with the enemy. What these cannonballs could do to a mast or a man was truly awe-inspiring. Facing this required extraordinary nerve. Timing was paramount, and in the event the fleet's coordinated movements failed to come off completely as planned. However, the French apparently were taken sufficiently off guard to gain the initiative for the British in the battle. This they would not relinquish.

Aboard *Bellerophon*, Blyth felt his ship come about just short of the French line of battle and engage in a murderous short-range duel with two French ships. The acrid smoke, the deafening noise, the shouts and entreaties of desperate men filled young Samuel's nose and ears. According to later accounts, in this "horrible scene of uproar and carnage," he "evinced the most dauntless courage and admirable conduct."[2] All youthful pretensions were stripped away and Samuel's character was laid bare for all to see. He kept his head. He was no coward. And then came news of the fall of Rear Admiral Thomas Pasley, the *Bellerophon*'s commander and Blyth's patron. Pasley suffered a grisly wound requiring immediate amputation of his leg. Blyth was nearby and was affected deeply by what he saw transpiring in front of him:

Painting "The Glorious First of June" (1794), Loutherbourg

. . . when he saw him lay—mangled and bleeding on the deck—it was almost by violence alone he could be kept away during the time the brave admiral suffered amputation of his leg.[3]

Blyth had to be beaten back from Pasley's side as the butcher was paid his bill. He had been on board ship less than one month. He was eleven years old.

THE "GLORIOUS FIRST OF JUNE" turned out to be a short-term strategic victory for the French, as the grain convoy reached French ports. However, in the long term, the French suffered a strategic defeat whose outcome would be challenged, but never overturned. The blockade stayed enforced. For his part, Blyth had passed his first test as an aspiring Royal Navy officer with flying colors. For the next four and a half years the *Bellerophon* would be his home. His tender age would have excited little comment in that era. Though officially the age limit was eleven, there would likely have been boys as young as seven aboard. Big "Billy Ruffian," as she was commonly known among the crew,[4] was an interesting home for a young lad: interesting, but certainly not comfortable. For one thing, Blyth would have shared quarters with his fellow midshipmen in the midshipmen's berth. Described as "a place where the light of the sun never penetrated,"[5] the young men and boys would have had no privacy and precious little space. Their quarters were but one cramped nook in a vast floating world that was home to more people than some of the villages the crew hailed from. The *Bellerophon*, for instance, was home to approximately 724 men,[6] the overwhelming majority of whom would have been common seamen. The novelist Patrick O'Brian described the *Bellerophon*'s crew on shore leave in Minorca:

> *... some wearing broad striped trousers, some plain sailcloth; some had fine red waistcoats and some ordinary blue jackets; some wore tarpaulin hats, in spite of the heat, some broad straws, and some spotted handkerchiefs tied over their heads; but they all of them had long swinging pigtails and they all had the indefinable air of man-of-war's men. They were Bellerophons ...*

The Bellerophons were clearly considered a competent lot. They came from a society that was arguably the most democratic in Europe. That said, Europe was not a very democratic place.

Samuel Blyth grew up in a world that was rigidly divided according to class. The hierarchy ashore that had its roots in the feudal era was transferred to the Royal Navy from its inception. The distinction between "gentlemen" and common seamen, even those with important responsibilities, was stark. Thus, any easy fraternization between Samuel Blyth and the Bellerophons described by O'Brian would have been very unlikely. Blyth's aspirations, and those of his paternal grandmother for her grandson, rested precariously on a combination of skill, timing (read luck), and "interest." The latter he did not possess in any significant measure. He had the intuitive sea knowledge inherited from his forebears, it is true, but hailing from a prominent family socially and politically counted for much more. And he did not. Blyth had to be very conscious of not being seen as fraternizing with common jack-tars—it was just too close to home. In any event, relations between Royal Navy seamen and their officers came to a head while Blyth was serving aboard the *Bellerophon*. The stark class distinctions had been rubbed raw and were now exposed in one of the more remarkable episodes in Royal Navy history.

THE MUTINY OF 1797 shook Britain in a very fundamental way. Assumptions that had gone unchallenged for decades had to be reexamined. For a brief moment, the men on whose backs rested the greatness of Britain's maritime empire rose up, threatening to upset the world order they made possible.

The roots of the mutiny lay in the low regard in which common seamen were held by the government, by their officers, and by the population at large. The irony in this was that Britain, as an island, had relied on its navy for defense for centuries. And however brilliant its officers might be, ships required crews. The largely nameless generations of Englishmen (and men of other nationalities) who served aboard their majesties' vessels made the Royal Navy function. But the dignity these men had earned was denied them. Within the navy men were subjected to physical punishment and harassment, which were considered by those in authority as necessary evils at sea. The most serious punishment, short of hanging, was to be flogged. This involved being stripped to the waist and bound hand and foot to a grating set up against the quarterdeck, where the officers and midshipmen kept their watches. One of the petty (noncommissioned) officers* applied the punishment with a cat-o'-nine-tails. This instrument could flay strips of skin out of a man's bare back with ease. Sentences normally varied anywhere from a half dozen to two dozen strokes for infractions, such as insubordination, fighting, neglect of duty, and, most commonly, drunkenness—though some sadistic commanders ordered as many as one hundred strokes, certainly sufficient to kill a man. Even so, "The dictum was more than once quoted that flogging ruined a good seaman and made a bad one incorrigible."[7] Added to this brutal practice was the more common, petty humiliation of being "started" by petty officers. This involved being struck on the back or around the head in order to get one to look lively and avoid loafing. To a large degree it was this latter practice that caused the deepest resentment.

As the third anniversary of the Glorious First of June neared in the spring of 1797, the seamen aboard the ships of the line moored off Spithead in the narrow strait separating the Isle of Wight from the mainland decided enough was enough. What had brought this to a head was not simply the brutality and petty humiliations, but, rather, that they had been increasing in frequency and intensity. This increasingly tense environment was largely due to the fact that the Royal Navy had increased its size to fight the war by essentially conscripting landsmen and sweetening the pot by offering them bounties. This led to large numbers of unseasoned recruits having to be absorbed into the ranks of the veteran Royal Navy seamen. The tension between the two was worsened by the fact that the bounties paid to new recruits were often more than an able seaman could earn in four years.[8] As competency aboard navy vessels declined with the injection of so many unskilled landsmen, starting increased, with blows often raining down indiscriminately. Better, or at least more just, treatment of seamen

---

*Boatswain's mates were usually responsible for doing the actual flogging.

became a rallying cry for those who, on April 16, in the narrow strait stated their intention to not bring their ships to sea if ordered to do so. The mutiny of 1797 had begun.

Interestingly (considering their grievances), the outstanding characteristic of the mutineers at Spithead was their moderation. The reasonableness of their demands caused the navy and government to reflect with some depth on how they had permitted a system to develop that was, to all but the most coldhearted, glaringly unfair. First, seamen were paid considerably less than their counterparts in the army— earning approximately eleven shillings per month less than soldiers.[9] This was not a question of discipline, but a question of equity. Second, the navy had allowed a system to evolve that permitted a ship's purser (essentially a seagoing bookkeeper) to keep two out of every sixteen ounces of ship's provisions for himself.[10] This led to seamen getting shorted on their rations. Added to this systemic inequity was the fact that sick or off-duty seamen convalescing from wounds received no pay. Shore leave in Britain also had become increasingly rare as the exigencies of war took precedence over any home life seamen may have had. The strain was enormous. However, under this strain violent acts by the mutineers were nearly nonexistent. Seamen kept Royal Navy discipline aboard the mutinous vessels, elected leaders, and presented their demands to the Admiralty.* They also made it clear they would put to sea if the French fleet came out and threatened Britain. There was some razzing of officers, but considering how much worse it could have been it was decidedly mild. That said, it was not lost on the Admiralty, Parliament, and the public at large how badly it *could* have gone. After all, Britons had only to look across the English Channel to France to see the consequences of an unchecked challenge to authority. These were revolutionary times.

Eventually by mid-May 1797, with sympathy running high for the

---

*The body responsible for running the Royal Navy.

mutineers even among senior officers, a deal was struck; "a bill was hurried through Parliament, the mutineers were given the King's pardon, and they carried Lord Howe, the admiral who had conducted the negotiations, shoulder-high through the streets of Portsmouth."[11] Common seamen had leveraged their collective power to form a new, more equitable relationship with the authorities. It was an important moment. Just up the coast at the Nore, astride the Thames River estuary, another group of seamen decided to duplicate the actions of their brethren at Spithead. In this instance, the challenge to British society was even more grave, as the mutinous vessels imposed a blockade on shipping in the Thames—London's main artery to the world. To add to the more provocative nature of the Nore mutiny, its leader, one Richard Parker, was openly sympathetic to revolutionary France and entertained ideas of carrying the mutinous vessels for that country. An impatient Admiralty dealt far more severely with the Nore mutineers than it had with those at Spithead. In the end, Parker and dozens of his fellow conspirators were executed.

The Royal Navy had been shaken, but it had held firm. Legitimate grievances had been addressed. Dangerous ideologies had been quashed. The navy in which the teenage Samuel Blyth was serving emerged from the storm and looked ahead to a decisive confrontation with its archnemesis, the French fleet.

Samuel Blyth had felt only the ripples of the distant mutiny that had taken place in home waters. The "Billy Ruffian" had been stationed off Cádiz in May 1797.[12] Eight months later, in January 1798, young Samuel left his floating home of three and a half years to serve aboard His Majesty's frigate *L'Aigle*. Though his time on *L'Aigle*'s muster rolls was brief, it was eventful. Stationed in the Mediterranean, *L'Aigle* was wrecked off the coast of Tunis. The North African summer sun would have been a trial indeed for the survivors of the wreck, the site of which was later described as "a desolate coast, inhabited by cruel barbarians."[13] Not yet fifteen years old, Samuel rose to the occasion. Even though he had lost "all his personal possessions, and had to sustain many severe privations," he did not despair and demonstrated that "his fortitude to endure afflictions, was equal to his courage in braving dangers."[14] Tunis (present-day Tunisia) was home to one branch of the famed Barbary pirates. Europeans, such as the teenage Samuel, could expect little aid or comfort there. In fact, enslavement was a distinct possibility. Sunstroke, thirst, hunger, and uncertainty about their common fate would have tested the mettle of *L'Aigle*'s officers and crew. Samuel Blyth was made of stern material.

Following his and his comrades' rescue, Samuel next was appointed to the *Centaur*. On this, his third ship, Blyth seemed to have a knack for finding action. He was involved in the capture of the Mediterranean base on the island of Minorca, as well as in the seizure of three French frigates.

Britain had managed to take the fight to France the previous year when a fleet under the command of Horatio Nelson cornered a French fleet at anchor in Aboukir Bay, Egypt. The "Battle of the Nile," as it came to be known, was a decisive victory for the Royal Navy. It was won largely by boldness. Nelson struck at night in shoal-filled waters. The French seemed to have been confident no one would try such a reckless act. They were wrong. Nelson once famously explained his philosophy as simply to "Never mind manoeuvres . . . Always go at them."[15] This mind-set seems to have spread to the entire navy, particularly among junior officers and aspiring junior officers, such as Samuel Blyth. Blyth would have recognized that boldness bordering on recklessness was the rule and not the exception in his chosen profession. The correlation between risk and reward could not have been more clear. It was not so much the fierceness and courage of young men like Blyth that stood out, but rather the breathtaking audacity with which they carried off their plans. The zest for combat they possessed seemed to have an almost fanatical edge to it.

And Britain needed heroes. France had found its military genius in the form of a short, wild-haired Corsican named Napoleon Bonaparte. In fact, the reason why a French fleet was anchored off Egypt in the first place in 1798 was because he had convinced his government to support an Egyptian expedition. Ostensibly launched to pressure Britain's Indian empire, it was more an exercise in political showmanship by the young general. It proved to be wildly popular back home. Napoleon, in fact, would use his celebrity to be named first consul of France. By 1802 he was consul-for-life. Two years later he crowned himself Emperor of the French. His armies were on the march. His ambitions were limitless. Britain needed heroes.

It was a remarkable feature of the Napoleonic era that naval officers took on a prominence in the public eye much like top professional athletes have in the twentieth and twenty-first centuries.* Their lives, loves, and most of all their exploits in combat captivated readers. Entire publications were devoted to satisfying the public's interest. This was a time when killing in the name of one's country had little of the moral uncertainty experienced by later generations of warriors. Samuel Blyth had entered an occupation capable of generating tremendous star power.

However, the public was fickle, and tended to have a short memory as well. Samuel Blyth possessed all of the necessary qualities, save one, to become a figure of public adulation: a genteel birth. The question facing him was simply whether his background would hold him back, not allowing him to achieve the kind of exploits that were his best, perhaps only, way to ultimately overcome it. Samuel Blyth needed an opportunity; Britain needed heroes.

As Samuel Blyth grew into manhood, his prospects were uncertain. Due largely to the 1802 Peace of Amiens, which halted hostilities between France and Britain, Samuel Blyth was a man without a job. As he had not yet taken his lieutenancy's examination, Blyth was stuck

---

*This comparison, however, does not extend to remuneration.

Commander Samuel Blyth, RN. This portrait captures the devil-may-care countenance he faced life with.

without any official rank (he was rated a midshipman and master's mate[16]) and thus was not eligible to draw half pay while off duty. Luckily for Blyth, and those ashore who had scrimped and saved to maintain him in his position and further his career, the peace was temporary. It turned out to be merely a breathing spell for Napoleon to consolidate his domestic reforms. When war broke out again in 1803, Blyth was ordered to serve aboard the *Rodney*; then, later, aboard his former vessel, the *Centaur*, in the West Indies. While again serving aboard the *Centaur* Blyth was "severely wounded cutting out a French privateer* from under the batteries of Guadaloupe."[17] "Cutting out" was one of the practices that junior officers and aspiring junior officers like Blyth relished. Put simply, it involved boarding an enemy vessel by stealth, then taking control of it from its crew and sailing it away. One could easily picture this kind of procedure taking place in an old Errol Flynn movie.

Now in his twenties, and no longer the boy in awe of the mighty battleships of the line, Blyth must have cut quite a swashbuckling figure in the Caribbean. To a certain extent men like Blyth had to possess a bit of the pirate's makeup mentally to succeed in these conditions. The potential for promotion and prize money also motivated them. Blyth, in fact, appears to have received an acting lieutenant's rank when he was given temporary command of the vessel he had captured. Yet an actual commission would have to wait until he had passed his formal examination. And command of one of His Majesty's vessels seemed as remote as ever. Blyth could not have helped but recognize that his best, again perhaps only, route to promotion and command would come as a result of valorous deeds. He would need to take risks to get noticed. But taking risks was the British way. These men were lions.

---

*Privately owned vessels authorized to make war through a document known as a letter of marque.

No one exemplified this ethos more publicly and forcefully than Horatio Nelson. His example has inspired generations of Britons, and has even led to the creation of a subdivision of British history known as Nelsonian Studies. His boldness and his patriotism marked him as an officer and as a man. Physically unimposing, the son of a vicar, Nelson did not necessarily look the part. But he certainly lived the part. By 1805 the forty-seven-year-old Nelson had attained the rank of vice admiral and had earned more decorations than nearly any officer in the fleet. A remark made by Prince William Henry, King George III's son, about Nelson came as close as any ever would to capturing the essence of what made him the great leader he was. The prince, serving as a midshipman, encountered Nelson and recorded his first impression:

> *There was something irresistibly pleasing in his address and conversation: and an enthusiasm, when speaking on professional subjects, that showed he was no common being.*[18]

No common being indeed. In battle, Nelson conspicuously wore the coat that had embroidered upon it all of the various decorations he had been awarded.[19] Thus, he made a rather conspicuous target for enemy marksmen in combat. And also by 1805, the right sleeve of that coat would have been pinned to the chest, as he had earlier lost an arm in battle in the Canaries. Nelson was an unconventional idol, but that he was an idol to Blyth and his contemporaries is beyond question.

Nelson's equivalent on land, the Emperor Napoleon, was frustrated by his inability to come to grips with Britain's army and crush the island's prickly resistance to his designs. Recognizing, much as Adolf Hitler would in a later generation, that invading Britain required gaining control of the English Channel (at least temporarily), he looked to his navy, and to that of his ally, Spain, to break the status quo that had been established over a decade before on the Glorious First of June.

The combined Franco-Spanish fleet presented a formidable challenge to the Royal Navy. In total, thirty-three battleships of the line lay at anchor off Cape Trafalgar in southwestern Spain. Ton for ton these vessels were considered to be of superior quality to the majority of the British vessels that opposed them. The question of what this combined Franco-Spanish fleet could do, would do, weighed heavily on the minds of those in charge of Britain's war effort. In the end, a preemptive strike was decided on with Nelson chosen to lead it. As he had at Aboukir Bay seven years earlier, Nelson attacked with very little deliberation once he had made visual contact with the enemy. His plan of action called for his outnumbered force of twenty-seven battleships of the line to split the Franco-Spanish line of battle and fight first one, then the other, wing of the divided enemy force. Leading from the front in his flagship, HMS *Victory*, Nelson signaled the fleet his famous admonition to do one's duty for king and country. In the ensuing battle, Great Britain won the most decisive naval engagement in its history. Twenty-one ships of the combined Franco-Spanish fleet were captured, and another was completely destroyed. Nearly four thousand men lost their lives, the great majority of them aboard French and Spanish vessels. Britain lost no ships, though Nelson's *Victory* appeared for a moment as if it might be carried by the French ship *Redoubtable*. The fighting was intense. At its peak Nelson was felled by an enemy marksman. He was carried below, and held on long enough to realize he had won. It was the end of an era. It was also the end of any plans Napoleon might have entertained to ever invade Britain.

Samuel Blyth missed the Battle of Trafalgar. The vessel he was serving on during this period, *L'Africaine*, had grounded off North Yarmouth, England, and lost her masts. Temporarily without a vessel to call home, Blyth spent a number of eventful months ashore. On February 5 he passed his lieutenant's examination at Somerset House. This was the former palace on the Strand, London, that housed the Navy Board. It had taken him eleven years from when he first boarded

"England Expects That Each Man Will Do His Duty," the famous semaphore hoisted aboard Nelson's flagship on the eve of battle at Trafalgar

the *Bellerophon* to achieve his commission. The following June he married
Delia Lea at St. George's Church in Hanover Square, also in London. The
circumstances of their meeting and courtship are unknown, but it would
seem likely that they met in London and enjoyed a springtime romance.
The many small parks that the capital was known for would have been
filled with blooming flowers and the songs of birds. News of war filled
the city's papers, adding a sense of urgency to the two lovers' plans. They
had each other, for a time. . . .

Marrying a naval officer was not for all women. The entire concept
of a steady home life, with husband and father reassuringly close, providing stability, was a mirage for those women who did. Delia Lea
must have at least considered this before she consented to marry Samuel Blyth. Or perhaps she hoped the lack of a vessel on which to serve
would keep her future husband out of a full-time job—and on land—at
least temporarily. Unfortunately, for any prospect they may have envi-
sioned of a stable married existence, from this point forward in his
career Samuel Blyth would experience some of the greatest adventures
of his life. But the price was many months at sea and in foreign lands,
and precious few months at home with his bride. It certainly is a reasonable assumption to make that this state of affairs may have had
much to do with the fact the couple remained childless.

Blyth, however, could not have known this when he boarded His

Britannic Majesty's frigate *Confiance*, commanded by Sir James Lucas Yeo, a man who would become one of his most staunch supporters. He was appointed first lieutenant, and thus second in command to Yeo. In this capacity Blyth was once entrusted with taking charge of the frigate during a voyage between England and the coast of Portugal. His own command, every naval officer's dream, must have seemed tantalizingly close. His reverie would have been broken soon after, however, when an officer his senior was appointed to the *Confiance*, suddenly relegating him to second lieutenant. For five years Samuel Blyth would be frustrated in his efforts to be given command of his own vessel. The old weakness in his résumé—the lack of "interest" or political ties—kept him back. To his credit, Blyth seems to have maintained a nearly carefree demeanor through all of the frustrations he endured. An anecdote from his earliest biographer, concerning an incident aboard the *Confiance*, says a lot about the man:

> *Whilst Blyth was in this frigate, and she was going at the rate of ten knots, this thoughtless young fellow leaped overboard in his boots and uniform! As soon as they could, the ship hove-to, and a boat lowered, but he fell so far astern, that he was totally exhausted, and on the point of sinking when he was picked up. We do not insert this anecdote as worthy of imitation, but as a trait of his impetuous and giddy disposition, and the little weight that prudential considerations had with him.*[20]

What possessed Samuel Blyth to do such a thing is not known. However, it is a vivid demonstration of a man who, though concerned about advancement, did not take life in general very seriously. This man liked danger and he liked to have fun. Sir James Yeo's mission to capture and destroy the French fortifications at Cayenne in French Guiana would afford Samuel Blyth an ideal opportunity to experience both.

French Guiana was (and is) France's only colony in mainland South America. Made famous in the Hollywood blockbuster *Papillon*, starring Steve McQueen and Dustin Hoffman, French Guiana would gain a somewhat sinister reputation as a penal colony: a place where convicts worked off their sentences in the equatorial sun. At that time it was a relatively isolated outpost of Napoleon's empire that invited attack. The British to the north in Barbados, and the Portuguese to the south in Brazil, both wished to reduce it as a base for any possible French military ventures in South America. By early 1809, when the attack was ordered, the Portuguese royal family had itself relocated to South America, making Rio de Janeiro the new, albeit temporary, capital of the Portuguese empire. Their transatlantic odyssey had been precipitated by Napoleon's invasion of their country in 1807. They had fled rather than submit. Now, both the Portuguese and their British allies plotted to drive the French occupiers out and reestablish Lisbon as the capital of the empire. Eventually they would succeed. But in the short term, French Guiana provided an opportunity for combined action that was much more near at hand.

On January 7, 1807, Samuel Blyth led the landing party given the responsibility to capture Fort Diamant. This was the main French fortification protecting the colony's capital, Cayenne. The buccaneer in Blyth shined under these circumstances. According to one account, he "landed at the very muzzles of the guns in defiance of a continual fire of grape and musketry and put the enemy to flight."[21] This took tremendous nerve, as grapeshot could blow a bloody cloud into an oncoming force at close range. It was essentially hundreds of small lead balls fired out of a cannon all at once, meant to scatter and inflict bloody wounds, if not kill outright. To literally face that took exceptional courage. It also was the kind of act that caused people to take notice. If he had to climb into the muzzle of a cannon to gain promotion, so be it.

In any event, Blyth achieved his objective. The fort was taken.

However, Blyth received wounds from a more primitive method of warfare—bow and arrow. The French in Cayenne used local Indians in the defense of their town. As Blyth's biographer explained:

> *The arrows are made of reeds as strong as small canes, they are*
> *nearly four feet long, with rough, coarse and barbed heads of iron.*
> *He [Blyth] received no less than five of those arrows in his arm,*
> *and from being barbed they could not be extracted but by the*
> *knife.*[22]

Considering the damage that could be inflicted by even one of these arrowheads, let alone five of them, it is some wonder Blyth did not lose his arm altogether. According to Blyth himself, "I was three days and nights with my wounds undressed and bleeding, before I procured medical assistance."[23] He continued in Nelson mode, ". . . but should it be my fate to return home mutilated in the service of my country, I shall not repine."[24]

This buccaneer-patriot next found himself temporarily occupying the estate of one of the colony's French planters, a figure of some consequence named Rival. Another side of Samuel Blyth manifested itself during this period. Described as having a "noble demeanor,"[25] Blyth demonstrated that he was as chivalrous and magnanimous in victory as he was undaunted and ferocious in combat. As an earlier biographer recognized, the letter that Monsieur Rival composed and gave to Blyth to keep on his person should he ever fall into French hands is worth reproducing, as it bears witness to the character of the man:

> *You will not, I am sure, refuse me this proof of your friendship,*
> *when you shall be acquainted with the motives which animate me*
> *to interest myself in behalf of that officer, who commanded a strong*
> *detachment sent against my estate, and made me his prisoner. His*
> *behavior to me on this occasion was of the most noble and*

generous nature; he kept up the most exact discipline, and the
utmost regularity was observed by his men; so much so, that none
of my property has been in the least injured or disturbed, and his
presence on my estate had more the resemblance of a family visit
than a capture. I feel a pleasure in bearing testimony in favor of a
man of such exalted sentiment, and polished manners; and ardently
wish an opportunity may occur of demonstrating my gratitude.
You, too, will be sensible to the propriety of returning such invalu-
able services to a man who, in fulfilling his duty as an enemy,
observes at the same time all the courtesies which polished nations
owe to each other.[26]

Samuel Blyth's quality was known among his enemies. It was also known among his friends. The Portuguese were impressed by Blyth's conduct at Cayenne, and over the next few months in 1809 showed themselves to be appreciative hosts. Samuel Blyth, now an invalid, headed south soon after taking leave of Rival. His destination: the new capital of the Portuguese Empire.

Rio de Janeiro is a natural wonder. Few if any cities in the world can match its breathtaking combination of green-breasted mountains seeming to rise like jewels out of Guanabara Bay, its necklace of sandy white beaches, and its sheltered lagoon. As he entered the bay, Samuel Blyth was confronted with startling beauty. But the fact that he was an ill man may have colored his first impressions. Blyth the invalid was a source of interest for the most powerful man in Brazil—the Prince Regent Dom João Braganza, the future king of Portugal. The prince's mother, the mad Queen Maria, was deemed incapable of ruling; thus, her son bore the weight of governing for his family. Dom João arrived in Rio in 1808 and quickly set about remaking the sleepy colonial outpost into an imperial capital. As Joseph A. Page explained, "He [Dom João] established a national library, an academy of fine arts, a royal school of medicine, a print shop, a national bank, a mint, and botanical gardens."[27] Interestingly, for a man so vigorous in remaking his new tropical home, the prince regent was very corpulent, obese even. According to Page this was the result of ". . . a royal gluttony fueled by an uncontrollable appetite for fried chicken."[28] His wife, Carlotta, was no less interesting a figure, one whom Blyth likely would have encountered in his time there. Carlotta was short and ugly, but sexually adventurous. Her affairs eventually caught up with her when she arranged the assassination of a rival and was temporarily sent to a convent by her husband. Brazil was not dull. It was also seen (as was all of Latin America) as a vast untapped market by the British. In exchange for British naval protection, early on in his stay in Brazil Dom João "signed a decree opening up Brazilian ports to foreign trade," and "lifted the bans on industry and foreign residents in Brazil."[29] For the next century Britain would play a dominant, if not dominating, role in Brazil's and Latin America's trade.

For Samuel Blyth, the most significant aspects of his Brazilian experience were that he recovered his health and that he received a great honor from Dom João. As was reported in London the following year:

> *His R.H. the Prince Regent, as a special and singular favor, not to serve as example or precedent, grants to Lt. Samuel Blyth, who was wounded in five places, the sum of 150 pounds for the purchase of a Sword or any other memorial of the conquest of Cayenne.*[30]

Having the future king of Portugal on one's side could certainly have been a sign Blyth had finally attained the political "interest" he had lacked his entire career. What he did with the 150 pounds is not known. Considering a lieutenant's pay was 8 pounds, 8 shillings[31] per lunar month,* it certainly would have been tempting merely to pocket

---

*There are thirteen in a year.

Dom João Braganza, as João VI, King of Portugal

the windfall and bring it home to Delia. And home he did come in the late summer of 1809. Covered in glory and not a few medals, Blyth may have entertained the hope that his actions in South America would translate into his own command. If so, he was mistaken. Once more, he would have to take ever-greater risks in order to achieve his goal.

Samuel Blyth was a fighter. By 1809 he had repeatedly demonstrated that he could take a punch, and that he could deliver a punch. Like the name of the vessel he would one day command off Pemaquid

Point, Samuel Blyth had entered the ring numerous times since he was an eleven-year-old boy, and had always emerged from it standing. The Royal Navy valued its fighters. But genteel British society had its rules. Social climbers, or "chancers" as they were known, could rise, but not nearly as easily as they could on the other side of the Atlantic. As Patrick O'Brian noted:

> . . . those young men who, having passed the Navy's examination for lieutenant, remained senior midshipmen or master's mates because they did not "pass for a gentleman," a mute, unwritten, unacknowledged examination whose result was announced only by the absence of a commission.[32]

By almost any measure Samuel Blyth had long since earned the right to his own command. Yet it did not come. A tour of duty in the West Indies soon after his return to England seemed to offer promising possibilities. He was put in charge* of the schooner *Laura* at one point, delivering dispatches to the commander of the British base at Halifax, Nova Scotia. Soon after, however, as a result of a change at the top of the Admiralty, Blyth found himself facing the fact that the "crisis of his hopes was fast approaching."[33] As his biographer explained:

> His ardent expectations of preferment [promotion] sought in the field of battle, earned at the muzzle of the enemy's cannon, and ultimately promised by the First Lord of the Admiralty, were at once blasted. Nor did his misfortunes end here: he was immediately superseded in the command of the *Laura* schooner, and set ashore at Tortola! thence he proceeded to the island of St. Thomas's, where he took passage to Europe in a merchant vessel, and

---

* "In charge," but not "in command." The latter came with the rank of master and commander, which Blyth did not attain in the West Indies.

arrived in England with disappointed hopes—his health greatly
impaired—and his pecuniary affairs much deranged.[34]

Samuel Blyth's next appointment, as First Lieutenant aboard the
frigate *Quebec*, would afford him another chance to "cut his way to
promotion."[35] The *Quebec* was part of a squadron whose purpose was
to cause mischief along the Dutch coast near Friesland. The formerly
independent United Provinces of the Netherlands had, by this time,
been incorporated into the French Empire. This empire now included
nearly all of Europe from Spain to Poland, from Italy to Denmark,
with once proud powers such as Prussia and Austria forced into
unequal alliances with the emperor. It was this seemingly impenetrable edifice that the Royal Navy looked to slash and harass, within the
limits of their reach. Napoleon and his lackeys would never be allowed
to rest easy anywhere near the sea. What this often meant was sending
smaller craft propelled by oars to do the dirty work: stealing, burning,
cutting throats. It was just this type of work that brought out the
latent pirate in all of the officers and seamen of His Majesty's Navy. In
fact, what they were doing was not so very different from what the
Vikings did along the English coast during Alfred the Great's time.

The inshore waterways between the chain of low-lying islands and
the Dutch mainland were guarded by flotillas of gunboats. These gunboats, though not particularly seaworthy, mounted long twelve-
pounder guns, as well as two smaller cannon. In the hands of
experienced artillerymen these guns could inflict severe damage and,
in the case of the twelve-pounder, at considerable range. The commander of the British squadron settled on a plan to capture or destroy
as many of the flotilla as possible. Samuel Blyth immediately volunteered to lead this dangerous raid. With his experience in successfully
cutting out a French privateer in the West Indies, Blyth must have
exuded confidence. "As soon as it became known, more officers and
men volunteered than could be accepted."[36] Blyth's reputation as a

fire-eater had preceded him. In the end, 117 men volunteered to join him. On August 1, 1811, Blyth's expedition, in ten boats, rowed into the channel, weaving between the islands of Wanger-oog, Spyker-oog, and Langer-oog. After clearing the last of these, Blyth and his men encountered their quarry. With each gunboat manned by twenty seamen and five French soldiers in addition to their cannon, the hunters could quite easily become the hunted, as they well recognized. Blyth ordered his men "to lay on their oars," and then spoke to his brother officer, Lieutenant Humphrey Moore of the Royal Marines. Their conversation would prove eerily prophetic:

Moore—"It is a hot day, and we shall have warm work of it."

Blyth—"Yes, they seem to be waiting for us; and, as the Scotch witch said who was going to be burned, there will be no fun till we get there."[37]

Blyth led his raiders to the headmost gunboat and "sprang upon the deck . . . killing one man and wounding two others in the struggle."[38] Instead of being satisfied with capturing his prize, Blyth immediately turned the gunboat's twelve-pounder against its sister vessels. Unfortunately for himself and his comrades, their unfamiliarity with French artillery led to a terrible accident. As William James explained in his *Naval History*:

There was a quantity of cartridges lying on the deck, covered by a sail, and from these the British loaded the gun, but could find no lighted match. The gunner of the Quebec, *having primed the 12-pounder from a French powder-horn, which, from its peculiar construction scattered a part of the powder on the deck, discharged the piece by discharging his pistol at the priming, when, the fire,*

communicating with the loose powder on deck, and thence to the
cartridges under the sail, caused an explosion that killed or
wounded 19 persons, including Lieutenant Blyth himself . . .[39]

Blyth received burns over much of his body, including on his face, hands, and feet. He was hurled by the force of the explosion into the sea, but then managed to swim to one of the friendly boats and return to the *Quebec* in great pain, but victorious. Following the accident on the foremost gunboat, its sister vessels had all been carried by the raiders, making a complete success of the venture. However, the raid was not without its tragedy, as Marine Lieutenant Moore was "dreadfully scorched" in the explosion, and died the next day. Two others suffering from severe burns joined him.

Many more were badly hurt in the Friesland raid. Blyth, obviously suffering himself, soon after composed a letter to his wife, Delia, in which he stated, "My share of the prize-money I intend to give to the wounded."[40] For an officer who was barely getting by, this gesture was in many respects the truest measure of the man. Blyth was a leader. He deserved to command. "He had been six times wounded. . . ."[41] This is worth pondering. Samuel Blyth had nothing left to prove in battle, at sea or on land. He had been a credit to his nation in his dealings with its enemies as well as its allies. He had never asked for compensation or notoriety, only his own vessel. His time had come.

It was Samuel Blyth's Portuguese connection that finally tipped the scales in favor of his promotion. His friend, the Chevalier de Souza Coutralvo, the Portuguese minister in London, contacted the Admiralty the same month as the Friesland raid. Capitalizing on his friend's recent success, the chevalier pressed them to act. On September 5, 1811, Samuel Blyth was officially promoted to the rank of master and commander. Now it remained only to find him a vessel to command. Blyth's countryman of a later generation, the novelist and naval historian C. S. Forester, commented on Blyth's predicament:

It is a curious aspect of total war as waged at that time that England, fighting for her national existence, should find herself allowing young and vigorous men (Blyth was twenty-nine) to remain unemployed for these long intervals as a result of having distinguished themselves.[42]

Curious indeed. . . .

Samuel Blyth's native Hampshire was home to a number of busy shipyards. At one of these yards, that of Hobbs & Hellyer in Redbridge, construction was under way on one of the least desirable classes of vessel in His Majesty's Navy. The brig-sloop-of-war (or "gun brig") was notoriously slow and lightly armed. According to one opinion, these vessels were "neither strong enough to fight an American sloop, nor fleet enough to escape by flight."[43] Yet, they were built and apparently deemed to be of some value to the Royal Navy. If nothing else, brig-sloops of this sort allowed younger officers with the rank of commander, such as Samuel Blyth, to gain a vessel of their own—their very undesirability leading, at least partly, to their increased availability. Strangely, given their poor reputation, "the British had 150 in commission at the beginning of 1813. Thirty of these were of ten guns and the others rated at fourteen, sixteen, and eighteen guns."[44] One of these brig-sloops built by Hobbs & Hillyer was christened the *Boxer*. Launched on July 25, 1812, she was rated at 182 tons carrying twelve guns, "ten carronades and two long sixes"[45] (soon augmented by an additional two carronades). Carronades were short, stumpy-looking cannon that were lighter and required fewer men to handle them. They also threw a heavy shot at the opponent. However, their range was very limited. In general, they were only effective in close action. The long guns, on the other hand, were heavier and required more men to handle them, but their range and accuracy were devastating in competent hands. A brig-sloop such as this would not have been Samuel Blyth's first choice, but he recognized that if he failed "to catch his tide," he might never have a second opportunity. Thus, this unremarkable vessel would become inextricably linked in history to its remarkable commander. And if nothing else, the *Boxer*'s name fit the man.

Blyth learned of his first command in a note dated August 15, 1812. It read, "Lord Melville presents his compliments to Captain Samuel Blyth, and has great pleasure in acquainting him that he is appointed to the *Boxer*."[46] Melville's referring to Blyth as a "Captain" was a term of command, but as Melville was well aware, not in reference to his rank. A captain in the Royal Navy was an officer holding the rank of post-captain. This was not only a higher rank than master and commander, it was also a sure track to becoming an admiral . . . if one lived long enough. Blyth had not yet achieved this status. His advancement beyond his present station was in no way guaranteed. Again, he would have to fight his way to promotion. But now he had his own vessel. Blyth realized he now enjoyed "a fine opening for a young man to gain the next step in his profession, or a place in the Abbey."[*][47] Less than a month after his thirtieth birthday, Samuel Blyth left England for the last time. What did he say to his wife, Delia, when they parted? Perhaps there were tears, but also perhaps a hopefulness that his time in command of the *Boxer* might lead to bigger and better things for them both. After a brief stopover in Cork, Ireland, where he had his portrait painted, Blyth crossed the Atlantic bound for the Canadian Maritimes. A strange war beckoned.

---

[*]Westminster Abbey, where Britain's heroes are entombed.

CHAPTER 4

The *Enterprise*

"enterprise"—*"Boldness, energy, and invention in practical affairs"*

Maryland's Eastern Shore has a long history of shipbuilding. Its forests of white oak, yellow pine, and cedar reaching down to the Chesapeake Bay have provided the raw material shipwrights need to build. Sturdy white oak for the hulls, workable yellow pine for the planking, less resilient cedar for inshore craft. Among these Eastern Shore shipbuilders, the Spencer family name carried particular weight at the close of the eighteenth century. Since the colonial era they had been involved in the trade and had built an enviable reputation. In 1799, young Henry Spencer received a commission from Baltimore's naval agent, Jeremiah Yellott, to build a schooner based on a design attributed to Benjamin Hutton.[1] This was a great opportunity to demonstrate to the government that Spencer workmanship was sound, timely, and cost-efficient. A site was chosen in St. Michaels Harbor, workmen gathered, and axmen ventured forth from the shore to cut trees. Somewhere in a Maryland forest the *Enterprise*, the vessel that William Burrows would one day command in battle off Pemaquid Point, was born.

The *Enterprise* was not the first U.S. Navy vessel to carry that name. A hastily constructed craft that fought in the delaying action against Guy Carleton's invading flotilla on Lake Champlain in 1776 bears the distinction of being the first. It was beached and burned soon

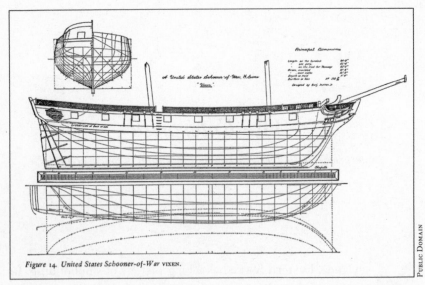

Figure 14. United States Schooner-of-War VIXEN.

Plans for U.S. schooner *Vixen* designed by Benjamin Hutton. No original
plans for *Enterprise* survive, but the *Vixen* was expressly desired by the
then-secretary of the navy to replicate the *Enterprise*.

after. The second *Enterprise* was an armed coastal schooner that operated in the Chesapeake theater of operations during the Revolutionary
War. Following the war's conclusion there is no further mention of this
second *Enterprise*. It was the third of the vessels that would carry this
name that would achieve the greatest fame. The impetus for the construction of the third Enterprise, as well as of a sister ship of very
similar design—the *Experiment*—was the undeclared quasi-war with
France, which was then taking its toll on American shipping. The
administration of President John Adams (1797–1801) was actively pursuing a more muscular naval policy and needed vessels to protect
American merchantmen and harass the enemy. When completed later
that same year, the *Enterprise* was rated at 135 tons; her keel measured
sixty feet; her deck, eighty-four feet in length, twenty-two feet six inches
in breadth. Her "bulwarks were pierced for 14 guns"[2] (though she was
rated as carrying 12 six-pounders). Finally, her hull was sheathed in

copper to prevent sea worms from burrowing into her underside. A naval officer of a later era described her thus:

> *She was not a fancy ship but from all accounts was an excellent example of the craftsmanship of the early Chesapeake ship-wrights . . . she had the sharp bow and sweeping lines favored by the Maryland shipbuilders.*[3]

The total cost of the *Enterprise* to the U.S. government came to $16,240.[4] The Spencer yards had produced a champion that would justify every cent that the government had invested in its construction.

AFTER BEING FITTED OUT at the head of the bay in Baltimore, the *Enterprise* was ordered south to join Thomas Truxton's West Indies Squadron. On December 17 the schooner headed for blue water under the command of Baltimore native John Shaw. One month later Midshipman William Burrows of Philadelphia put to sea aboard the corvette *Portsmouth* under the command of Daniel McNeil. The *Portsmouth* has been described as "something of a madhouse, the captain (McNeil) full of inexplicable caprices."[5] Midshipman Burrows was fourteen years old and painfully aware of his shortcomings as a seaman and as an aspiring officer. His silk-stocking background must have ill prepared him for his life at sea. As Mary Powers Anderson noted:

> *A midshipman was on the lowest rung of the naval officer's career ladder—senior only to the ship's cat. He was appointed by warrant and not commissioned, but was expected to climb into the commissioned ranks. It was an extremely hard way of life.*[6]

The Naval Academy at Annapolis did not yet exist; thus, young unseasoned officer candidates had to learn their craft "on the job," so to speak. Their lives were also lived in a degree of isolation (more socially and professionally than physically, as the cramped world of a man-of-war permitted little or no privacy). The entire system was in fact not very systematic at all. A young man like Burrows would have found "A midshipman's duties were usually anything the captain thought he ought to do. They were, as potential officers and gentlemen, quartered separately from the enlisted men, and were between the two worlds of officers and men, included in neither."[7]

One of the marked characteristics of William Burrows's naval career was the importance he attached to his standing among common seaman. As a teenager aboard the *Portsmouth* in his first Atlantic crossing, Burrows likely would have looked on with no small degree of awe at the skill with which the navy tars completed their tasks. Their ability was something he would never lose respect for. Their approbation was something he valued. Their care and comfort would become one of his priorities as an officer. Their concerns, and the very lives they led, would become a source of great interest for him as a man. Burrows was clearly a person who wanted to earn the right to lead from the bottom up. The standing his family enjoyed in Philadelphia held little influence aboard ship, in a world that was both limitless and claustrophobic at the same time. What the common seamen aboard the *Portsmouth* thought of the young midshipman is not known. However, in time, his reputation would grow among the tars.

And who were these men? In the Philadelphia of William Burrows's youth they were "far and away the single largest group of working men in the city."[8] Helping to build and protect an Atlantic future for the new republic, they tended to be disproportionately patriotic and Jeffersonian. They also tended to be shorter in stature than average American males, by nearly two inches.[9] Often living on the margins of polite society, seamen were proud, if often poor, and self-consciously aware of the elite skills they had mastered and the many tribulations they had endured. Bent (often literally) but unbowed, seamen represented the most independent nature in the new American man. This said, not all seamen made a career of the life. Many tried it on for a number of years before eventually settling down to pursue a living ashore. Some shipped out only seasonally, some only on a lark. One of the more remarkable features of maritime communities in eighteenth- and nineteenth-century America was the ease with which many young men (many only boys) signed on for voyages to distant fishing grounds and ports of call. The very ordinariness with which the practice was viewed surprises the modern reader. However, this had far-reaching consequences for the development of both the American maritime economy as a whole and for the American navy in particular. As Theodore Roosevelt explained:

> *On the New England seaboard but few of the boys would reach manhood without having made at least one voyage to the New-foundland Banks after codfish; and in the whaling towns of Long Island it used to be an old saying that no man could marry till he struck a whale. The wealthy merchants of the large cities would often send their sons on a voyage or two before they let them enter their counting-houses. Thus it came about that a large proportion of our population was engaged in seafaring pursuits of a nature strongly tending to develop a resolute and hardy character in the men that followed them.*[10]

Thus, the United States could draw upon a deep reservoir of men accustomed to life at sea and often possessing highly sought-after skills. Aboard the *Portsmouth* on Burrows's first cruise he would likely have found a mix of professional, lifelong seamen, and some who were more temporary. In either case, however, the life of a common seaman was tough, even brutal, with few comforts. Salt pork and salt beef were standard fare aboard ship, along with the dried peas and the infamous "hardtack" sea biscuit, which was so hard that it often first needed to be soaked before being bitten into. Clean drinking water was nonexistent. The "scuttlebutt" located at the bow end of the crew's quarters contained "sweet" water, but it was as likely to make one sick as not, if one's stomach was not accustomed to it. The single comfort permitted was the daily ration of rum mixed with lime juice and sugar ("grog"), but this was a mixed blessing. Alcohol consumption on the job is something few would recommend, let alone alcohol consumption on a job that requires often death-defying maneuvers aloft at dizzying heights on a heaving sea. Add to this the fact that sleep deprivation was a matter of course, and one could see how the consumption of grog could be deadly indeed. In the navy of that time it was expected that a seaman would work (or at least be at the ready) in twenty-hour shifts. This left only four hours for sleep. Any doctor could point out that this type of sleep deprivation would have severe consequences. However, on the three-, six-, sometimes nine-month-long cruises vessels would make, this was a necessary evil. The space for an individual to sling their hammocks and sleep was extremely limited. Furthermore, most vessels carried more than their assigned contingent of men in order to man hoped-for prizes. Simply put, the number of men on a ship far exceeded its capacity to provide sleeping quarters for them. Particularly on brigs, such as the one William Burrows would one day command, men often had to sling their hammocks in two layers—one above the other—leading to an unappealing nose-to-rear-end arrangement. Privacy was nonexistent. Men urinated and defecated directly into the sea from the "head" located at the bow. In rougher seas a seaman relieving himself in this manner might receive a not altogether unwelcome bidet.

Seasickness was a bane of newcomers, though interestingly some had to battle it their entire careers. Certainly, young William Burrows must have dealt with this condition at some point in his first voyage. A naval officer of a later era explained how on his initial shakedown cruise the older petty officers walked around the ship with sardines sticking very visibly out of the corners of their mouths during a patch of rough seas simply to torment the struggling junior officers.[11] This type of anecdote almost certainly had parallels of one sort or another in Burrows's era, and was just as likely to be seen in a humorous light. But one must keep in mind that for one enduring a bout of seasickness it is not at all funny. In extreme cases if one cannot keep down food and drink for an extended period, malnutrition and dehydration, even death, can ensue. For seamen, getting one's sea legs was a necessary development in order to function aboard ship. Whether this was primarily a conditioned or learned response, or whether genetic factors were most decisive, is inconclusive. Interestingly, the era's greatest naval hero, Horatio Nelson, was widely known to have been "sick in bad weather all his life."[12]

The seaman's life left its mark on the bodies of the men who made a career of it. Simon P. Newman described one such seaman:

> *Reading's small stature, his "brown" tanned complexion, distinctive clothes, and rolling gait, and especially the scars and tattoos that marked his body all proclaimed the fact that this man was one of the city's many seafarers . . . several inches shorter than was average for native-born white men. His visibly broken left elbow and the vivid scar on his right wrist illustrated the toll that seafaring could take.*[13]

Given the difficulties of this life, a seaman's greatest attribute may well have been what Patrick O'Brian referred to as his "power of living intensely in the present, with little or no regard for futurity." An approach that O'Brian termed "a feckless attitude, but one combined with uncommon fortitude."[14]

Broken bones, disease, rheumatism—all were far more common in seamen than in their fellow citizens on land. In dealing with these afflictions they turned to their shipmates for support. The loving hands of one's mother or sweetheart were far away, and one's mates, though a poor substitute, were all one had. Bonds between seamen could be very strong, even intimate to a certain degree. This was unsurprising given the smallness of the world they inhabited at sea. Homosexuality and life at sea have often been associated, perhaps most famously in Anthony Montague Browne's stinging assessment of the Royal Navy's propensity for "rum, sodomy, and the lash."* To refute this characterization to some degree goes against common sense, which reasons that placing large groups of young, virile men together in close quarters for extended periods of time without female companionship is bound to lead to at least some homosexual activity. That said, given that there was no privacy aboard a man-of-war, and that seamen only had four hours off each day during which they likely would have slept like dead men, it is hard to visualize when they would have had the time, space, or energy to engage in homosexual trysts.

What was characteristic for American jack-tars held true for their British cousins as well, though, in fact, on balance the Britons had it a bit worse. Rations were a little more scanty, and the harsher aspects of discipline were applied a little more liberally. And in the end, the Yankees were all volunteers—the same certainly could not be said of the Britons.

As WILLIAM BURROWS made his way across the Atlantic, the vessel he would one day command sailed into the aquamarine Caribbean Sea. The fighting in these waters oscillated between preying on weaker foes and flying from stronger ones. The French navy and French privateers had been loosed on Yankee shipping by the republican

---

*This quote has been widely misattributed to Winston Churchill, Browne's employer.

government in Paris, in no small measure out of French pique at the American government's unwillingness to extend and honor its earlier commitments to the now defunct Bourbon monarchy. No formal declaration of war had been made, but President Adams recognized the fighting at sea for what it was: a challenge to the United States as an independent power.

The *Enterprise*'s first encounter in this struggle occurred when, en route to St. Kitts, she fell in with the merchant brig *Polly* out of Wiscasset, Maine, which had been taken as a prize by a French privateer. The brig's captain, a seaman, and a boy who had been allowed to stay on board the *Polly* had successfully overpowered the eight-man French prize crew, and had regained control of their vessel. Lieutenant Shaw graciously volunteered a dozen of his own men to help this intrepid trio bring their brig into a friendly port.

During the remainder of the quasi-war, the *Enterprise* acquitted herself well—taking a number of prizes without becoming victim herself to more heavily armed vessels. Her greatest triumphs in the Caribbean came against the French privateers *L'Aigle* and *Flambeau*. In the engagement with *L'Aigle*, the *Enterprise* raked her opponent's stern with a broadside before carrying her with a boarding party. The *Flambeau* was taken only after a desperate struggle whose ferocity inspired Navy Secretary Stoddert to award the schooner's crew double prize money.[15] She also gained a reputation among her larger sister ships: "The logs of various frigates often noted that in rough seas with strong winds *Enterprize* had difficulty keeping up but in calm seas and light winds she could out sail them all."[16] The naval historian Fletcher Pratt summarized the *Enterprise*'s record in the quasi-war as thus:

> *All told,* Enterprise *took eighteen ships with a total of forty-two guns and three hundred prisoners, killed and wounded sixty-one of the enemy—no poor record for a ship of 12 guns and seventy men.*[17]

Eventually a treaty was negotiated between the United States and France, ending a war that never officially took place. The American envoys who brokered this peace had sailed aboard the *Portsmouth* along with Midshipman Burrows. His experience in France seems to have convinced him that his neglect of his studies of the French language as a boy would become a handicap to him as an aspiring naval officer. He also recognized his deficiency in mathematics and navigation (to a large degree one and the same thing on board a man-of-war). Granted a furlough of several months upon his return to the United States, Burrows aggressively pursued his studies in both French and navigation, achieving fluency in the first and an increasing confidence in the second. Even so, he wore the mantle of his status as an aspiring naval officer uncomfortably, and it was only "with great difficulty that he could be persuaded to wear the uniform of the navy."[18] His reasons appear to have been an exaggerated sense of humility, mixed with a genuine feeling of being unworthy to "exercise authority over the aged and veteran sailor, whom he considered his superior in seamanship."[19] No one was tougher on William than William. How much his father's status as commandant of the Marine Corps influenced the younger Burrows's career at this time is not altogether clear. The U.S. Navy was noted for its meritocratic ethos, as Paul Johnson noted:

> *On the high seas, American warships, both regulars and privateers benefited from the fact that their officers were appointed and promoted entirely on merit—one genuine advantage of republicanism—rather than on interest: as in the Royal Navy.*[20]

It is unlikely the elder Burrows interfered much, then, if at all. He understood all too well the life his son had chosen and could only hope he would serve under commanders of merit who also took their duties as teachers of midshipmen and junior officers seriously. In Edward Preble, his hopes would have been fulfilled.

Preble, commodore of the Mediterranean fleet and commander of the *Constitution* (nicknamed "Old Ironsides" for its seemingly impenetrable hull constructed of live oak), was a giant in the service. After completing his furlough and serving aboard the *Philadelphia* for a time, Burrows was ordered to the Mediterranean as a midshipman on Preble's flagship in 1803. The commodore has been described as having had "a violent temper," but also as being "a dynamic leader . . . adept at bringing out the capabilities of his subordinates."[21] The latter was certainly the case with William Burrows. Finally, in the heat and adventure of the wars against the Barbary pirates, Burrows came into his own, "under the approval of the frosty old demon on *Constitution*'s quarterdeck, he began to live the life he wanted, and his character opened out and developed."[22]

Burrows was mastering his craft and asserting himself as never before as he reached his nineteenth birthday far from home. He was living the life he had chosen, and he was doing better than merely surviving—he was beginning to excel. Preble, having taken an active interest in the young man's career (often inviting him to dine with

Enterprise vs. *Tripoli*, 1801

him), recommended Burrows for an acting lieutenant's commission. Considering that Preble had singled out and advanced the careers of the brightest stars in the youthful U.S. Navy, his recognition of Burrows was quite significant. Without the crucible of the Barbary pirate wars, however, Burrows's superior qualities might not have had a chance to blossom. To a certain extent, then, William Burrows had the pasha of Tripoli to thank for his turn of good fortune.

THE PASHA AND HIS FELLOW North African potentates along the Barbary Coast had for decades essentially terrorized any Westerners who ventured into the Mediterranean. Though their religion was Islam, and their victims were primarily Christian, their motive was monetary and not religious. Fair-skinned, fair-eyed captives could be sold for a handsome profit in the slave markets of the Arab world, or ransomed home for even larger profits. Over time, a less labor-intensive system was developed whereby Western governments simply negotiated an annual tribute payment to avoid attacks on their nationals. This was humbling, but practical, for countries like the United States, who had an increasing volume of merchant shipping in the Mediterranean region. But the agreements were shaky, and often entered into in something less than good faith. Matters finally reached a head in 1801 when the pasha of Tripoli, jealous of the rival Algerines' agreement with the United States, demanded equity. When this was not forthcoming, he ordered the flagpole in front of the U.S. consulate cut down and declared war.

The war between the pasha of Tripoli and the United States was in many ways a blessing for the U.S. Navy. It was able to demonstrate its usefulness to a presidential administration that was fundamentally hostile to maintaining a navy in the first place; it built up a mythology and tradition for the navy among the general public; and finally, it proved to be a most effective school in graduating top-caliber junior officers who would one day assume senior rank in a war against a more formidable foe. One of the vessels that proved to be at the center of the action during the conflict was the Maryland-built *Enterprise*. It was the only vessel not rated a frigate that made the transatlantic crossing in 1801, to "show the flag of the young Republic" and to "act as a deterrent to the ambitions of the rulers of the Barbary states."[23] These were dangerous waters, even for a swift schooner like the *Enterprise*. Andrew Sterett, the vessel's new commander (another Baltimore native), was given permission to fly whatever ensign he deemed wise to run up, although he was given strict orders not to fire his guns under any flag but the Stars and Stripes.[24] This disguising of vessels in order to avoid a fight or gain the element of surprise was a common ruse in naval warfare at the time. Thus, the *Enterprise* was flying the British Jack when it came within hailing distance of the Tripolitan vessel *Tripoli* of fourteen guns, commanded by Mohammed Sous. Sous complained he had been cruising for American vessels and regretted he had not come alongside any yet. Suddenly, Sterett ordered the British flag lowered and the American ensign raised. Marine marksmen opened up on the *Tripoli*, which replied with a broadside. The ensuing battle was a testament to the determination and courage of both sides. On three separate occasions the Tripolitans attempted to board and were repelled.

> For three hours the Enterprise *pounded away at her. Twice she struck and twice she treacherously opened fire again. The third time the Tripolitan commander threw his flag into the sea and begged for quarter. When the* Enterprise *took possession, the boarding officer, Lieutenant David Porter, found twenty dead and thirty wounded on her decks. The* Enterprise *had suffered no loss.*[25]

William Burrows's teacher and patron in the U.S. Navy,
Commodore Edward Preble

For his victory, Sterett was voted a commemorative sword by Congress, while his crew was voted an extra month's pay (apparently, though, no funds were appropriated for either[26]). Lacking the authority to take prizes, Sterett sent the *Tripoli* home in disgrace. Her commander, Mohammed Sous, was "ridden through the streets backward on a jackass and then bastinadoed[*] to show what the Tripolitans thought of anyone who gave up to an American."[27]

---

[*] Punishment or torture in which the soles of the victim's feet are beaten with a stick.

The reputation of the "lucky little *Enterprise*" was growing. It had demonstrated, both in the Caribbean and in the Mediterranean, the capacity to subdue any vessel its equal or its inferior in armament, while also demonstrating the capacity to outsail and avoid vessels that were its superior. Furthermore, in this, the first round of fighting in the Barbary pirate wars, she had been "the only United States naval vessel to engage the enemy."[28] In a fighting navy this was a significant mark of distinction. The *Enterprise*'s first tour of duty in the Mediterranean ended in the autumn of 1802, when Sterett was ordered to sail for her home port of Baltimore. However, by March 1803 the *Enterprise* was back at her station, swiftly navigating from one end of that ancient sea to the other as the war between Tripoli and the United States expanded.

By 1803 the other Barbary states (Morocco, Tunis, and Algiers) were in league against the United States, along with the pasha of Tripoli. They correctly sensed that if American defiance of Tripoli's increased demands was allowed to stand, they all would then be diminished in consequence. When Edward Preble assumed command he correctly surmised, however, that Tripoli was the main enemy and would have to be brought to heel first. In time the others would follow. Preble's inclination was to take the fight directly into Tripoli's well-fortified harbor, as well as to blockade it. During this time Burrows drew the attention of his frosty commander for his ability to work the main and main topsail braces, "a post for a seaman and probably the most important a midshipman could have."[29] Shortly thereafter Burrows was transferred to first the *Vixen*, then to the *Siren*, as sailing master responsible for each vessel's propulsion. Preble had clearly marked him out as a junior officer to watch. Not only was his seamanship of the highest caliber, his fearlessness was also manifest. In one incident during the war, he "rushed into the midst of a mutinous body, and seized the ring-leader, at the imminent hazard of his life."[30] Controlling hard men takes a hard man. The dreamy, brooding, pampered young Philadelphian had toughened into someone who could lead men, someone of substance. Burrows exhibited the characteristics (selflessness, daring, physical courage) that made many of his contemporaries and his immediate superiors stand out from the crowd: men such as Henry Wadsworth, Isaac Hull, Stephen Decatur, and David Porter. In fact, it was Decatur in command of the *Enterprise* in late 1803 who captured the ketch *Mastico* bound for Constantinople with a cargo of female slaves to fill the Sultan's harem.[31] Renamed *Intrepid*, the ketch was used in the most daring operation of the entire war, in which the captured U.S. frigate *Philadelphia* was burned by Decatur and a party of raiders to deny its use by the pasha's navy. No less than Horatio Nelson himself called Decatur's raid "the most bold and daring act of the age."[32] Considering the source, and the age, that is quite a statement. The *Intrepid*'s luck ran out when Preble ordered a skeleton volunteer force to sail the ketch between the pasha's castle and his fleet and blow it up after rowing away. The plan failed to come off when the *Intrepid* exploded prematurely, killing all hands, including young Henry Wadsworth. Boldness had its pitfalls, but these were considered acceptable in the aggressive climate Preble had cultivated. On five separate occasions in the late summer of 1804 Preble attacked the castles of Tripoli, with the *Enterprise* playing a significant supporting role. By 1805, the pasha had finally agreed to terms. The war was over.*

WILLIAM BURROWS HAD PLAYED a full part in what were increasingly being seen at the time, both inside and outside the navy, as the glorious and adventurous days of the Barbary pirate wars. But what had he

---

*The Tripolitans' neighbors, the Algerines, instigated a further war in 1807, which was not completely won by the United States until 1816.

missed? In the time he spent in the Mediterranean both his mother and father had died, and his elder sister Sarah had married. And what did they know of his heroics on the other side of the world? Apparently very little, or at least only what could be gleaned from others, as Burrows refused to present himself as anything other than competent, and that grudgingly. In 1815, only two years after his death off the Maine coast, his biographer Isaac Bailey commented on "the striking fact that none are more ignorant of the personal exploits of this officer than his own immediate relatives."[33] But perhaps this was also a symptom of living a life on another level of intensity than that lived on land. As another of Burrows's early biographers, Washington Irving, perceptibly commented:

> *The details of a sailor's life are generally brief and little satisfactory. We expect miraculous stories from men who rove the deep, visit every corner of the world, and mingle in storms and battles; and are mortified to find them treating these subjects with provoking brevity. The fact is, these circumstances that excite our wonder, are trite and familiar to their minds. He whose whole life is a tissue of perils and adventure, passes lightly over scenes at which the landsman, accustomed to the security of his fireside, shudders even in imagination. Mere bravery ceases to be a matter of ostentation, when everyone around him is brave; and hair breadth escapes are commonplace topics among men whose very profession consists in the hourly hazard of existence.*[34]

In the years immediately following the war, Burrows served on board the light frigate *Essex*; then, upon finally returning home to the United States in 1807, he was given command of a gunboat, no. 119, posted in Delaware Bay. The purpose of these gunboats was essentially to enforce an unpopular embargo on trade with Europe. This was a far cry from storming the battlements of the pasha's castles. For a young man like Burrows brimming with ability and ambition, to be placed in this situation was at best an oversight, and at worst a provocation. Then president Thomas Jefferson's secretary of the navy, Robert Smith, had earlier developed an adversarial relationship with Burrows's father, the elder William Ward Burrows. This had its origins in the elder Burrows's staunchly Federalist politics, which aligned him with the minority party at that time in Washington. Smith shared the view of many in Jefferson's administration that a blue-water navy was to a certain degree undesirable. The Marine Corps that the elder Burrows had worked diligently to build was therefore also largely expendable. In 1804, as the elder Burrows looked to his retirement, Smith penned a note in which he cast aspersions on the elder Burrows's character:

> . . . as there is a large balance to your debit on the books of this department, it is expected that you will without delay repair to this place for the purpose of settling this balance.[35]

"The balance" turned out to be a total of $9,428—an amount nine times the elder Burrows's salary as Marine Corps commandant. A congressional investigation indicated no wrongdoing on the elder Burrows's part, but recommended changes in how the Marine Corps kept track of future expenditures. It was an embarrassing end to a distinguished career, and was most likely intended to be so. The naval historian Fletcher Pratt, in *Preble's Boys* (1950), made the assertion that with the elder Burrows's death in 1805, the sins of the father were then visited upon the son. His evidence, though circumstantial, is compelling, in that of all of the junior officers Edward Preble singled out for swift promotion, Burrows alone failed to rise rapidly. Whether Navy Secretary Smith had a vendetta against the Burrows family or not, the feeling on the part of the younger Burrows that he had been unfairly passed over for promotion began to eat away at him. His propensity for withdrawing inwardly and for donning common seaman's garb and secretly exploring "all the dives of the seaport towns in search of matters of interest"[36] increased. What this says about Burrows as a man is open to conjecture. Perhaps as the scion of such a prominent family his behavior was simply an extension of his earlier rejection of the Philadelphia elite, their tastes and values. Or possibly it allowed him to do things that he could not do as an officer and a gentleman. He clearly had far too much respect for the common seamen under his command to merely have been "slumming" it in order to amuse himself at their expense. He looked up to these men, not down on them.

Certainly, William Burrows was unusual in his decision to immerse himself so intimately in the haunts of these men. What would he have found there? Alcohol for one—seamen liked their rum, but were not averse to beer, wine, and other spirits. Song—though men-of-war were technically silent when under way, the folk rhythms of maritime life were never far below the surface and gushed forth ashore as seamen boasted, pined, and made merry to lyrics that most often came from within their own ranks. And finally women (or boys dressed as women). Some were prostitutes, some were hangers-on, many were the underemployed and destitute widows or discarded sweethearts of other seamen. The incidence of venereal disease among seamen was significantly higher than the average at that time in America.[37] William Burrows, the grandson of a South Carolina planter, would also likely have been rubbing shoulders with blacks as well as whites. By one estimate better than one in five seamen were of African-American or African descent.[38] In donning common seaman's garb he was crossing lines not only of class, but likely of race as well. Certainly, if he had been recognized by his shipmates, it is reasonable to assume a degree of awkwardness must have been felt, but either he avoided the haunts favored by men from his own vessel or they avoided talking about it. Port culture was a culture between, with the life of the sea and that of the shore coexisting on more or less equal terms. Its nature was also to a large degree temporary, with an intense debauch of hours, or days at most, followed by months of separation. If nothing else, as a result of his forays Burrows gained an insight into the lives of those under his command few if any officers ever had. As Fletcher Pratt explained:

> *He spoke the language of the seamen, understood their agitations and, when they had any, their ambitions; was always ready to get them out of trouble, and did so on numerous occasions. No officer but Decatur had so good a reputation with the lower deck.*[39]

With his own kind, Burrows came off as subdued on the one hand, and droll and brimming with anecdotes on the other. As Isaac Bailey noted based on interviews with those who served with Burrows, "between mock solemnity and uncontrollable mirth, lieutenant Burrows was pre-eminent."[40] His sense of humor was dry, his sense of discretion noteworthy. It was remarked of him that he was "zealous in the performance of secret and important services for those to whom he was attached."[41] What these "secret and important services" were will likely remain unknown, but they add a certain mystique to the man. He was trusted, that much is clear. A letter from this period from Burrows to Commodore Rodgers concerning a vessel's cargo displays handwriting that is elegant yet strong.[42]

Following his depressing turn in Delaware Bay, Burrows was transferred to the frigate *President*, then to the sloop *Hornet*. In one of the few surviving accounts of Burrows's exploits during this period, his brother officers aboard the *Hornet* "during a violent and dangerous gale . . . attributed the preservation of the ship entirely to his presence of mind and consummate seamanship."[43] The latter was something that Burrows took great pride in. He had come a long way indeed from that first green cruise to France in 1800. But his ability was not matched by promotion. With Preble's death in 1807 from tuberculosis, Burrows had lost an important patron. His father's staunchly Federalist politics seemed to continue to dog him, and those who had been his juniors now leapfrogged him in the service. For a man who had given everything to the navy—who defined himself by it—this was a moment of personal crisis. As Washington Irving remarked:

> *Men of gayer spirits and more mercurial temperament, may readily shake off vexation, or bustle it away amid the amusements and occupations of the world; but Burrows was scanty in his pleasures, limited in his resources, single in his ambition.*[44]

Though he had risen to become first lieutenant under James Lawrence aboard the *Hornet*, he coveted his own command. Finally, in 1811, he submitted his resignation to Secretary of the Navy Hamilton.

LIKE THE YOUNG OFFICER who was one day destined to command her off Pemaquid Point, the *Enterprise* also entered a period of crisis following her early successes. Lieutenant Thomas Robinson, in command of the vessel in 1805, reported her laid up for repairs in Venice, Italy. He remarked that "she was almost completely rotten."[45] Time and tide had done what her enemies had failed to accomplish. However, by the spring of that year Robinson could report, "SIR The *Enterprise* was returned to her Ellement in the same handsome stile & masterly manner with which she withdrew from its embrace."[46] A return to service, then a return home, followed by a third Mediterranean tour continued to wear on the "lucky little *Enterprise*." In 1811, hauled into dry dock at the Washington Naval Yard across the Chesapeake from the shore of her birth, the *Enterprise* was "cut in two and lengthened by about twelve feet."[47] It was almost as if a new vessel was being built, as she was "completely rebuilt from the floor-timbers up."[48] The reasons for this Frankenstein-like transformation were essentially to remake the *Enterprise* into a more heavily armed brig capable of carrying a larger complement of men. The trim schooner that had arisen in the Spencer shipyard was no more. As Sherwood Picking observed:

An immaterial increase in armament had been obtained at the expense of a decrease in speed. Most enemy vessels were still superior to her in gun power and now she no longer had the legs to run from their overwhelming superiority in guns.[49]

On April 8, 1811, Johnston Blakely took command of the *Enterprise.* Ordered south into the Gulf of Mexico, she was stationed there during the early part of the War of 1812 between the United States and Britain. On January 2, 1813, Blakely left New Orleans en route to Portsmouth, New Hampshire, arriving there approximately five months later. Portsmouth was a substantial town possessing a strong sense of its colonial history and its maritime traditions. The embargo and the war, however, had drained the town of its lifeblood of sea trade. Blakely set about trying to clear the New Hampshire–Maine coast of enemy privateers, capturing the *Fly* as a prize soon thereafter. In August 1813 word reached Blakely he was to be given command of one of the new sloops that had recently been built, the *Wasp.* Thus, the *Enterprise* was set to receive a new commanding officer, her eighth since she was launched in 1799.

William Burrows looked ahead to an uncertain future in the U.S. Navy. His resignation had been refused by Secretary of the Navy Hamilton. No promotion to command his own vessel was forthcoming, and war with Britain—the one possibility to rise quickly—seemed remote. Following the voyage in which he had saved the *Hornet* in a hurricane, he remarked that he "was convinced the government would never get up the backbone to do anything about the long-continued British aggressions."[50] Burrows clearly saw Britain as the instigator, but this was more an objective rather than passionate observation on his part.

In March 1812 he applied for, and was granted, a furlough to serve as first mate of the merchantman *Thomas Penrose* bound for Canton, China. The *Thomas Penrose* was part of Philadelphia's great commercial fleet, which had penetrated so deeply into the Asian market in the decades of the 1780s–1810s. This was potentially a golden opportunity for Burrows to switch tack midcareer and pursue a more lucrative, if less illustrious, occupation as an officer in the merchant marine. Venturing farther abroad than he had ever done, Burrows rounded the Cape of Good Hope aboard the *Thomas Penrose* and sailed into the Indian Ocean. However, by the time he had navigated up the Pearl River Delta to Canton with its large foreign settlement and its distinct Chinese sights, smells, and attractions, war had been declared. For a man like Burrows, the return voyage must have been torturously slow as he realized with anticipation and anxiety that he might finally have the chance to make his name. To make matters worse, the *Thomas Penrose* was taken as a prize off the West Indies by the British, and he and his fellow crewmates were held as prisoners in Barbados, awaiting exchange and unable to reach home. This process, in which the honor of the exchanged was indispensable, meant that Burrows and his compatriots were eventually permitted to take passage home on the understanding that they would not take up arms against Britain until one of their opposite numbers in American detention was formally swapped for them. In Burrows's case this did not take long. Finally, he faced Navy Secretary Hamilton, who held in his hand orders for Burrows to report to Portsmouth, New Hampshire, with all due haste to assume command of the U.S. brig *Enterprise*. Hamilton's admonition to "take that brig and fight yourself into notice!"[51] certainly did not fall on deaf ears. Burrows had every intention of doing just that, then telling the navy to go hang—confiding to a friend "that he would serve during the war, and that he would then dash his commission in the fire."[52] This was not a man fueled by an overwhelming sense of outrage at Britain's deprivations; this was a professional who recognized that this was perhaps his one and only opportunity to show what he could do in command.

The Portsmouth Naval Yard* sits on an island in the Piscataqua River from which the docks and lights of Portsmouth, New Hampshire, can be easily seen. Now spanned by a number of bridges, the Piscataqua at that time could only be crossed by ferry. William Burrows arrived on the Maine side of the river in a rowboat and reached the navy's most recent acquisition (a farm being converted into a navy yard) to report to its new commander, Isaac Hull. Hull had served with Burrows in the Mediterranean and had commanded the *Enterprise* for a time as well. It must have pleased him to see a worthy and deserving officer being given command of a vessel to which he was sentimentally attached. In point of fact, the *Enterprise* was out at sea when Burrows reported for duty but returned the following morning, anchoring off Kittery Point in Pepperell Cove. It was here that William Burrows took command of a man-of-war, in a time of war, for the first time. It was here that the *Enterprise*, no longer the trim schooner of yore, was taken command of by the man who would bring to her name more fame than had ever previously been attached to it. All in a war that the local people, for the most part, curiously, did not support. Why was this so?

---

*The yard's actual location is in Kittery, Maine, not Portsmouth.

CHAPTER 5

The War

As Samuel Blyth and William Burrows made their ways inexorably toward their common fate off the Maine coast, the war that had drawn them into its vortex was carried on in a confused manner by two oddly paired antagonists. Why were Britain and the United States fighting each other? This is not just a question for scholars today. It was a question being asked by people on both sides of the Atlantic at the time.

The War of 1812, which in fact lasted until 1815, is one of the least understood conflicts either the United States or Britain has ever been involved in. For Canadians it registers of far greater weight historically, largely for nationalistic reasons, yet to a large degree is equally misunderstood. That it was a war of choice fought to achieve multiple and sometimes conflicting aims on the part of the United States has added to this general cloudiness about the war. The United States at that time could be compared to a big, ruddy, raw-boned youth full of energy and promise, but also somewhat uncouth and lacking polish. The generation that had come of age after the Revolution produced political leaders like Henry Clay who were half statesman and half huckster. It was these men more than any others, along with the leader of France, Napoleon Bonaparte, who wanted the war to happen. Like many wars before and since, the full consequences of going to war with Britain in 1812 were not anticipated by Clay and his fellow war hawks. In the end the conflict brought on a national crisis that the youthful United States barely escaped from in one piece. The war also, to a very large degree, created another nation. Canada could be taken by the Kentucky Militia alone according to Clay.[1] As it turned out, it could not be; and not by the regular U.S Army, either, such as it was. For Britain the war was a bloody, aggravating sideshow to an even bloodier and more desperate struggle, without which, perhaps, the War of 1812 would never have happened at all.

THE AMERICAN REVOLUTION OF 1775–1781, and the French Revolution that followed in 1789, altered the balance of powers in the world in ways those same powers were still sorting out as the nineteenth century began. This altered balance of power was not simply between countries and empires, but between classes within the countries and empires themselves. The old order was giving way to a new, more inclusionary system of governance. Whether this transition would be orderly and gradual or sudden and violent was at the heart of the conflict between Britain and France. The former had seen the cost of disallowing an orderly and gradual transition to a more equal relationship with its American cousins and had lost a sizable portion of its empire as a result. The lesson stung, but it had been learned. The latter had embraced a more radical vision of the future that the British found fundamentally disturbing. And even more disturbing, the French were looking to export it. In any event, these two revolutions were truly earth-changing. As the noted British historian L. C. B. Seaman wrote:

> *The American and French Revolutions proclaimed two astonishing facts, new in the experience of European man. The first was*

that men could wage war successfully against their rulers. The colonists had by violence freed themselves from the King of Britain. The French had by violence freed themselves from the House of Bourbon and gone on to overthrow or humiliate the ruling dynasties of all Europe. Such a thing had never happened in European history. There had been wars between dynasty and dynasty, between turbulent feudal lords, between city-states and empires, or between Christians and heathen peoples such as Arabs, Moors, Turks, and American Indians. But the idea that subjects could make war successfully against their hereditary rulers was to open up possibilities in the field of politics as awe-inspiring as those presented to a later age by the discovery of nuclear fission.[2]

In the end then, the War of 1812 was to a large extent about Britain's attempt to halt the onslaught of France's revolution, while for America, it was an attempt to consolidate, even expand, the gains of its own.

Perhaps no other American encapsulated this tumultuous, contradictory age as much as the third president of the United States. Thomas Jefferson embraced the French Revolution during his time in Paris representing the United States, but cautioned against the "tyranny of the majority."[3] He wrote of "liberty" as an "unalienable right" yet owned a vast plantation worked by slave labor. He opposed the expansion of the youthful U.S. Navy, yet used it to exert American muscle in support of American claims thousands of miles from its home waters against the Barbary pirates. He loathed Britain, yet was very much a member of the landed gentry of Virginia, which had been consciously modeled on that of Britain. He firmly believed that wars of conquest were wrong, yet fully supported the absorption of Canada if the opportunity presented itself. His party, founded in defiance of George Washington's appeal to avoid such a political system, rose to power on a wave of public disenchantment with the administration of the second president of the United States, John Adams. Adams had adopted Draconian measures to silence political opponents and to limit or eliminate foreign influence on the American body politic. This foreign influence was seen as French radicalism, and it was associated with Jefferson and his supporters. The Jeffersonians countered with claims of Adams posturing as a European-style monarch—too conservative, too closely aligned with Britain and the commercial interests wedded to Britain. Jefferson wanted a revolutionary America, one that would stand as an isolated experiment if necessary. He did not want an alliance, even of a commercial nature, with Britain. Nor could he ignore the rise of Napoleon and the new liberal empire of the French he had proclaimed. In Jefferson's presidency (1801–1809) lay the seeds of the War of 1812. The United States was both uncertain of itself and its place in a world at war. Britain had no such qualms.

To the British, Napoleon was merely the latest in a succession of threats arising from the European continent aiming at hegemony. Philip II's Spanish Armada, Louis XIV's wars of conquest and succession, and now Bonaparte, fighting in the name of liberalism and nationalism, but in reality a familiar enemy. What made this old opponent in its newest incarnation more toxic was its insistence of having history (that is, the French Revolution) on its side. Great Britain as it chose to see itself, the embodiment of restraint, political and otherwise, felt a historical obligation to meet and defeat this old/new threat. In this war its two greatest assets were its economic muscle and its naval muscle. However, in exerting these it placed itself on a confrontational course with its former colonies.

One of the great facts, often overlooked, of early American history is the significance of the United States' maritime culture. The historian Frederick Jackson Turner shaped the thinking of generations of his countrymen when he proclaimed his "Frontier Thesis" at a meeting of the American Historical Association in 1893. This thesis focused on the westward expansion of the young nation, and the frontier's seminal importance in shaping and creating American values. It also raised the troubling question of "what next?" as the frontier line had officially been declared indefinable three years earlier by the U.S. Census Bureau. What Turner's thesis overlooked, however, was the role the Atlantic and the seas generally had played in defining American identity. Both the fisheries and the merchant trade were of far greater importance in the early years of the United States, and in the colonial era that had preceded it, than expansion into the interior of the continent of North America. It was the aggressive expansion of Yankee merchant vessels into European and Asian markets that generated the greatest wealth and forced the new nation to confront an unstable world. Handsome profits could be made trading with both sides in the European war, but it was a tricky balancing act. Eventually, first France then Britain forced the issue by in essence declaring trade with the enemy by neutral vessels a hostile activity. Napoleon's Berlin and Milan decrees, and the British Orders in Council, were used as a justification for seizing ships and cargoes. Unsurprisingly, American ships and American cargoes were hit hard. If it had only been property that was being seized, however, the intensity of feeling that at least partially led to the war would have been averted. Unfortunately, the Royal Navy was not just seizing property.

"IMPRESSMENT" WAS ONE OF THE ugliest terms that came out of this period. To Americans, particularly seamen, it stood for everything they disliked about Britain. Arrogance, high-handedness, brutality—all were associated in the American mind with this term. For Britons, too, it had a negative connotation. Basically, the Royal Navy had an enormously large number of vessels to be manned and did not have enough able-bodied men to man them. In a country at war, located on an island, relying on its overseas trade and empire for prosperity, this state of affairs was little short of a crisis. Press gangs from British ships were notorious for essentially kidnapping any likely-looking fellow who had the misfortune to be on the wrong street at the wrong time in the wrong port town. But these actions could be justified as a necessary evil to contain Napoleon. It was not a time for half measures. American seamen could be found in almost any port in Europe at that time, either temporarily ashore from the merchantmen they were serving aboard or temporarily out of work and looking to sign on with a new outfit. That some would be swept up in the dragnet was nearly inevitable. They spoke English, they looked English, in some instances they had been born in the British Isles, and moreover they were skillful mariners, making them a highly valued commodity. To be forced aboard a Royal Navy ship and be subject to Royal Navy discipline was no small matter. Lemuel Norton, a seaman and Maine native, recalled the dread of the press gang:

Portsmouth is one of the largest naval stations in England, and is generally thronged with men-of-war of the largest class—such as are termed line-of-battleships. Here, too, expeditions are often fitted out in time of war in great haste. On these occasions press gangs patrol the streets by night and by day, utterly regardless of whom they meet, if hand is hard, which they immediately ascertain by feeling of his palm. Whether he be English, Dutch, French, or American, it makes no difference—away he must go to the watch house and be examined, and if unable to prove his identity or satisfy the recruiting officer that he is not an Englishman, protection or no protection, he the next morning is marched down to a boat and taken on board some ship-of-war, and ere finds

himself on the high seas in the midst of battle and war, surrounded
by death and carnage.[4]

This took an even more sinister turn when American seamen were
pressed directly off American merchant ships during inspections and
seizures by the Royal Navy. Theodore Roosevelt, in his *Naval War of*
1812, argued forcefully that this was the main cause of the war:

> *Any innocent merchant vessel was liable to seizure at any*
> *moment; and when overhauled by a British cruiser short of men*
> *was sure to be stripped of most of her crew. The British officers*
> *were themselves the judges as to whether a seaman should be*
> *pronounced a native of America or Britain, and there was no*
> *appeal from their judgment. If a captain lacked his full comple-*
> *ment there was little doubt as to the view he would take of any*
> *man's nationality. The wrongs inflicted on our seafaring country-*
> *men by their impressment into foreign ships formed the main cause*
> *of the war.*[5]

That this was indeed *the* main cause of the war is debatable, but it
certainly was *a* main cause. Another debatable point in Roosevelt's
thesis is his assertion that these were "innocent merchant vessel[s]."
To British eyes, neutrality in the tense climate that existed in Europe
was a dangerous luxury, and one Americans could do little to uphold
regardless. It is also important to keep in mind that the overwhelming
majority of seamen pressed in the Royal Navy were in fact British
subjects. In his novel *Beat to Quarters*, C. S. Forester's commander
Horatio Hornblower muses on his predominantly British crew:

> *... three quarters of them had never been sailors until this com-*
> *mission, and had no desire to be sailors either ... He had*

*waggoners and potters—he had even two draper's assistants and
a printer among his crew; men snatched without notice from their
families and their employment and forced into this sort of labour,
on wretched food, in hideous working conditions, haunted always
by fear of cat* or . . . rattan, and with chance of death by drowning or by hostile action to seal the bargain.[6]*

British subjects bore the brunt of the press gangs' reach, not Americans. But those Americans, or foreign-born seamen, serving aboard
U.S. merchantmen who were "pressed" cared little for this distinction.[†]

Ultimately, however, were the British right? Was impressment
simply the ugly but necessary stepchild of the island's noble struggle
with continental tyranny? What if the blockade, begun when Blyth
was still a boy ashore, had not held? What if Napoleon had been confident enough to launch his splendid army into transports to cross the
Channel and invade England? What then? Would the United States
have become Napoleon's next target? Was then Britain being unfairly
maligned, when in fact through her considerable exertions she was
doing what she had to do to keep the wolf at bay, not just from her own
door but from the United States' door? The answer is clearly yes.
Whatever Napoleon's legion of admirers may want to claim about their
hero, the fact remains he had more in common with Adolf Hitler than
with any other figure in European history. Both had unlimited aims
and the mind-sets of conquerors. Britain's methods may have been
questionable, but her ultimate purpose justified them. Americans at the
time, however, could be forgiven for not recognizing this.

For his part, Jefferson's attempt to limit the intercourse of

---

*Cat-o'-nine-tails, the whip used to punish seamen.
†To the modern reader, impressment may sound too unjust to be believable, but
that's how it was—it was not unlike the child soldiers one reads about in places like
Uganda in our own time. It seems so unjust that it cannot be true, yet it is.

Americans with Europeans via an ill-conceived embargo in his second term as president was unsustainable given the aforementioned significance of the maritime economy to the United States. What could be done then? Jefferson may have looked into the continent's interior for answers, imagining an idealized farmer-citizenry practicing self-government removed from Europe's corrupting influence and hazardous entanglements. However, even in the interior conflict beckoned and proved this insulated vision a mirage. Later generations would call this "isolationism." But as it was forced to relearn again in 1917 and 1941, a country with the United States' vast territorial and overseas market-driven ambitions could not have its cake and it eat too.

Caught in the middle of this were the interior's native peoples, or "First Nations," to adopt a Canadian term. These First Nations (Ottawa, Wyandot, Winnebago, Potawatomi, Mohawk, Miami, Shawnee, and others) laid claim to much of what now comprises part or all of one Canadian province and six American states. The North American "cake" had been divided by treaty twice (1783, 1794) between the United States and the British Empire. On both occasions the First Nations felt their interests had been abandoned by their British benefactors. Since Pontiac's rebellion some four decades earlier, the reaction to the seemingly endless flood of American settlers onto native lands had been intensely violent. In many respects the roots of the War of 1812 can be found in both Britain's attempts to support their native allies, and in American attempts to isolate the First Nations from the British and essentially pick them off one by one, by force or by treaty. Though the phrase "Manifest Destiny" had yet to be coined, the powerful feelings behind it were already there—in fact, had been there since the earliest settlements. If a fight was coming ostensibly over maritime rights, why not take advantage of it to deal a crushing blow to British power in North America? At the very least, the native threat could be eliminated once and for all in the old Northwest, and the seizure of Upper Canada (today's Ontario) could be used as a bargaining chip in negotiations if not annexed outright. It was these aims that motivated men like Clay, as well as the future seventh president of the United States, Andrew Jackson, though in Jackson's case his territorial ambitions for his country ran to the southeast into the Creek nation and Spanish Florida. Thus, the causes of the war in which Samuel Blyth and William Burrows would find themselves on opposite sides were not absolutely clear-cut. The one certainty was that the war was a war of choice on the part of the United States; whether primarily to assert its rights at sea or to consolidate its territorial expansion in the northwest and southeast was the question being asked then, and one debated by historians of the war since.

TO PREPARE PUBLIC OPINION FOR WAR, and convince the public's representatives to vote for it, is not a simple matter in a country that has not been directly attacked. Perhaps isolated settlers, victims in a raid by native peoples, who had seen loved ones killed, might need little convincing. Otherwise, the war Clay and his fellow hawks were pushing was an abstraction to most Americans. France was seen by many to be as much or more of a potential threat than Britain. And why war in 1812? Why not in 1807 when HBMS *Leopard* fired into the USS *Chesapeake* at point-blank range in an act of unprovoked, naked aggression? The simple answer was that Thomas Jefferson was still president and wanted to keep his country well clear of a European war. The British reprimanded the *Leopard*'s commander and made official apologies and compensation, but in the end there was no war because there was no will to war on the part of Jefferson, and by extension the party he led. This party, interchangeably referred to as both Republicans and Democratic-Republicans in the press of the day (though neither of the present-day parties in the United States can legitimately trace their roots to

Jefferson's party), had gained new leadership, however, by 1812. In both the Congress and in the White House, Republicans with more assertive policies vis-à-vis Britain were in charge. The *situation* had changed little from Jefferson's presidency, but the *will* for war had changed.

When finally put to a vote in 1812, on the eve of both congressional elections and a presidential election, the measure for war passed 79–49 in the House and 19–13 in the Senate. Thus, the decision to go to war with the greatest naval power in the world was approved by percentages of less than two-thirds each (61 percent in the House, 59 percent in the Senate). Moreover, as the historian Donald Hickey pointed out:

> . . . *the vote on the war bill was essentially a party vote. About 81% of Republicans in both houses of Congress voted for the measure (98–23), while all the Federalists voted against it (39–0).*[7]

Rarely has a war been embarked on with such lack of national solidarity as the War of 1812, and never in American history. Proof of this can be seen in the highly charged decision by President George W. Bush to go to war with Iraq in 2003. In the congressional vote in late 2002 that authorized Bush to make war on Iraq if diplomacy failed, the measure passed 296–133 in the House and 77–23 in the Senate.[8] Like Britain, Iraq had not attacked the United States, but also like Britain it had been accused of arming and instigating nonstate actors to attack the United States on its home soil, with a suggested association with al-Qaeda and the 9/11 attackers* in place of hostile American Indians on the warpath. However, in comparison, the percentages in favor of war with Iraq were 68 percent and 77 percent, respectively. The polarizing nature of the War of 1812 domestically in the United States was there from its inception. Just as the Iraq War divided a later

---

* It is worth recalling that this association was, ultimately, unfounded.

generation of Americans, the War of 1812 divided an earlier one. The results were equally painful, and perhaps more so.

Toward the end of the war a group of Federalist politicians representing the remnants of John Adams's old party gathered in Connecticut's state capital to draft a document calling for revisions to the U.S. Constitution. The first of seven proposed amendments called for "a two-thirds vote in Congress to declare war. . . ."[9] Though branded traitors by many of their opponents, and to a large degree subsequent generations of Americans, one could argue that they were onto something.

One of Clay's biggest problems in the push for war was his inability to explain the compelling reasons for it in a cogent manner. His president (and Jefferson's successor), James Madison, found it equally difficult to explain. This being the case, one could well reach the conclusion that if one cannot convince a sizable majority of his or her countrymen of the overwhelming reasons to go to war, then perhaps one should not go to war. To fight and kill, to lose an eye or an arm or a testicle, to lose one's life in a war in which one's political leaders cannot even explain the reasons for it in a direct fashion, this must have tested a man. Many did kill, many were dismembered, and many did die. The war had everything: fiasco, furious hand-to-hand combat, daring raids, treasonous smugglers, massacre, and sea combat at a level of skill unprecedented in the Age of Sail. It had everything but a winner in the usual sense, though it certainly had clear-cut losers.

THE UNITED STATES' PLAN FOR winning the war rested on two assumptions: (1) that Canada was there for the taking, and (2) that Napoleon would keep Britain busy in Europe and thus unable to bring her full force to bear on the United States. Both of these turned out to be wrong. Canada, with its relatively small population and overstretched

British garrison, was invaded in three places in 1812–1813 by U.S. forces: north across the New York State–Lower Canada (Quebec) frontier; west across the Niagara River; and east across the Detroit River. The first was a fiasco; the second was a tough, drawn-out fight that lasted well into 1814; and the last was an initially shocking humiliation that, however, the commander of a second attempt managed to salvage a major victory from. This latter battle was the Battle of the Thames in today's Ontario, in which the would-be leader of a grand First Nations alliance was cut down. This man was Tecumseh, and his nemesis was the governor of Indiana Territory, a Virginian by birth like Jefferson and Madison, William Henry Harrison. Harrison's victory stood in stark contrast to his predecessor, who surrendered his fortified position at Detroit on American soil to a force inferior in size, but certainly not in nerve. The British commander who captured Detroit, Isaac Brock, became a figure of almost mythical significance to later generations of Canadians. Throughout the early period of the war, he showed himself to be both daring and resourceful. He also understood the value of psychological warfare, writing Detroit's American commander a note urging surrender, but suggesting something darker as an alternative to surrender:

> *It is far from my intention to join in a war of extermination but you must be aware, that the numerous body of Indians who have attached themselves to my troops will be beyond control the moment the contest commences.*[10]

This was no idle threat, as the American garrison and their families at Fort Dearborn (Chicago) had been nearly wiped out by native warriors at this time after receiving orders to abandon their post. Brock fell to American bullets a short time later defending the Niagara frontier, but in the process became a martyr to Canadian nationalism vis-à-vis American aggression. The irony to a certain degree was that

Canada's great national hero of the war their nation "won" (as Malcolm Gladwell notably claimed)[11] was not Canadian at all. Neither were the great majority of Canada's defenders on land or on the Great Lakes. As the prominent Canadian military historian J. Mackay Hitsman explained:

> *The British regular bore the brunt of the fighting and suffered the heaviest casualties throughout the war. . . .*[12]

Hitsman continued:

> *The exploits of [Canadian] militia flank companies which accompanied Brock to Detroit and those which fought as auxiliaries at*

Isaac Brock, intrepid British Army officer who became
a Canadian national hero

The War

Queenston Heights, stalwart as they were, were soon exaggerated by local patriotism and seem to be the basis for the hardy myth that Canada in this war was successfully defended by the militia, with only small help from the British Army.[13]

If "winning" the war meant keeping Canada part of the British Empire and not part of the United States, then Canadians can certainly claim victory. But this victory was won for them, not by them.

IF THE ATTEMPT TO CONQUER Canada was a frustrating failure, the hope that Napoleon would keep Britain preoccupied was equally disappointing. Following his hubris-filled attempt to conquer Russia and dictate a peace to its czar, Napoleon was consistently on the defensive. With his defeat and abdication as emperor of the French in early 1814, Britain could now concentrate her forces to punish the United States. These sentiments were shared by a vocal segment of the British press. The *Morning Post* expressed the view that the American government needed to be "beaten into a sense of their unworthiness and their incapacity." The *Times* opined, "They are struck to the heart with terror for their impending punishment . . . Strike! chastise the savages for such they are."[14] Certainly the most famous of the British attempts to punish the United States was the raid on Washington on August 24–25, 1814. Boldly and ably led by the British army officer Robert Ross, the raid made Washington a perfect victim not of British arms, but of American lack of preparedness. The secretary of war abdicated his responsibilities; the commanding general was incompetent, and the government was in paralysis. The idea that the British, who marauded throughout the Chesapeake Bay region with relative impunity, would be so audacious as to march a force into the interior and attack the capital never seemed to have been taken very seriously by those in positions of responsibility. To their credit the British burned only public buildings on the raid, not private homes. Looting was restricted, though the White House was a prime target of British vandalism. Another interesting Canadian myth about the war was that Canada burned Washington in retaliation for the burning of York (Toronto) by U.S. forces in 1813. Again, it was British soldiers and marines who made the raid; not a single Canadian unit took part. Furthermore, the American raid on York had already been avenged in retaliatory raids on Buffalo and Black Rock in western New York State. The burning of private homes in Newark, Upper Canada, in December of 1813 was actually the worst example of American misbehavior on Canadian soil, as it primarily impacted civilians left homeless in wintertime, not York, in which the majority of victims were American soldiers killed in an explosion of an armory. Among those killed was the explorer and army officer Zebulon Pike, a great loss for his country.

Overall then, by the summer of 1814 the war, for the United States, had become a battle "not for free trade and sailors' rights, not for the Conquest of the Canadas, but for our National Existence," according to Republican Joseph Nicholson.[15] British forces occupied Maine east of the Penobscot River and turned Castine into a major hub for illicit trade with the interior. Two large armies were formed out of crack British units that had fought in Portugal and Spain. One was sent to the St. Lawrence River Valley to invade northern New York State, the other to the mouth of the Mississippi River to capture the port of New Orleans. Basically, Britain's leaders had decided that the war should be continued long enough to favorably revise British North America's borders with the United States in favor of the former. In particular, they hoped to annex the U.S. naval base at Sackets Harbor on Lake Ontario and Fort Niagara on the eastern (American) shore of the Niagara River. They also hoped to acquire a more direct line of communication and commerce between the Canadian Maritimes and Lower Canada by annexing northern and eastern Maine. They even went so far as to require a loyalty oath of Maine residents living under occupation. Last, they hoped to overturn the result of Harrison's victory and carve out a gigantic buffer territory for the First Nations north of the Ohio River. For its part, the government in Washington was thoroughly discredited by its ignominious flight from the British, with its organs functioning in only a limited and uncertain fashion. In addition to this state of affairs, the largest enemy force ever to invade American soil marched south across the New York State–Lower Canada frontier in late summer 1814.

FAR REMOVED GEOGRAPHICALLY FROM THIS dire situation for the United States, a team of American negotiators was making the first tentative moves toward a settlement. Interestingly, one of the men sent by President Madison to negotiate peace was the notorious war hawk, Clay. He was joined by John Adams's son, John Quincy, as well as the Swiss-born ex–treasury secretary, Albert Gallatin, among others. The team was, as it turned out, exceptionally gifted. This was particularly so in contrast to their British counterparts, who were recognized mediocrities. The dominant figure in Britain's government, the Irish peer Lord Castlereagh, was not inclined toward continuing the war much longer. His main focus at this time was the Congress of Vienna. This months-long meeting was called to determine the future state of Europe. Napoleon's conservative enemies, Britain chief among them, worked to undo as much of the damage (as they saw it) of the French Revolution and Napoleon's adventurism as they could. Also, in the larger historical context, Castlereagh was insisting on a balance of powers in continental Europe in which no one power wielded inordinate muscle. This policy, which was consistently Britain's foreign policy from the early eighteenth century to the early twentieth century, was being challenged at Vienna by Russia's vain young czar. Czar Alexander I had more "boots on the ground," to borrow a contemporary term, in Europe than any other leader at the congress. As a result, he was less inclined to compromise, especially concerning the future disposition of Poland, which he felt was Russia's by right of conquest. Britain made overtures to the other powers to form a united front against Russia diplomatically, and even militarily (or at least this was implied). Due to this tension, Castlereagh was certainly more open to winding up the North American war as soon as possible on the best terms Britain could get if not necessarily dictate. Clay, Adams, Gallatin, and their colleagues could not have known this. The bad news from home seemed only to weaken their hand. Added to this was the sectional divide symbolized by Adams's insistence on upholding the access of Americans to the North Atlantic fisheries so central to Britain's two earlier treaties with the United States; and Clay's insistence on getting Britain to concede its rights of navigation on the Mississippi. Clay was a westerner from Kentucky. Adams was an easterner from Massachusetts. Furthermore, it was Adams's father who had negotiated the original concession from Britain over fishing rights and access to Canadian shores for American fishermen. He was not about to sacrifice one for the other. Fortunately for the United States, events significantly altered the equation and Clay and Adams were able to move beyond their differences.

The British army and accompanying Canadian militia crossed the New York State frontier in September 1814. Henry Adams claimed, "Great Britain had never sent to America so formidable an armament. Neither Wolfe nor Amherst, neither Burgoyne nor Cornwallis, had led so large and so fine an army."[16] This force, under the command of Canada's military governor, George Prevost, was first heading toward the American base on Lake Champlain at Plattsburgh. It was supported by a fleet under the command of George Downie. Their goal was to destroy the American fleet, reduce the town's fortifications, and then continue their march. The purpose of this was not, as it had been in Washington, to raid. It was a war of conquest meant to force

Thomas Macdonough. His victory at Plattsburgh Bay in the
most important battle of the war saved the United States from
an ignominious peace.

a dictated peace in which much of the United States' Great Lakes territory would have been annexed. The tables had been entirely turned
from 1812. The commander of the American fleet at Plattsburgh Bay
was Thomas Macdonough. Macdonough, though largely forgotten
now, was perhaps the greatest war hero to come out of the War of 1812
on the American side (with the exception of Andrew Jackson). Macdonough used the bay's geography to his advantage and forced the
British to attack him on his terms. In the middle of the fight he

employed an intrepid maneuver that he earlier had anticipated would be necessary. This involved using hand-winched cables instead of wind power to turn his flagship, *Saratoga*, on a dime and pour in a devastating broadside to his opposite number at the critical moment. Downie was killed, Prevost lost his nerve, and Britain's mighty invasion force marched back the way it had come. The date was September 11. No battle of the war had as much significance. As one of the British peace negotiators admitted, "If we had either burned Baltimore or held Plattsburgh I believe we should have had peace on our terms."[17] Those terms would have emasculated the United States.

Castlereagh, concerned by the latest news from America and by the czar's increasing megalomania, informed his men to make peace based on the *status quo ante bellum*, the state of affairs before the war. In those days before the telegraph was invented, he could do little about the other large force that he had already dispatched to the Gulf of Mexico. The Battle of New Orleans, fought after the war had officially been terminated by the Christmas Eve Peace, is probably the most famous episode of the war in American popular memory. Generations of schoolchildren (including that of the author) could be forgiven for reaching the conclusion that the War of 1812 was won by the United States, due to the emphasis placed on the final battle of the war by teachers and textbook authors. It inspired films and popular music. That it was a convincing victory against the odds appealed to American pride. It catapulted the victorious commander, Andrew Jackson, to political prominence. But on balance it was an overrated action. Castlereagh did not inform his negotiators to change tack due to Jackson's victory, but he did do so due largely to Macdonough's victory.

THE PEACE WAS GENERALLY GREETED with relief on both sides of the Atlantic. The war had been unpopular, and it had, disturbingly, taken on the character of a quasi–civil war. As Theodore Roosevelt pointed out:

> *It must always be kept in mind that the Americans and the British are two substantially similar branches of the same great English race, which both before and after their separation have assimilated, and made Englishmen of many other peoples. The lessons taught by the war can hardly be learned unless this identity is kept in mind. It was practically a civil war, and was waged with much harshness and bitterness on both sides.*[18]

A return to the *status quo ante bellum* appealed to the public at large. However, for the First Nations this was unsustainable and they, as well as their opponents and their supporters, understood this. For them the war's outcome meant an accelerated process of isolation and assimilation, if not outright exploitation. Turner's frontier line moved farther west, and within two generations the abandoned American post of Fort Dearborn (Chicago) had grown to become the second largest city in America after New York. There were clear losers in this war. And they were not the British or the Americans.

THERE WAS ONE OTHER FACTOR that played a prominent part in convincing the British government to seek a status quo peace. This was the tremendous success of American privateers preying on British shipping, in British waters.

In Britain, the equivalent of New York's Financial District is a neighborhood called the City of London, or simply the City. It was, in the era of the war and up until 1914, the most dynamic financial market in the world. Fortunes were made and lost within its confines. As the war dragged on into its third year, the merchants of the City began to be directly impacted by its continuance. Cargoes and the vessels that carried them were being either stolen or sunk at an alarming rate. Though not officially connected with the navy, the privateers did more damage to Britain than the official navy did. As is often the case in history, insight can often be found following the money trail. Henry Adams focused, for instance, on insurance rates to better explain the impact of the privateers:

> . . . *underwriters at Lloyd's [of London] could scarcely be induced to insure at any rate of premium . . . for the first time in history a rate of 13% had been paid on risks to cross the Irish Channel. Lloyd's list then showed eight hundred and twenty-five prizes lost to the Americans. . . .*[19]

Simply put, British maritime trade, even, and perhaps especially, close to home, was becoming nearly impossible to conduct in any normal manner. Something had to be done. The City's powerful business interests began to place enormous pressure on the government. In the end, it was easier and less costly for Britain to simply terminate the war than to continue it. The effort the Royal Navy put into escorting convoys and in hunting down the actual privateers themselves was significant, but proved, in the larger context, to be ineffective.

American shipbuilders were adept at producing schooners that were ideal for privateering. The standard procedure for these privateers was to capture any weaker opponent, and fly if one met a stronger opponent. American schooners were marveled at by the British for their ability to do just that. In fact, the maritime culture of the United States in general earned a respect it had lacked before the war. The sailing quality of its ships, the skill and bravery of its seamen, and the intrepid nature of its captains made a lasting impression. To a very large degree this was the most important result of the war, though nothing in the treaty ending the war made any explicit mention of it.

The War

In fact, the silence in general about the war in both London and Washington following its conclusion is the most telling characteristic of its outcome. With the exception of Andrew Jackson, politicians distanced themselves from the whole sordid affair with a forward-mindedness that was breathtaking. Those who had died or who had been maimed for life as a result of the decisions these politicians made did not have the same luxury.

CHAPTER 6

The Maritime War

On June 28, 1814, the U.S. Navy sloop *Wasp* spotted a sail on the horizon. It belonged to HBM brig *Reindeer*. The *Reindeer* was one of several ships on the lookout for American privateers and a new menace—the *Wasp*. Commanded by Irish-born Johnston Blakely (one of the *Enterprise*'s former commanders), but manned almost entirely by New England–born Yankees, the *Wasp* had burned or sunk five British merchantmen in the mouth of the English Channel in a three-week period. The audacity and skill it took to carry this off were the very qualities that had made its adversary, the Royal Navy, great. No one better exemplified this spirit than the *Reindeer*'s commander, William Manners.

Though Manners realized soon enough that he was facing a larger, better-armed opponent, he made clear his intentions to fight rather than fly. The British fired first and accurately as the Americans patiently maneuvered into position. Then, with less than twenty yards between the two ships, the Americans opened up a terrific concentration of fire on the *Reindeer*. Manners encouraged his men to return it in kind, but the difference in overall weight of metal was too great in favor of the *Wasp*. He then rammed his ship into the *Wasp* in the hope that he and his men could board her and carry the day by the sheer ferocity of their attack. He was bleeding to death. Both of his calves had been shot away and he had been wounded by grapeshot in both thighs, and yet he led his men from the front hoping to inspire them to meet the equally ferocious Yankees. The boarders were boarded. Cutlasses hacked, pikes impaled, marksmen found their mark. Manners was felled by two direct shots to the head. It was over in twenty-seven minutes.

Theodore Roosevelt, who would himself go on to achieve fame in combat, wrote as a student almost enviously of Manners:

> . . . *still clenching the sword he had shown he could wear so worthily, with his face to the foe, he fell back to his own deck dead, while above him floated the flag for which he had given his life. No Norse Viking, slain over shield, ever died better.*[1]

The *Wasp-Reindeer* engagement was remarkable in its intensity, but it was not out of the ordinary when looking at the whole of the maritime theater of the War of 1812. It was maritime, and not strictly blue-water, due to the fact that a significant proportion of the fighting took place on the Great Lakes. Along with Macdonough at Plattsburgh Bay, the only other multiple-vessel battle of note of the war was also on the lakes. On the high seas, single-ship actions were most commonplace. But regardless, the fighting involving seamen at sea and on the lakes, and, perhaps somewhat surprisingly, even on land, was particularly noteworthy for its ferocity and the resolute nature of the men involved. It also was particularly noteworthy for the high percentage of officers killed or wounded in action. Aboard the *Reindeer* that day in 1814, among the officers, only the ship's clerk was left standing at battle's end.

When war was declared on June 18, 1812, the U.S. Navy faced what on the surface appeared to be a Herculean task. The Royal Navy had hundreds of vessels at its command. In North American waters alone it boasted seventy-nine men-of-war. This included three ships of the line and twenty-three frigates. In opposition the U.S. Navy could muster only twenty vessels total, five of which were laid up for repairs. Of the remaining fifteen, five were frigates, three sloops, and seven brigs (including the *Enterprise*).[2] Thus, the U.S. Navy in its home waters was outnumbered over five to one by the Royal Navy at the war's outset—and outnumbered more than four to one in vessels with the rating of frigate. Any dent the outnumbered American navy could make against the greatest naval power in history up to that time would come as a surprise, albeit a pleasant one, for James Madison's government.

From the American perspective, 1812 was certainly the best year of the maritime war. The British blockade had yet to tighten to the extent that it would later, and American naval vessels were able to slip out of port and make cruises. The frigates *Constitution* and *United States* under the command of Isaac Hull and Stephen Decatur, respectively, won major engagements with British vessels of equal or nearly equal caliber. Hull's victory over HBM frigate *Guerriere* was probably the single-most famous American naval victory of the entire war. Hull outmaneuvered his opponent, and his gunners to a very large degree hit what they were aiming at. This was not as true of the British seamen on the other side. In a pattern that would hold true throughout the war, with rare exception, the accuracy of American fire notably exceeded the accuracy of British fire. Why was this so? One school of thought points to simple training and repetition. British crews, on average, simply were not drilled at their guns to the extent American crews were. However, another possibility exists. In the United States of the early nineteenth century it was common for young men to handle firearms; in early-nineteenth-century Britain it was not, for commoners. Though wealthy Britons indulged in hunting and the shooting of game birds recreationally, this was only for an elite few. In the United States this was simply not the case. To be fair, handling a gun as heavy as a modern-day sport utility vehicle is not the same as

USS *Constitution* vs. HBMS *Guerriere*

shooting a musket, but marksmanship is still the deciding factor in determining the effectiveness of both.

Hull's victory also came at a time when American fortunes elsewhere had gone badly. The invasion of Canada had been a dismal failure and the capture of Detroit by Brock a national shame. That Hull was nephew to Detroit's disgraced American commander added symmetry to the victory as well. And if proof was required of the validity of American claims against the Royal Navy, one needed to look no further than the fact that the *Guerriere*'s commander had graciously permitted "the ten Americans on board to go below, so as not to fight against their flag." Impressment mattered a great deal to the American seamen engaged in battle. Perhaps this also helped steady their aim. As Theodore Roosevelt explained:

> . . . *the American seaman was very patriotic. He had an honest and deep affection for his own flag . . . Whether he lived in*

*Maryland or Massachusetts, he certainly knew men whose ships
had been seized ... Some of his friends had fallen victims to the
odious right of search, and had never been heard from afterward.
He had suffered many an injury to friend, fortune, or person, and
some day he hoped to repay them all ...*[3]

Roosevelt went on to estimate that approximately twenty thousand
American seamen were, in fact, impressed.[4] Even if this number was
inflated, a conservative estimate of 25 percent of that total would still
represent more men than were actually serving in the entire U.S.
Navy.[5] Seaman Lemuel Norton recalled his sentiments upon returning
to his own American merchantman when he once barely eluded
impressment onto a British man-of-war. Norton's words are worth
emphasizing here because to a large degree they provide insight into
the motivation of Americans fighting at sea:

*... the boatmen at the oars brought us once more to our own ship,
at whose masthead the stars and stripes were floating in the gentle breeze. Never did they look more precious to me than at that
moment. We felt as though we could cheerfully die in their defense.*[6]

Stephen Decatur's victory over HBM frigate *Macedonian* two
months later was, to a certain extent, even more impressive than Hull's
victory over the *Guerriere*. This was due in large measure to the fact
that he brought the frigate into New York as a prize—the only instance
of a Royal Navy vessel of that rating ever being brought as a prize into
an American port. Decatur himself had fired the first gun in the
engagement. It is some wonder the *Macedonian*, in fact, did not sink.
Its hull had taken one hundred direct hits from American guns.[7] Interestingly, the *Macedonian*'s commander, unlike the *Guerriere*'s, refused
to allow his American contingent to go below during the battle. Three
of the eight Americans aboard were killed by their own countrymen.[8]

An incident of this sort would have particularly galled Decatur. He was well known for his resolute nationalism. After the war, he famously toasted, "Our country! In her intercourse with foreign nations may she always be in the right; but our country, right or wrong."[9]

Decatur's country was certainly beating the odds at sea in 1812. The last of the marquee victories that America's frigates would earn took place off the northeast coast of Brazil on December 29. The *Constitution*, now under the command of William Bainbridge, engaged HBM frigate *Java*. In a repeat of its earlier success, the *Constitution* was able to bring a heavier concentration of fire to bear, more accurately, than its opponent. Henry Adams characterized it as "slaughter." The *Java's* commander was mortally wounded; forty-eight others were killed outright or died soon after of their wounds.[10] The British press and public were astonished at these collective reversals at sea, a theater of war where they were accustomed to winning. Coupled with this was a feeling that the Americans were decidedly second-rate. As the historian Donald Hickey pointed out, "Given this contempt, the American victories went down hard."[11] It is also important to keep in mind that Britain's prestige was directly affected by these defeats. The Royal Navy's mastery of the seas was aided in no inconsiderable degree by the aura of invincibility that had grown up around it. The threat of losing this aura could have very real consequences if Britain's opponents, and not just the Americans, became emboldened all at once. Thus, as 1812 gave way to 1813, the U.S. Navy had the early edge. That said, it was not decisive. Nor could it be, given the disparity in numbers between the two navies.

THE FOLLOWING YEAR the Royal Navy was more assertive in establishing its domination of the American coastline. British vessels tended to sail in small- to medium-sized packs to ensure victory over any American vessel they might encounter. Thus, engagements became less frequent. The battle between Blyth's *Boxer* and Burrows's *Enterprise* was one of the few fought that year, though it followed the pattern of those fought in 1812—a single-ship action. However, the most famous battle of 1813, and Britain's greatest victory at sea of the entire war, was another single-ship engagement between HBM frigate *Shannon* and the USS *Chesapeake*, commanded by James Lawrence. The *Shannon*'s commander, Philip Broke, knowing the *Chesapeake* was in port in Boston, issued a formal invitation to Lawrence to do battle. This was hardly necessary, as Lawrence was eager to engage the enemy, though he was concerned about the quality of his new crew. Many of them were untried, while others were discontented over disputed prize money. Broke's crew, however, was top-rate. They had been together for a considerable amount of time and were, on average, much better trained in gunnery than most Royal Navy crews. They certainly demonstrated their mettle and skill against the *Chesapeake* on June 1, 1813.

To be fair, the *Chesapeake* was disabled early in the engagement. A crucial line, or "sheet," was shot away by one of the *Shannon*'s guns. This momentarily made it difficult for Lawrence to maneuver properly. But as any student of battles can certainly confirm, moments are oftentimes all that are necessary to bestow victory upon one antagonist or the other. And this was no chance shot. British commanders often preferred to disable their opponents in just this way.

For her part, the *Chesapeake* inflicted considerable damage on the *Shannon* with her fire, but the *Shannon*'s fire was, if not more accurate, more intense. With the *Chesapeake*'s stern drifting toward the *Shannon*, "every gun in the British broadside swept the American deck from stem to stern, clearing the quarter-deck and beating in the stern ports, while the musketry from the *Shannon*'s tops killed the men at the *Chesapeake*'s wheel, and picked off every officer, sailor, or marine in the after part of the ship."[12] It was devastating. A hail of lead made rallying the crew to board the *Shannon* nearly impossible. Instead, it was Broke who led a boarding party to seize the *Chesapeake*. That he did so personally was, as previously emphasized, in no way out of the ordinary. As it turned out Broke and his fifty boarders were in as much danger from the continuing fire from their own vessel as from the Americans rallying to resist them. In fact, of the fifty, "not less than thirty-seven were killed or wounded," including their commander, who received a cut on the head from a broadsword.[13] But they carried the day. Lawrence, mortally wounded, is claimed to have cried "don't give up the ship" to his men. But it seems those that could hear him chose to ignore him and fled below; and those who could not were below manning their guns and failed to fully recognize the significance of what was transpiring above their heads.

That the British chose to board, and with numbers seemingly inadequate for the task at hand (the *Chesapeake* had a crew of 379 at the battle's outset; 61 were killed or died soon after of their wounds, and another 85 received nonmortal wounds, which still left 233 healthy men aboard) was also in no way out of character for the Royal Navy.[14] Boarding was a preferred means of sea combat among its officers and crews. Much as the ancient Romans had perfected the method against their ancient Carthaginian foes, the British appeared to relish the opportunity of turning a sea battle into a land battle with grappling hooks, albeit a more desperate one, as there was no possibility of retreat. Close-in combat with axes, pikes, and cutlasses was, frankly, medieval. Pistols were discharged and marine marksmen took their deadly aim, but in the end it was steel against steel, and steel against flesh and bone that commonly decided the matter. The description "decks awash with blood" became almost cliché when referring to battles involving the Royal Navy during this era. There was a reason for this.

Broke received a baronetcy from the crown for his brilliant performance: a performance that assuaged to some degree the wounded pride of the Royal Navy and the British people following the reverses of 1812. The joy with which the news of his victory was greeted in

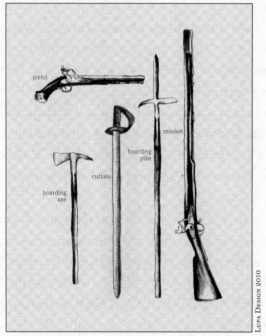

Arms commonly used in sea combat of the Napoleonic era

Halifax was out of all proportion to its military significance. But Broke could not share in the celebrations; the head wound he had received leading the boarding party left him an invalid and prevented him from active service thereafter. He was never the same man again.

Lawrence and his command were taken prisoner, and the *Chesapeake* was made a prize and brought into the Royal Navy's base in Nova Scotia. Lawrence died at sea en route. He and his second in command, Lieutenant Ludlow, were given a funeral with full military honors by the victors. Among those who volunteered to serve as a pallbearer for Lawrence's coffin was Samuel Blyth.

THE LOSS OF LAWRENCE WAS keenly felt among his fellow U.S. naval officers. And his final moments in command passed into myth. Among those who drew inspiration from Lawrence was the American commander on Lake Erie, Oliver Hazard Perry. J. Mackay Hitsman described Perry as "Representative of the small but superbly well-trained American naval officer corps."[15] Perry had been sent to the Great Lakes region weighted with a daunting task. His responsibility was to create a fleet out of nothing in what was still a howling wilderness in northwestern Pennsylvania and northern Ohio, man it, and gain control of the lake for the American side. The lack of skilled workers and seamen, and the prevalence of disease, made this task harder still.

Control of Lake Erie had been a crucial factor in Isaac Brock's success at Detroit. Without command of it Britain risked losing touch with its far western bases and posts around the upper Great Lakes. From his flagship *Lawrence*, Perry flew a blue banner bearing the words "don't give up the ship." His opposite number on the British side, Robert Heriot Barclay, commanded a small fleet and was furiously trying to get a new flagship of his own completed, the *Detroit*. Barclay, like Britain's great naval hero of the Napoleonic era, Horatio Nelson, had one arm, having lost the other in combat. He had, in fact, been with Nelson at the Battle of Trafalgar eight years before. Both men in command on the lake were warriors in the truest sense.

The Great Lakes are a wonder to coastal dwellers the first time they are seen. The fact that bodies of water of that size exist so far into the interior of the continent forces a reorientation of geographical understanding about North America. It is as if there were an inland sea, or seas. Navigating southwest up the St. Lawrence River, early French explorers recognized the value of it as a highway leading directly into the watery heart of the continent. Their colony, New France, was built on its banks. Its wealth came from the furs trapped on the St. Lawrence's tributaries, and from the territory around the Great Lakes. Britain inherited this colony as a result of the French and Indian War. Now, in 1813, they were defending it from the Americans.

Lake Erie was the key because control of it meant one could support land operations on one's own side while severing the supply lines of one's opponent. Victories and reverses on the upper Great Lakes, whose waters fed into Erie, would mean little without control of the latter, because they could not be sustained. Thus, in a strategic sense the battle between Perry's and Barclay's squadrons exceeded the significance of the other major naval engagements of the war, with the single important exception of Macdonough's September 11, 1814, victory.

On September 9, 1813, Barclay sallied out of his frontier town–base at Fort Malden on the Detroit River. Barclay knew Perry was in the vicinity and chose to pick a fight, because not to do so would likely mean Malden could not be reprovisioned in time to prevent widespread hunger, most particularly among the large number of native hangers-on depending on British rations to feed their families. As he himself acknowledged in a letter to his superior, "the Risk is very great I feel very much, but in the present state of this place, without provisions, without stores,—& without Indian goods it is necessary."[16]

Perry had stationed his force in a group of islands located near the mouth of the Sandusky River. The following day the two squadrons found each other and Perry gamely bore in on his opponent. That he clearly expected an intense fight is demonstrated by his "spreading sand on his decks to prevent his men from slipping on the water that would be splashed up or the blood that would be spilled."[17] The British had the advantage of possessing more long-range guns, which could be used to hit the enemy from a greater distance without being damaged in return. Perry, however, was able to close and bring to bear his squadron's greater overall firepower at close range. The respective commanders' flagships poured one broadside after another into each other, with the *Lawrence* getting the worst of it. Its officers and crew sustained 80 percent casualties. Perry, undaunted, was rowed from his now entirely disabled flagship to the *Niagara*, which he then took immediate command of and turned directly into the British squadron. The ferocity and determination he exhibited seemed to be transmitted to the remaining American vessels and their crews as they devastated their opponent. When the Americans finally boarded Barclay's *Detroit* they found its commander with his one good arm mangled, and a "pet bear lapping up blood on the decks."[18]

In a note to William Henry Harrison stationed nearby with his army, Perry gained a modest immortality for penning the words "We have met the enemy and they are ours."[19] Not only was Barclay's squadron beaten, but the outnumbered British force and their First Nations allies on land were also strategically checkmated by Perry's victory. As Harrison ascended the Thames River from Lake St. Clair in pursuit, Perry's force supported his advance with gunboats on the river, and furthermore ensured that his army could be supplied. When the gunboats reached a point where the Thames was no longer navigable, "Captain Perry himself continued as a 'volunteer.' "[20] The man clearly relished a good fight. In the larger scheme of things, his victory was

Perry transferring his flagship from the *Lawrence* to the *Niagara* at Lake Erie, September 9, 1813

really two victories, as Harrison's would not have been likely, perhaps not even possible, without Perry's.

THE EXTENT OF THE MARITIME war between Britain and the United States was not confined to the Atlantic and the Great Lakes. David Porter, commanding the USS *Essex*, had rounded Cape Horn at the extreme southern tip of South America in 1813 and began wreaking havoc on enemy shipping in the Pacific Ocean. The cruise of the *Essex* was one of the great naval achievements of the entire era. Much as Francis Drake's *Golden Hind* had brought the war to colonial New Spain's unprepared coastal settlements and shipping in the Elizabethan Age, Porter performed a similar service for his country. Theodore Roosevelt underscored this when he wrote:

> *The cruise was something sui generis in modern warfare, recalling to mind the cruises of early English and Dutch navigators. An American ship was at a serious disadvantage in having no harbor or refuge away from home; while on almost every sea there were British, French, and Spanish ports into which vessels of those nations could run for safety. It was an unprecedented thing for a small frigate to cruise for a year and a half in enemy's waters, and to supply herself during that time, purely from captured vessels, with everything—cordage, sails, guns, anchors, provisions, and medicines, and even money to pay the officers and men! Porter's cruise was the very model of what such an expedition should be, harassing the enemy most effectually at no cost whatever.*[21]

The *Essex* had among its crew a boy named David Farragut, who would later go on to lead the Union Navy to victory in the Civil War. Farragut is perhaps best known for his command to "Damn the torpedoes [and proceed] full steam ahead" at the Battle of Mobile Bay in

1864.[22] One could argue the mentality that produced that type of response to danger had been ingrained fifty years earlier in Farragut the boy, aboard the *Essex*. One area, for instance, Farragut personally recalled as being a point of emphasis on board was hand-to-hand combat: "I have never been on a ship where the crew of the old *Essex* is represented but that I found them to be the best swordsmen on board." He added, "They had been so thoroughly trained as boarders that every man was prepared for such an emergency with his cutlass as sharp as a razor, a dirk made by the ship's armorer out of a file, and a pistol."[23] The *Essex* was up to the task. That it was performing this task on borrowed time to a large degree made the success all the sweeter.

When a small pack of British men-of-war finally caught up with the *Essex* off the Chilean coast and took her as a hard-won prize, the small frigate had already convincingly staked the United States' claim to be a power in the Pacific. Though it would take a couple of generations for this to occur, it did occur. The man arguably most responsible: Theodore Roosevelt.

Perhaps the finest example of the fighting qualities of seamen and their officers on the American side in the conflict occurred at the Battle of Bladensburg on August 24, 1814. Seamanship, however, mattered little at Bladensburg, as not a single vessel was involved. Bladensburg was fought on land along the main north-south road running into the District of Columbia. Overall, it was one of the most shameful episodes of the entire war for American arms. It also could be argued that it placed in stark contrast the commitment to the fight of Americans at sea in comparison to the commitment to the fight of Americans on land.

Joshua Barney, a Revolutionary War veteran and ex-privateersman, had been given command of a flotilla of gunboats to defend Chesapeake Bay's western shore. Given the length of the coastline and the number of his enemy, this was a nearly impossible task. As a prelude to Ross's raid on Washington, the British navy looked to capture or destroy Barney's flotilla in the Patuxent River. Instead of surrendering, Barney and his men removed the five 24-pounder guns from their craft and burned the flotilla themselves rather than see either fall into British hands. They then moved northwest to rendezvous with the confused defense being assembled by General William Winder. Initially detailed to defend the Washington Navy Yard, Barney protested to the secretary of the navy to be released to meet the enemy outside the city. Winder's force was composed largely of local militia, who, though they outnumbered the British raiders coming down the road, certainly were not of the same caliber as their opponent. With President Madison himself looking on, Barney's seamen and their five naval guns took up position astride the road with primarily militia to their right and left. As the battle began, the untried militiamen, unlike those of 1775 at Concord Bridge, first hesitantly, then in near panic, retreated back down the road toward their nation's undefended capital. The retreat swiftly degenerated into a rout. Madison himself nearly blundered into being captured. If one could have enjoyed a bird's-eye view of the battle, however, one would have seen one unit at the center standing their ground as the rest of their countrymen melted away.

Four hundred men faced four thousand. This American "Thermopylae," though little known now, and to a large degree even in its own time obscured by the shock of the sack of Washington, stands as the finest hour of American seamen under fire. Three frontal assaults were driven back by Barney's seamen, the accuracy of their naval gunnery exacting a bloody toll on the attackers. This was followed by an attempt to turn their right flank in an open field. American marines held the position, but once British troops got into their rear the situation was hopeless.

Prominent among Barney's band were a significant contingent of

African-American seamen. The irony of these men defending Washington so heroically must have occurred to some: a city being built almost entirely by the toil of their enslaved brothers and sisters. Why fight? What drove them on? Henry Adams, a Washingtonian, wrote of his adopted city's darkest hour and its handful of defenders:

> *The British themselves were most outspoken in praise of Barney's men. "Not only did they serve their guns with a quickness and precision that astonished their assailant . . . but they stood till some of them were actually bayoneted with fuses in their hands . . ."*[24]

This type of fortitude in the face of hopeless odds was in many respects the truest measure of American seamen: fighting like cornered tigers, when all they needed to do to save themselves was to follow their fellow Americans' example and run away. Their commanding officer was, again unsurprisingly, wounded. Taken captive by Ross, Barney remarked that he was treated "with the most marked attention, respect, and politeness as if I was a brother."[25] A tiger knows a fellow tiger. The British raiders recognized and respected valor and grit. Unfortunately for the city of Washington, most of the Americans at Bladensburg possessed neither.

Seamen also, both from the U.S. Navy schooner *Carolina* and from the vessels of Jean Lafitte's Baratarian pirates, played a critical role in manning Andrew Jackson's artillery in the series of engagements collectively referred to as the Battle of New Orleans in 1814–1815. Edwin Pakenham, the British commander, tried to carry Jackson's makeshift fortifications by artillery duel, then by direct frontal assault. Both failed, and the latter was little short of catastrophic, with both Pakenham and his second in command dead on the field of battle. Just as at sea, Americans tended to hit what they aimed at.

The Maritime War

———

ULTIMATELY, the results of the maritime war were indecisive. The commerce of both nations suffered immensely. Britain's blockade turned once-thriving port towns into ghost towns awaiting better days. American privateers in turn imposed a de facto blockade around the British Isles that by war's end was equally as effective at disrupting trade on a national scale. The former gave rise to what Clay would later term the "American System," in which the government began to play a role in protecting and stimulating domestic manufacturing, as the war had exposed a large vulnerability within the American economy. The latter, at least partially, forced Britain into making peace on much more favorable terms than the United States would have received otherwise. But for all that it was great theater as well. Particularly for American citizens, the stories of derring-do and expertly fought maritime victories inspired both pride and interest in the U.S. Navy. The American eagle had challenged the mighty British lion in its element of greatest strength and had not only survived, but in some instances triumphed. It was heady stuff.

The British for their part took the maritime war in stride for the most part (with the single important exception of the business community). Though there was consternation at some of the Royal Navy's defeats, it must be kept in mind that since the Battle of Trafalgar in 1805, the British had ostensibly ruled the waves unchallenged and were unaccustomed by 1812 to either losing or fighting. That the Royal Navy had lost its edge somewhat, particularly as regards training in naval gunnery, seems clear in hindsight. And, frankly, the British just didn't take the Americans seriously enough. This changed. One major result of the maritime war was the increased respect members of the U.S. Navy received, not only as seamen but as fighting men. Michael Scott, the Scots author of *Tom Cringle's Log*, wrote after the war:

I don't like Americans. I never did and never shall like them . . .
I have no wish to eat with them, drink with them, deal or consort
with them in any way; but let me tell you the whole truth—nor
fight with them, were it not for the laurels to be acquired by
overcoming an enemy so brave, determined, and alert, and every
way so worthy of one's steel as they have always proved.[26]

Scott continued:

In the field or grappling in mortal combat on the blood-slippery
quarter-deck of an enemy's vessel, a British soldier or sailor is the
bravest of the brave. No soldier or sailor of any other country,
saving and excepting those damned Yankees, can stand against
them.[27]

What then did the Americans receive out of their conduct in the
maritime war? Again, respect. Though impressment was nowhere
mentioned in the document ending the war, the practice, at least
inasmuch as it affected Americans, essentially was quietly discontin-
ued. The United States also had made it clear to its former mother
country that it was a power in its own right, and not a British satellite.
This was the significance of the maritime war.

CHAPTER 7

Home Front

At sea one war raged, while at home another war was being fought in the press, the streets, and the pulpit. In this war, Americans railed against their brethren and provided aid to their enemies. Before it was all over, the United States faced an existential crisis, one that was almost entirely of its own making.

A common misperception among Americans of the baby boom and subsequent generations is that the 1960s ushered in a new, more confrontational relationship between the American people and their government. This relationship had been particularly strained by the Vietnam War of 1965–1973, in which many Americans refused to be drafted to serve in a war they did not support. It is true that within living memory, by the time the turbulent sixties dawned, Americans could look back on an apparently unbroken record of national unanimity in time of war: the Korean War, both World Wars, and as far back as the Spanish-American War. However, what this interpretation of American history failed to take into account was the intense feeling, even violence generated by the U.S. government's decision to go to war in 1861–1865, 1846–1848, and 1812–1815. Just as in the 1960s and early 1970s, the issue of conscription (i.e., the draft) was politically divisive and led to civil unrest. The first attempted draft led to the New York Draft Riots of July 1863, which were comparatively greater in scale and intensity than the April–May 1992 Los Angeles riots, for instance. The 1846–1848 war with Mexico was, much like the War of 1812, motivated largely by expansionist goals. In both, the sectional or regional divisions over the wisdom—even the morality—of these policies was stark. Abraham Lincoln, who led the United States into the Civil War in 1861–1865, and was the first president to preside over a national draft in 1863, was, in 1846, staunchly opposed to both the war with Mexico and any discussion in the House of Representatives of voting conscription to fight it. Similarly, in the War of 1812, Federalists as well as Republicans threw cold political water on any talk emanating from Madison's government to implement a draft. This, even though many regular army units were fighting at only partial strength. The war was so unpopular as to invite treason in much of the country. Thus, the Vietnam War era was not so out of character and groundbreaking in the broad sweep of American history as it often is perceived to be. The division of opinion, civil unrest, and trafficking with the enemy characteristic of the United States that William Burrows and his crew were defending rivals or exceeds that of any comparable period in the history of the nation. The United States was not united.

WHEN WAR WAS DECLARED ON JUNE 18, 1812, it came as a shock to a significant portion of the United States population. For years, their country had walked a diplomatic tightrope between the larger powers on the other side of the Atlantic, and had avoided being drawn into a war that was not theirs. There had been numerous war scares, and tough talk, but no war. This had lulled the general population into assuming that talk of war would never translate into actual war. As historian Donald Hickey explained:

Everywhere people were taken by surprise. Ever since 1805 the
nation's leaders had talked of war, and yet always the result was
more commercial restrictions. Many people—Republicans and
Federalists alike—assumed war would again be averted, that
some excuse would be found to continue diplomatic negotiations.[1]

None appeared. Even news of Parliament's June 23, 1812, decision
to lift the contentious Orders in Council was not enough to steer the
nation away from the abyss. Clay and his hawks wanted war. Declaring
it, and then backing off, would smack of bluffing. That, perhaps, may
have been President Madison's intention all along. But if it was, he
played his hand poorly. Events seemed to have gotten away from the
White House to a certain extent, and he was not a strong leader. His
party, on the other hand, recognized the tremendous political capital
that could be gained by politicizing the war domestically. The Federalist opposition who had voted against declaring war could be painted
as unpatriotic British sympathizers, thus handicapping them at the
upcoming November elections. The Republican press eagerly took up
this theme. The *Augusta Chronicle*, for instance, asserted that "The
Rubicon has been passed, he who is not for us is against us."[2] The
Washington National Intelligencer took a preemptive shot at the opposition by claiming, "This is no time for debating the propriety of a war."[3]

For their part, the Federalists were initially divided about how to
approach the war. Some rallied round the flag. Others staked out their
ground in opposition to the war in no uncertain terms:

A president who has made this war, is not qualified to make
peace . . . Organize a peace party throughout your country, and let
all party distinctions vanish.[4]

Few wars in American history have been so closely associated in
the public's mind with a president as much as the War of 1812 was with

The fourth President of the United States,
Virginia-born James Madison

Madison. Perhaps only the Iraq War of the early twenty-first century
has been more closely associated with a specific president. The prob-
lem with a war being personalized in such a way in the public's mind
is that it distances that same public from responsibility for the conflict.
As the war dragged on this became exceedingly dangerous for the
youthful United States. If a nation cannot defend its own capital from
a force inferior in numbers, then something is terribly amiss. As a
marine of a later generation explained:

> it will be necessary to accept one's responsibilities and to be willing
> to make sacrifices for one's country—as my comrades did. As the
> troops used to say, "If the country is good enough to live in, it's
> good enough to fight for." With privilege goes responsibility.[5]

These sentiments were shared by a relative few in the United States during the war. Some, to be sure, felt their responsibility was to end an unjust and unconstitutional war; others, however, put profit ahead of country, while still others were fair-weather patriots willing to support a war of expansion as long as it entailed no personal sacrifice on their part. The degree to which William Burrows and his fellow officers and crewmates aboard the *Enterprise* recognized this is worth pondering. After all, the ship was stationed in New England at the time—a hotbed of antiwar fervor and illicit trade with Canada.

William Burrows's great-grandfather, Dr. Thomas Bond Sr., had warned of the consequences of a government placing political expediency ahead of sound judgment. In 1782, he had addressed the American Philosophical Society in Pennsylvania's State House on the "Rank and Dignity of Man in the Scale of Being." His oration eventually settled on the topic of national character:

> *Military fame may be won or lost in an hour . . . The national Character of any country, can only be known abroad through the medium of its Government . . . for it is the Character of the Government that fixes the Character of the Country . . . The fame of America must rest on a broader basis than that of arms alone . . . [it] depends on our preserving a noble, generous and unspotted Character at Home.*[6]

From 1812 to 1815, the "national Character" was decidedly compromised. Bond's great-grandson was going to risk his life following the orders of the government that had compromised it, led by men who had undermined if not his father personally, at least then much of what he had stood for.

For their part, the British recognized the polarizing nature of the war and hoped to cultivate it to their gain. George Prevost, Canada's military governor, wrote:

I consider it prudent and politic to avoid any measure which can in its effect have a tendency to unite the people in the American states. Whilst disunion prevails among them, their attempts on these Provinces will be feeble.[7]

He added insightfully:

. . . the government of the United States, resting on public opinion for all its measures, is liable to sudden and violent changes; it becomes an essential part of our duty to watch the effect of parties on its measures, and to adapt ours to the impulse given by those possessed of influence over the public mind in America.[8]

What this meant in practical terms was the imposition of a partial blockade only in the first year and ten months of the war, in which New England's trade would be unobstructed. Trade with the Canadian Maritimes, as well as with Lower Canada (Quebec), was to be encouraged. According to John Sherbrooke, commanding in Nova Scotia, it was his "wish and desire that the Subjects of the United States, living on the frontiers, may pursue in peace their usual and accustomed Trade and occupations, without Molestation."[9] For the most part they did just that. Smuggling was a lucrative and often open enterprise. Maine merchants and Vermont and northern New York State farmers and ranchers were the most flagrant, but they were certainly not alone in trading with the enemy. Prevost himself famously claimed that "two thirds of the army in Canada are at this moment eating beef provided by American contractors, drawn principally from the States of Vermont and New York."[10] Not only was Britain's army in North America being supplied by Americans, so was Britain's army fighting Napoleon's forces in Portugal and Spain. As Donald Hickey pointed out, Madison's government itself was complicit in the latter:

The export of American flour to this region [Portugal and Spain]
had mushroomed from 105,000 barrels in 1809 to 939,000 bar-
rels in 1812. Since this trade was vital to American agriculture,
the government was careful not to obstruct it.[11]

The *Enterprise*'s nemesis, the Royal Navy, also was willingly provided with fresh produce by farmers and traders who not only sold but delivered food for profit. A report in a Maine newspaper attested to this:

A gentleman at my house, who left the Ramilies *yesterday, and*
who had been a prisoner on board about three weeks says that the
sloop Endeavor, *of Newport, which the officers said was an <u>old</u>*
<u>acquaintance</u>, was, on the 24th or 25th of August, voluntarily
alongside the Ramilies, *and he saw them put on board potatoes,*
onions, corn, and other vegetables, and a plenty of fruit.[12]

New Englanders not only trafficked in produce and imported British goods, but also in information. Stephen Decatur, bottled up in New London following his great victory over the *Macedonian,* was convinced his movements were being observed and reported to the enemy. He remarked, "the weather promised an opportunity for this squadron to get to sea . . . In the course of the evening two blue lights were burned on both points at the harbor's [New London] mouth as signals to the enemy."[13] The British took full advantage of Americans' willingness to provide anything for cash, but were privately appalled at such behavior. One exclaimed, "Self the great ruling principle [is] more powerful with Yankees than any people I ever saw."[14]

Certainly, New Englanders had every reason to feel the war had been imposed on them by a different region and different party dominated by the so-called Virginia Dynasty in the White House (Washington,

Jefferson, and Madison all hailed from this state). Through trade and interest, New England was closely tied to the British Isles. There was also considerably less sympathy in New England for the French Revolution and Napoleon. Conservative middle-class New Englanders and Britons were of a like mind about the threat these posed. There was also a suspicion that the war was being fought by land-hungry westerners to expand into Canada. Then, as now, New Englanders and their Canadian neighbors had a largely profitable and friendly relationship. Many shared the sentiments expressed by U.S. Representative Samuel Taggart of Massachusetts:

> *Canada has issued no Orders in Council . . . She has not impressed our seamen, taken our ships, confiscated our property, nor in any respect treated us ill. All the crime alleged against Canada or the Canadians, is that, without any act of their own, they are connected with, and under the protection of a nation which has injured us on the ocean.*[15]

New England states also refused to send their militias to take part in the invasion of Canada. Individual militiamen and militia units from states that did send troops often also refused to cross the frontier, claiming they had signed up to serve on their home state's soil only— or at least not on foreign soil. Whether these sentiments were motivated by self-preservation, lack of commitment, or principle is open to debate. What is clearly not debatable is the fact that the war produced the first antiwar movement in American history. The arguments made cogently at that time carry a special resonance now.

"IN A democracy, to get anything done that is costly in lives & treasure, requires the support of the great majority of the people."[16] William Westmoreland, the United States' supreme commander in Vietnam during the first three years of that conflict, made this remark in an interview reflecting back on his country's defeat. His words are highly relevant when studying the War of 1812. J. Mackay Hitsman, who, like Westmoreland, came of age during the World War II era, and witnessed his country's, and other countries', mobilization for total war at that time, was startled by the conclusions he reached from his research concerning the War of 1812:

What is surprising is the total lack of anything resembling a national war effort on either side. Life went on as usual, unless there was imminent danger from an immediate enemy. Both Americans and Canadians were willing to leave the real fighting to professionals and to the patriotic or adventurous minority who volunteered their services.[17]

In Britain, too, the war failed to resonate with the great majority of the population. Certain elements of the press were rabidly anti-American, but the public as a whole was not. The Atlantic Ocean separated them from the war in North America. Only the English Channel, and the Royal Navy, separated the British people from Napoleon's armies and secret police. The contrast was lost on few. When the editor of the *Edinburgh Review* called on Madison in the midst of the war and was pressed by the president to comment on public opinion in Britain, he replied, "Half the people of England do not know there is a war with America, and those who did had forgotten it."[18]

Given this seeming indifference, one could be excused for thinking that the war generated little passion among the citizenry. In the United States, however, this would be a mistaken assumption. In comparison to Britain, the passions aroused in the United States by the government's decision to go to war were white hot. Though most were unwilling to risk their lives trying to kill British soldiers, some were willing to kill their fellow citizens for holding different opinions. Some did kill their fellow citizens. The issue at stake for those opposed to the war on principle was that it was being fought under false pretenses (maritime rights) to expand the country—much as a later generation of antiwar agitators would claim the Iraq War was being fought not to disarm a dictator and implant democracy, but rather to acquire oil. The president's defenders, then as in the early twenty-first century, often retreated into patriotism and by implication painted opposition to the war as opposition to the country. This could be very effective, but it undermined to a large degree the basic tenets of democratic society. Simply put: For democracy to function the citizenry must first agree to disagree, and with a certain amount of civility. Democracy is not consensus. Partly because the United States republic was young, and partly because there had been a degree of dissembling on the part of the hawks, this façade of civility showed major cracks, if not outright breaches.

The most disturbing of these were the Baltimore riots of July 27–28, 1812. This port town on the Chesapeake Bay had a sizable Republican and anti-British majority (often one and the same in that era). However, the state of Maryland in which it was located was strongly Federalist in opinion. Newspapers such as the *Baltimore Federal Republican* on the one hand and the *Baltimore Sun* on the other railed at each other in print as the buildup to declaring war that summer spilled over into actual war. The editors of the *Federal Republican* took a strong stand not merely against the war but against the intimidation many of the war's opponents were being subjected to:

> *a war would put the constitution and all civil rights to sleep. Those who commenced it, would become dictators and despots.*[19]

Needless to say, the paper came out strongly against the war when it was declared less than three weeks later. This would not stand in the Baltimore of 1812. Its offices were attacked, its employees mobbed, its readers cowed. Apparently, freedom of speech and press did not give one the right to criticize one's government in time of war. Ironically, it was the editor of the rival *Baltimore Sun* who brought a cannon to bear on the *Federal Republican*'s offices at the height of the riots. Only the intervention of a troop of cavalry stopped the cannon from being fired. Eventually the Federalists barricaded inside were convinced to surrender themselves to the protection of the authorities and marched off to the relative safety of the town jail. In one of the lowest moments for American democracy, a gang of hooligans was permitted entrance into the jail the following day and proceeded to beat and torture the Federalists they caught trying to flee. Donald Hickey, in his comprehensive account, explained:

> *Nine of the Federalists . . . were severely beaten and deposited in a heap in front of the jail. Over the next three hours, they were repeatedly beaten. When they showed signs of life, they were stabbed with penknives and hot candle wax was dropped into their eyes to determine if they were alive. Women who were present reportedly cried out, "Kill the tories," while children exulted at the awful scene, clapping their hands and skipping for joy.*[20]

Antiwar politicians and citizens were, however, emboldened, not cowed, by news of the atrocities in Baltimore. In the 1812 congressional elections the Federalists made significant gains. Though they ran no candidate of their own in the general election, the Federalists backed the governor of New York, DeWitt Clinton, who represented a splinter faction within the Republican Party. In the end, Madison was reelected, but it was no landslide. Clearly, the country was divided. Again, it was New England in particular that stood out strongest against the war. At a level equal to the pro-war intimidation in Baltimore was the stifling of any pro-war sentiment in much of the New

England region. The preacher David Osgood warned his fellow New Englanders in no uncertain terms:

> *[E]ach man who volunteers his services in such a cause, or loans his money for its support, or by his conversation, his writings, or any other mode of influence, encourages its prosecution . . . loads his conscience with the blackest crimes.*[21]

Political polarization of the type associated with the Vietnam and Iraq wars was, if anything, worse during the War of 1812. No event highlighted this more than the Hartford Convention of late 1814. Each of the five New England states as they then were (Maine was part of Massachusetts until 1820) sent delegates to this meeting called ostensibly to make common cause for constitutional reform. Above all they wanted to avoid a repetition of 1812, when, in their view, one party and one region had forced war on the entire nation. Their motivations were not unique in American history certainly. In 1937, isolationist congressmen concerned over President Franklin D. Roosevelt's warnings about wars in Spain and China spreading proposed and nearly voted into law the Ludlow Resolution. This bill would have required a national referendum among all citizens in favor of declaring war before taking any action. One could argue that had this resolution been law in 1812 the war could have been avoided. Perhaps, perhaps not. Most likely one would have seen high vote counts in favor in certain regions, and the opposite in other regions, with war still being declared without national unanimity.

The proposals made by the conventioneers at Hartford were actually quite moderate in relation to the shrill tone among much of the public in the states represented. As previously referred to, the convention's proposal to require a two-thirds majority vote in both houses of Congress before issuing a declaration of war could have prevented the War of 1812. Where the convention trod on thin ice, however, was in its support of states' rights to the exclusion of a strong national government. As would be the case in 1860–1861 in the Southern states, this smacked of disunion. The call for a New England Confederation, in fact, anticipated the formation of the Confederate States of America by forty-six years. What many of the conventioneers and their supporters, however, would come to realize after the peace was signed was that, as Donald Hickey explained, "Opposition to the war was popular during the conflict but not afterward. . . ."[22]

John Kerry's 2004 bid for the U.S. presidency could be used for comparison's sake as a proof of this remark as a historical maxim. Kerry, a decorated veteran of the Vietnam War, returned home and became a prominent figure within the growing antiwar movement. One could argue that this was politically expedient, as the war had become deeply unpopular, and a young man with political ambition could capitalize on this. The turning point for Kerry in the 2004 election was in Ohio, the location of Kent State University campus, the site of a battle between antiwar agitators and local National Guardsmen that resulted in four deaths in 1970. Thirty-four years later Kerry would have become the forty-fourth president of the United States if he had been able to carry the vote in that state. He did not. His fellow veterans, who should have been firmly in his camp, were divided. Even those who felt "he earned the right" to criticize the war admitted, "veterans were still upset with him" about it.[23] Another opined that "it absolutely hurt him, not a doubt," and that "if he had built credibility, instead of making statements that were not credible" when he returned from Vietnam, he likely could have relied on the solidarity of his fellow veterans in the voting booth.[24]

Hartford became associated with treason. Jackson's victory at New Orleans placed an exclamation point on this sentiment. In Maine, where Burrows and the *Enterprise* would meet their destiny, treason also was in the air. However, it was more by accommodation than principle.

When William Burrows took command of the *Enterprise* in late August 1813, the brig was stationed at the Portsmouth Naval Yard, located in Kittery, Maine. The *Wasp*'s future commander, Johnston Blakely, had been cruising the coast looking for enemy privateers and merchantmen. Though the war had been going on for over a year by that time, shipping in the coastal waters of Maine, New Brunswick, and Nova Scotia was doing brisk business. With word of the *Boxer*'s entry onto the scene, however, Maine merchants and shipowners had become increasingly anxious. The capture of the merchantman *Industry* at the mouth of the Sheepscot River on August 2 had sent a shiver through the business community. The *Boxer*'s young commander clearly was looking to shake things up a bit, and possibly realize some profit by seizing prizes. It was the job of the *Enterprise* to put a stop to this.

Maine was in an awkward yet advantageous position when war broke out. On the one hand, its border with Canada was by far the longest of any state. This placed pressure for its defense on the Massachusetts state government in Boston, and on the national government in Washington. Both were, in relative terms, far away and focused on more pressing concerns elsewhere. This then placed Maine's citizens in the position of being next to the enemy, but without adequate means of defending themselves from raid or invasion. So long as Britain chose to cultivate trade and fraternization between Maine and the Canadian Maritimes, as was the case throughout most of the war, this proximity could be seen as an advantage rather than a liability. Samuel Blyth's buccaneering behavior in the summer of 1813 threatened to upset this arrangement.

But was this arrangement treason? According to Article III, Section 3, of the United States Constitution, treason consists of "adhering to their [the United States'] enemies, giving them aid or comfort."[25]

Enriching British traders and textile manufacturers by importing British cloth, selling flour and cattle to the British military, which otherwise would have had to import food to North America to feed its troops—would these then qualify as aiding or comforting Britain? One certainly could make a strong case that they were. This is not to imply that all Maine citizens were trafficking with the enemy. The state had its own Federalist/Republican divisions, to be sure, but patriotism was not in short supply. However, illicit deals were not in any way extraordinary at that time, either, in Maine. In fact, it was one of these deals that, indirectly, brought the *Boxer* to the attention of Burrows's *Enterprise*.

The status quo changed in Maine in April 1814 when Britain's Admiral Cochrane imposed a full blockade of the American coastline. This was followed by a seaborne invasion of eastern Maine in September. The towns of Eastport, Machias, Castine, Bangor, and Belfast were all captured. This territory was meant to be permanently annexed to British North America. Its residents passed into a state of legal limbo—technically they were U.S. citizens living under occupation, but with the imposition of a loyalty oath to the monarchy, Britain's military leaders on the ground in Maine appear not to have recognized this. After the Revolution, no part of the United States, with the exception of the islands of Kiska and Attu in the Aleutian chain during World War II, was ever subjected to foreign occupation—that is, except eastern Maine in 1814–1815. What would that have been like? Americans in the twentieth century became accustomed to having their husbands, sons, and brothers occupying foreign lands. What if it had been the other way around? Apparently in this instance it was not the insufferable burden one might assume. As J. Mackay Hitsman pointed out:

> *inhabitants could take either the formal oath of allegiance [many did] or a lesser oath, "to behave peaceably and quietly, and while*

*inhabiting and residing within that country, not to carry arms, or
in any respect act hostilely against His Majesty, or any of his subjects." The inhabitants acquiesced in the new regime and no hostile
acts were committed against the considerable British garrison at
Castine or the small one on Moose Island. The people of Maine
were too busy resuming the interrupted trade with New Brunswick and Nova Scotia to care about a war they had not wanted
in the first place.*[26]

According to Henry Adams, Maine citizens living under occupation
"showed no unwillingness to remain permanently British subjects."[27]
The occupation authorities sweetened the pot by offering commercial
privileges to those who took the more formal oath to the crown. Talk
of an expedition of Massachusetts militia retaking the lost territory
came to nothing; and the Royal Navy dominated the waters off the
coast with the seventy-four-gun ship of the line HBMS *Bulwark* leading
her own marauding force. The residents of the Pemaquid Peninsula who
had witnessed the fight between the *Boxer* and *Enterprise* were, one year
later, living on the front line between British-occupied Maine and the
rest of the state. It was a tense time. Cannon were placed at the villages
of Pemaquid Falls and Round Pond on the peninsula to deter raiding
parties. On the morning of June 30, 1814, one raiding party of three
barges attacked the village of New Harbor on the peninsula's eastern
shore, within sight of Monhegan. Villagers who had watched the sea
duel between the *Boxer* and the *Enterprise* now faced down British seamen and marines in a pitched battle of their own. One William Elliot
claimed "he had been having the best sport he ever had in his life shooting Englishmen."[28] Most, however, living in those uncertain times in
that exposed area were less exuberant and more anxious:

*The people of Bristol [Maine], as well as other adjacent towns,
well understood the disasters that portended them; but we, their*

172

descendants, cannot now well appreciate the feeling that for many weeks pervaded the public mind.[29]

Invasion and occupation, then, were not welcomed or accommodated by all Maine citizens. It seems those living in eastern Maine, and thus closer to the Canadian frontier, were more inclined to accommodate, even embrace, British rule, while those living west of Penobscot Bay were of a more patriotic complexion. There is no doubt that Burrows, his officers, and his crew would have approved of the latter without reservation.

CHAPTER 8

The Battle

As William Burrows assumed command of the USS *Enterprise* on August 22, 1813, Britain's blockade of the New England coast north of Martha's Vineyard had not yet been implemented. The strip of coastline for which he and his crew were now responsible was essentially an open maritime zone where merchantmen and privateers from both sides sailed at their leisure . . . and at their peril. Word of the *Boxer* and its commander, Samuel Blyth, prowling Maine waters had added a new element to the mix. In short order he had snapped up five merchantmen prizes—the *Two Brothers*, *Friendship*, *Fairplay*, *Rebecca*, and *Fortune*. To assert American sovereignty and protect American shipping was Burrows's duty. Blyth's presence was a direct provocation on both counts.

It took ten days for the *Enterprise* to get under way and ride the ebb tide out of the Piscataqua River, which divided New Hampshire from Maine, to the open sea. From this point, a northerly wind made the voyage north-northeast to Portland slow going. Burrows's standard practice of appearing on the quarterdeck* in civilian clothing rather than in uniform may have elicited some comment from the crew

---

*The stern area of a ship's upper deck reserved for officers on watch.

concerning their new commander. However, it was not entirely out of the ordinary for a naval officer to do so at sea.

Burrows, the Philadelphian, had no experience with Maine or its long, serrated coastline. Much of his time before getting under way, and on the voyage to Portland, was spent familiarizing himself with nautical charts. His life and the lives of his crew might depend upon mastering them. Prominent on these charts, Portland Harbor was one of the most important ports along the Eastern Seaboard of North America. In a later era, during World War II, it served as the base for the U.S. North Atlantic Fleet fighting the Battle of the Atlantic against Hitler's U-boats.

In the early 1800s, the town apparently had a less than savory reputation among seamen. This was partly because it was rumored to be the source of much of the U.S. Navy's detested salted beef. A well-known naval ditty of the day exclaimed:

> *Old horse! Old horse, what brought you here?*
> *From Sacarap to Portland Pier*
> *I've carted stone this many a year;*
> *Till, killed by blows and sore abuse,*
> *They salted me down for sailors' use.*
> *The sailors they do me despise;*
> *They turn me over and damn my eyes;*
> *Cut off my meat and scrape my bones*
> *And pitch me over to Davey Jones.*[1]

On the headland at Portland Harbor's entrance, a lighthouse, commissioned by President George Washington in 1791, heralded the city's location. A necklace of wooded islands insulated the harbor from all but the most severe Atlantic gales. Founded in 1632, Portland, or Falmouth, as it was known through 1786, grew into Maine's premier port town. Most of its exports—boards, barrel staves, small boats, and house frames, all bound for the West Indies—were made of wood. So was most of the city. In living memory of many Portlanders in 1813 was the raid conducted by British forces under Henry Mowat in 1775 that left the port in ashes. Now, with Maine at war with Britain again, there was genuine fear of a repetition of this calamity. Fort Preble, commanding the harbor's entrance, provided the town protection. However, much of its garrison had been sent west to do battle along the Great Lakes, thus reducing the fort's defenders to a skeleton unit. There was reason for concern.

The arrival of the *Enterprise* on September 3 galvanized the town and its port. Seeing an American man-of-war flying the Stars and Stripes in their harbor gave Portlanders a much-needed boost in confidence. Their sense of isolation and vulnerability certainly would have been lessened, if not broken, by its appearance.

Lieutenant Burrows came ashore and made a point of meeting with the town's naval agent, Samuel Storer, as well as with the famous "Captain" Lemuel Moody, who had built the town's signature structure, the Portland Observatory, atop a grassy hill on the town's eastern outskirts. His tower was completed in 1807, painted a dull red, and equipped with a Dollond telescope imported from London. This device enabled Portland's merchants and shipowners to expedite commerce and cargo by supplying information on incoming vessels some time before they actually docked in the harbor.

Stevedores and their foremen could anticipate what labor would be needed where, and be ready to handle cargo shortly afterward. The maxim "time is money"* proved a boon for the port, and for Moody, who for a fee supplied the information to his subscribers, who in turn found it to be a sound investment. The captain relayed his information via semaphore, a system using different-colored flags and symbols arranged in certain patterns. The Royal Navy had been using a similar system, quite effectively, for some time.

---

*First attributed to Benjamin Franklin in "Advice to a Young Tradesman," 1748.

The Portland Observatory

Shortly after his arrival, Burrows climbed the observatory's steps and took in the breathtaking view of Casco Bay to the east, the town and port below to the west, and, perhaps, if the skies had been particularly clear, the peak of Mount Washington far to the northwest. Though it was his first visit, Burrows had personal connections to Portland. In the wars with the Barbary pirates he had served under the renowned Commodore Edward Preble and had been a messmate of Henry Wadsworth aboard the *Constitution*—both Maine men and Portland natives; both now dead. Wadsworth's young six-year-old nephew, Henry Wadsworth Longfellow, and his parents were living in the city, but Burrows would not have time to call on them. However, the events of the next few days would deeply affect the little boy. Though he never met Burrows, he would remember him.

An important concern of Burrows's was employing a native pilot to advise him and his officers about Maine's inshore waters. The naval agent, Storer, contacted a local man of ability on short notice and arranged a meeting. Samuel Drinkwater, a native of North Yarmouth and a Revolutionary War veteran, had fished and navigated the Maine coast for decades. He was seventy-one years old in 1813.[2] Having recently lost his vessel to a British privateer, he was both available and motivated. For Burrows, bringing on a man with Drinkwater's degree of experience could give the *Enterprise* an edge against Blyth, though to be fair, Blyth had slightly more experience in Maine waters than Burrows, who had none. The other men Burrows would rely on also would prove to be a competent lot. Only William Harper, his sailing master and a Portland native, would fail to rise to the occasion. First Lieutenant Edward McCall, Second Lieutenant Thomas Tillinghast, Master's Mate John Aulick, and Midshipman Kervin Waters would all prove themselves worthy of their posts under fire. All were under twenty-three years of age.

As for the enlisted seamen, some had only recently been recruited from Portland's waterfront during a previous visit by the *Enterprise*, and thus were returning briefly to their hometown. Of the other members of the crew, some were seeing the town for the first time, while the rest had been there before under their former commander, Johnston Blakely. During this port call earlier in the summer, Blakely had purchased seventy yards of bunting, one quire* of paper, two flasks of oil, a shark hook, ten balls of shipping twine, a deep-sea line of 150 fathoms, and a barrel of tar from a local chandler.[3] Having the navy in town was good for business.

How many of the crew enjoyed the haunts of Portland is unknown. There was an undeniable buzz on the streets and in the grog shops. If

---

*Approximately two dozen sheets.

rumors of one of His Majesty's brigs out there somewhere to the east were accurate, then a fight was likely coming. For a crewman this could mean prize money. It could also mean combat and death. If one had the opportunity to come ashore and down a pint or two, it certainly would not have been a bad time to do so. And there likely would have been no shortage of well-wishers to buy a round.

For his part, Samuel Blyth, with an eye for personal gain, had made a deal with a syndicate of Maine merchants recently arrived in St. John, New Brunswick. Charles Tappan and his associates had purchased a large consignment of British textiles for import into the American market. To facilitate this they registered their vessel, the *Margaretta*, under a neutral Swedish flag to ensure its safe passage. The *Margaretta*, however, needed additional protection. As Tappan himself later said, "All we had to fear was American privateers."[4] Blyth would provide the protection in exchange for a £100 bill of exchange with the merchants' London banker. This type of arrangement was entirely in character with the war along the Maine-Canadian frontier. For Blyth, it seemed a thoroughly favorable situation. A Royal Navy officer's pay was relatively small, and he certainly could use the extra money. If Americans wanted to purchase British protection for British goods, so be it.

For part of the voyage the *Boxer* towed the *Margaretta*, but as they neared the waters at the mouth of the Kennebec River, they attempted to give the impression that they were strangers. In Pemaquid Harbor the *Boxer* and the *Margaretta* rendezvoused one last time,[5] and reached agreement on having Blyth stage a mock attack on the *Margaretta* in order to demonstrate to any onlookers that the two vessels were not acting in concert. Blyth was comfortable enough, even with the *Boxer* being in enemy waters, to permit two midshipmen, a convalescing army officer, and his ship's surgeon to go ashore at nearby Monhegan

Island for some shooting and exploring. It seems clear that if he had suspected the *Enterprise* was only forty miles away he would not have been so cavalier, particularly about his surgeon. To be fair to Blyth, however, the island's small population of fishermen had sent a boat out to the *Boxer* and requested the surgeon's assistance with a crippled islander who had taken ill. His visit was not entirely recreational.

Ironically, it was the mock fire from the *Boxer* on the *Margaretta* that drew the *Enterprise*, like a shark smelling blood. A local fisherman witnessed the sham attack from a distance and made for Portland, arriving Saturday morning, September 4. He immediately reported what he had seen and heard to the officers of the *Enterprise*. They responded swiftly. Due to the contrary tide at that hour, sweeps (essentially giant forty-foot oars) were used to row the brig out of the channel leading into the harbor. Like a Roman galley, the *Enterprise* used manpower to take itself to war rather than wait for a more favorable current. There was not a moment to lose. The hunt was on.

THERE IS NO DOUBT THAT William Burrows and his men already knew something of Samuel Blyth. The *Boxer*'s commander had gained a reputation not just for his depredations on merchant vessels in Maine waters, but also for his chivalrous nature. As Theodore Roosevelt later recounted, he "had not only shown himself to be a man of distinguished personal courage, but was equally noted for his gentleness and humanity."[6] Blyth's decision to serve as a pallbearer for the *Chesapeake*'s fallen commander, Lawrence, had earned him respect and gratitude, while another escapade had shown his lighter, more gallant side. Earlier in the summer he had captured a barge full of ladies on an excursion off of West Quoddy Head. After a short and not unpleasant captivity, the party was released on the American side. One of the ladies' husbands was the commanding officer of U.S. troops stationed along the frontier. He later wrote a personal note to Blyth:

Colonel Ulmer, commanding the American troops on the north eastern frontier, improves with gratitude the earliest opportunity of acknowledging the politeness shewn to his Lady and the Ladies accompanying her, by Captain Blyth, commanding his Britannic Majesty's ship Boxer, when taken by his barge near Westquoddy, and for the gentlemanly manner in which he released Colonel Ulmer's barge.[7]

Blyth seems not to have been expecting a fight as Sunday, September 5, dawned, but that he was ready for one regardless was a given. After spending the evening at anchor in Pemaquid Harbor, the *Boxer* made for the open sea near daybreak and its rendezvous with its company ashore on Monhegan. Blyth undoubtedly felt pleased with the transaction he had made with Tappan & Co., as he placed the bill of exchange in his breeches pocket.[8] But just as it left the harbor, the *Boxer* was sighted by the *Enterprise*, and with this the complexion of Blyth's morning changed in a literal blink of an eye.

The *Enterprise* had the advantage in guns (16 to 14 total—14 eighteen-pound carronades and 2 long nine-pounders to the *Boxer*'s 12 eighteen-pound carronades and 2 long six-pounders).[9] It also had a larger complement of men aboard to man these guns, operate the vessel, and form boarding parties if necessary (102 to 66 by one account[10]). Though there is some dispute as to the number of men aboard the *Boxer* that morning, even more generous estimates of the *Boxer*'s total number of officers and crew still place the *Enterprise* with a manpower advantage.[11] Drinkwater knew the waters around John's Bay and Pemaquid Point expertly, thus providing another important advantage for the *Enterprise*. Essentially, Burrows was faced with a battle he should win. However, victory was in no way a foregone conclusion. Both vessels were considered relatively cumbersome craft. Also, as gun brigs, they were of a type that C. S. Forester once referred to as

"Eggshells armed with hammers . . . the fragile sides . . . could be torn to pieces in no time by the smashing fire of heavy carronades at close range."[12] Carronades* were "ugly, stumpy little weapons . . . but they did terrible execution at close quarters, they took little room, and they could be handled by many fewer men than the long cannon."[13] Thus, the *Enterprise*'s advantage in manpower was less significant than if both ships had been armed primarily with long guns. Finally, Blyth was a dangerous opponent who had built a career taking bold, risky gambles and succeeding. There was no reason he could not do so again.

One must not forget that James Lawrence's ghost hovered over the two vessels as they sized each other up in the brilliant sunshine of that September morn. Blyth had carried his casket. Burrows had counted him a friend. Every American seaman was keenly aware of his loss. If Britain could reimpose its considerable mystique by winning a series of single-ship actions, then what would the U.S. Navy have left? It could not hope to counter the Royal Navy's quantitative advantage, and if it could no longer claim a qualitative advantage, then its purpose as a morale booster would have been neutralized. Burrows needed to win, because America needed a win.

The morning was clear and the seas calm. The wind was light, from the north-northwest. Events unfolded in a deliberate, slow-motion-like manner. Blyth certainly recognized that short of running away he was in for a fight, and, given the man he was, he immediately dismissed the option. Indeed, he fired first at approximately 8:30 a.m. As Blyth certainly anticipated, no harm came to the *Enterprise* as the cast-iron cannonball ricocheted harmlessly across the water. The shot was meant as a challenge, as were the three Royal Naval ensigns, or flags, Blyth had ordered nailed to the mast and rigging. His

---

*Named for the Carron ironworks in Falkirk, Scotland, where they were invented.

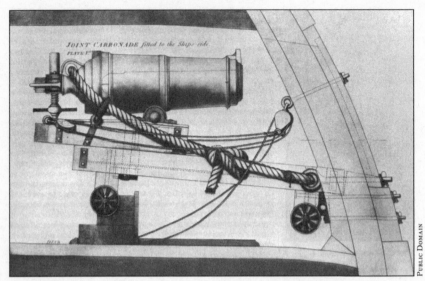

Carronade (ineffective at any considerable distance, it was, however,
particularly lethal at close range)

instructions were that "they should never be struck while he had life
in his body."[14] According to Henry Adams, "With such odds against
him the British captain might have entertained some desperate hope
of success, but could not have expected it."[15] And what of his midshipmen and surgeon on Monhegan? They would have to fend for themselves, and Blyth would simply have to fight without them.

Even with Blyth having fired off a challenge to his American pur-
suer, Burrows was in no hurry. According to Drinkwater, the wind
would shift to a more advantageous southwesterly breeze in the afternoon. His prediction proved to be spot-on. Though some of the crew
and Harper the sailing master grumbled anxiously about this slower,
more deliberate approach, Burrows was not about to rush the opportunity a more advantageous wind would present to him. As C. S. Forester remarked in one of his novels about an officer of the same rank
as Burrows, "If after all these years of service he had not learned to

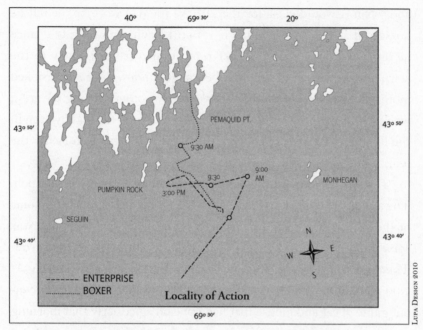

Map depicting general scene of battle and each vessel's movements
(after Sherwood Picking's *Sea Fight off Monhegan*)

wait patiently through a dull hour for an inevitable crisis, the navy had
not taught him even his first lesson."[16] Burrows waited. He now was
on the brink of what he had wanted all of his life. Sherwood Picking
wrote of him:

> *This was what he had lived for—the aim and object of every
> naval man—to command his own vessel in a fair fight with an
> equal and an honorable enemy. Nothing could take this moment
> from him.*[17]

Burrows tested his vessel's sailing attributes in comparison to
those of his quarry, attempting to gain the "weather-gauge" whereby
the *Enterprise* would have the wind at its back and could dictate where

and when it would close for the kill. As the day wore on, he felt he possessed a sufficient advantage, yet still leaving nothing to chance he ordered a long nine-pounder repositioned from the bow to the stern and aimed the weapon out his cabin window.[18] This occasioned more anxiety on the part of Harper and some others among the crew, who mistakenly believed Burrows intended to turn tail and fly even in the face of an inferior opponent. Why else position a gun facing the rear?

The seamen aboard the *Enterprise* were piped to dinner at noon. The anxiety at the mess tables likely was all but unbearable. For some of the men it was their last meal. But seamen knew that food was something you never turned down; it might not be there tomorrow. The crew of Burrows's *Enterprise* would fight on a full stomach. At 2:00 p.m. battle stations were manned. At 3:00 p.m. the long, drawn-out game of cat and mouse that had gone on since early that morning ended when the *Enterprise* finally came abreast of the *Boxer.*

A HALF A PISTOL SHOT away* stood Samuel Blyth and his men, their starboard broadside primed and ready. What goes through a man's mind when facing imminent combat? How does one overcome the natural inclination to seek cover? Drill certainly plays no small part in keeping men steady. But drill alone is not sufficient. Is an inner strength of character necessary? Or is the simple fear of letting down one's comrades in arms the most important factor? Only those who have been there know for certain, and Samuel Blyth and his men were now facing such a moment.

Each side was ready to deliver punishing blows. On the gun deck each gun's crew completed the procession of tasks that transformed

---

*Approximately ten yards in 1813.

their cumbersome monster into a truly terrifying weapon. Patrick O'Brian's description of this process is unequaled:

> . . . *with the gun run in and held by the breeching and the train-tackle, the sponger took the cartridge, a flannel bag with six pounds of powder in it, from the powder-boy, rammed it down the muzzle until the (gun) captain felt it in the breech with the priming-iron that he thrust through the touch-hole and cried "Home!" Then the 18-pound shot went down followed by a wad, both rammed hard: the men clapped on to the side-tackles and ran the loaded gun up, its muzzle as far out as it would go. The [gun] captain stabbed the cartridge with his iron, filled the hole and the pan above it with powder from his horn, and the gun was ready to fire . . . by a spark from a flint-lock or by a slow-match . . . At the word "Fire!" the [gun] captain stubbed the red end of the match into the powder on the pan, the flash ran through the touch-hole to the cartridge and the whole thing went off with an almighty bang. The shot flew out at 1,200 feet a second, the entire gun leapt backward with terrible force until it was brought up by the breeching, and the air was filled with dense, acrid smoke. The moment it was inboard the [gun] captain stopped the vent, the men at the train-tackle held the gun tight, the sponger thrust his wet mop down to clean the barrel and put out any smouldering sparks, another cartridge, shot and wad were rammed home, and the gun was run up again, hard against the port.*[19]

The men cheered lustily and fired. A deafening explosion of sound broke the late afternoon calm. Firing off the first broadside certainly could be a significant advantage, but of course, firing an accurate broadside was more so. The British crew fired high and inflicted minimal damage. Burrows and the crew of the *Enterprise* replied instantaneously. With three cheers, they poured their larboard (port) broadside into the *Boxer*.

Engagement Between the U.S. Brig "Enterprise" and H.M.S. Brig "Boxer",
Michel Corné, circa 1815

Samuel Blyth, who all of his life had heard stories of naval heroes falling gloriously in battle, lost his life in that moment. An eighteen-pound cast-iron cannonball exploded out of one of the *Enterprise*'s guns, hit Blyth in his midsection, and kept going. Flesh and bone is obviously no match for that kind of force, and valor counts for nothing. Blyth was nearly torn in two. The ensigns he had ordered nailed in place still waved above him in the stinging smoke, and the desperate fight continued. But his life slipped swiftly away, and he was gone.

In a testament to both the training of the crew of the *Enterprise* and the devastating accuracy of their first broadside, they were able to fire another before the crew of the *Boxer* could get in a second broadside of their own. Aboard both vessels, iron struck wood and flesh. Jagged splinters flew at harrowing angles and speeds. From above, spars and tackle crashed to the deck.

As history records, men can do odd things under the pressure of combat. Aboard the *Enterprise*, eighteen-year-old Master's Mate John Aulick recalled writing out instructions to his messmate on a bulwark. He wanted him to know what to do with his personal effects if he should fall. However, "a shot from the first broadside struck just over his hand and he dropped his lead pencil and didn't pick it up again."[20] Hard as it may be to believe, Aulick also recalled a member of one of the *Enterprise*'s gun crews by the name of Jordan who grew so impatient at the rate of fire that he used his own forearms to ram the shot home before it was discharged!*

Sailing Master William Harper at one point went round the deck of the *Enterprise* collecting spent grapeshot from the *Boxer*'s guns and stuffing it into his pockets. This odd behavior was only part of the story, however. After the battle, Harper had to defend himself against accusations that he had hidden behind one of the masts during the fighting, and he was in fact later charged with cowardice. Obviously, a naval officer was always expected to stand tall on the deck under fire.† (Nonetheless, across the way, three of the *Boxer*'s crew and Master's Mate Hugh James were in fact found hiding belowdecks as well.)

The two ships sailed slowly on, paired in a death struggle. Following the third broadside from the *Enterprise*, Lieutenant Burrows, exposed to enemy marksmen as well as cannonballs, helped haul a gun back into place that was functioning poorly. At that moment, with his left leg positioned on a bulwark, he was struck in the groin by a musket ball. The ball "passed up into his body, and out of his back, cutting off the neck of the bladder."[21] That it was a mortal wound was apparent immediately to both Burrows himself and the ship's surgeon, Dr. Washington, who had been called topside by Second Lieutenant Thomas Tillinghast. Dark blood spilled onto the wooden deck. Tillinghast was uncertain about what to do: fetch First Lieutenant McCall to assume command, or remain in command of his battery of guns. Burrows, in tremendous pain, gritted through his teeth to Tillinghast

---

*Curiously, however, no Jordan was listed on the *Enterprise*'s muster roll.
†Found not guilty of the charge at his court-martial in 1814, Harper nonetheless resigned from the navy.

that he would remain on deck. He had waited all of his life for this moment. He would see it out. McCall appeared at his commander's side with Harper the sailing master nearby, along with the ship's carpenter, Joseph Robinson. This was the crucial moment. Slowly, the effect of the *Boxer*'s fire was making it increasingly difficult to maneuver the *Enterprise*. McCall consulted Harper, his senior in years, but not in rank. According to later testimony before a court-martial, Harper responded, "you had better pull down the colors or we'll all be killed. The braces are all shot away, the Captain is killed, and that brig is going to rake us."[22] Yet the captain was not killed and the ship's carpenter, Robinson, reminded McCall of Burrows's earlier instructions not to surrender under any circumstances. What would he do?

Defeatism is like a disease. Harper's doubts threatened to infect the junior officers and the crew as a whole. To his everlasting credit, McCall ignored Harper's advice and heeded Robinson's. Burrows kept his head clear enough to provide McCall with a recipe for victory— outsail the *Boxer*, get ahead of her, cross, and fire on her bow, then

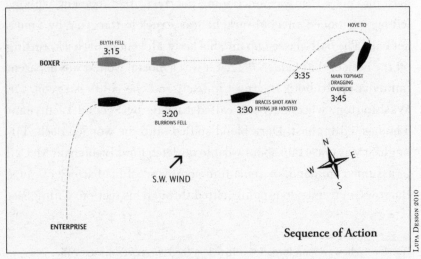

Map depicting Burrows's plan of action, which and he and his officers indeed executed (after Sherwood Picking's *Sea Fight off Monhegan*)

heave to and come about and rake her with a fresh starboard broadside. The danger would be greatest in the moments when the *Enterprise* would cross in front of the *Boxer*'s bow. It would then be most vulnerable to being rammed, boarded, and taken. And one could not underestimate the Britons' appetite for just this type of sea warfare. Only two months before, Broke had taken Lawrence's *Chesapeake* in a similar manner.

Though the "lucky little *Enterprise*" was no longer the swift craft of earlier days, her luck held. Just as it seemed the *Boxer* might successfully ram the *Enterprise* and force a battle of boarding parties, the *Enterprise* slipped past her bow. The nine-pounder sticking out of Burrows's cabin found its mark as she did so. Finally, the devastation of her starboard broadside being brought to bear on the bloodied, lumbering *Boxer* as she turned decided the matter.

The British ceased firing and called out to the *Enterprise*, but their ensigns, nailed in place, still flew. Fortunately for the remaining crew of the *Boxer*, the *Enterprise* did not fire further, and a patient and understanding Second Lieutenant Tillinghast sent John Aulick to cut down the British Jacks. The battle was over. It was not yet four o'clock in the afternoon. For William Burrows it had been his hour. Blyth's second in command, Lieutenant David McCrery, came aboard the *Enterprise* and presented the victor with his fallen commander's sword. Burrows politely refused it, with a request to return the sword to Blyth's family in England. Finally, before consenting to be carried below to what would be a lingering twilight death, Burrows exclaimed, "I am satisfied, I die contented."[23] He was twenty-seven years old.

THE RESIDENTS OF THE PEMAQUID PENINSULA waited for some news, some sign of victory or defeat. Families huddled on the headland strained their necks to see. The noise from the dueling guns would have frightened and excited the children as it rolled across the sea, while their parents would have anxiously tried to discern some sign of the battle's outcome, now obscured by the smoke from the burning gunpowder. Regardless of whose flag flew over which vessel, the direction the two vessels took would provide the answer. At first, somewhat ponderously, then picking up speed, the *Enterprise* and *Boxer* headed southwest toward Portland, and away from Nova Scotia. It was a powerful moment that would be etched in the collective memory of the peninsula's residents for generations. Pemaquid's residents were the first to know: Lawrence's defeat had been avenged. Little did they know the price that had been paid to do it.

Meanwhile in Portland, news of the battle was relayed down from the observatory by Captain Moody, then on down the hill by word of mouth to the town. With his powerful Dollond telescope, Moody could make out the smoke from the antagonists' guns, but not the result.[24] Regardless of Henry Wadsworth Longfellow's later recollection to have heard the ships' guns firing as a young boy, no such thing was in fact possible because the distance was too great.[25] The anxious throng on the hillside had to resign themselves to returning home without knowing who had won. Darkness then set in.

Though victorious, the officers and crew of the *Enterprise* were not in a celebratory mood as they returned to Portland. That night was more of a wake than a victory march. William Burrows, son of Pennsylvania, the boy who learned to love the sea by drawing ships, drifted into delirium below and never woke. The deep sleep of the forty fathoms rocked the dying man gently in its embrace. And then he too was gone.

As Sherwood Picking explained, by tradition, one of the first tasks following the trauma of what had occurred was to erase any trace of it:

> *Decks were scrubbed down, giving special care to tell-tale brown spots. Gear was laid up neatly. They were entering port. What of it that they had seen Hell; it must not show.*[26]

In all, the *Enterprise* lost three men killed, including its commander, along with fourteen wounded. The *Boxer*'s losses were significantly higher, but how much higher has been disputed ever since. The most reliable estimate appears to have been as many as twenty-five killed, including Blyth, and approximately half again wounded.[27] Some reports claimed the *Boxer*'s crew had heaved overboard numbers of their dead before actually surrendering, thus depressing the final total. Whatever the case, clearly the *Enterprise* had inflicted much higher casualties on its opponent. The damage to the *Boxer* itself was extreme. That it even stayed afloat on its voyage west to Portland is a testament to the craftsmanship of its builders back on the Isle of Wight and to the skill of Aulick and Harper, sent aboard to bring it into Portland Harbor. According to one eyewitness account from a mariner who had inspected the prize soon after, "there was no place on one side of the *Boxer* where he could not reach two shot holes at the same time by extending his arms."[28] A London newspaper later reported that "the *Boxer* was literally cut to pieces, rigging, spars, and hull; while the *Enterprise* was in a situation to commence a similar action immediately afterward."[29] The latter half of this remark may have been an exaggeration, but that the *Boxer* had been devastated by American fire was indisputable.

Up in his tower, Moody kept a keen eye on the eastern horizon still looking for a sign of the battle's outcome. The vessels soon appeared with the American ensign flying above the *Boxer*'s British ensign. Moody hurried to inform the town and port of the news. For Portlanders it must have been an exciting morning:

> *Three signals were hoisted: the American ensign, the British ensign, and a black ball. An American man-of-war was entering our harbor with a British man-of-war a prize!*[30]

This excitement, however, was of course tempered by news of Burrows's death, which McCall brought ashore with him when he proceeded to the offices of naval agent Samuel Storer. It spread quickly through the town. Isaac Hull, commanding at the Kittery naval yard, received word from Storer soon after in a note dated September 6, 1813. He began:

> *I have the happiness to inform you that another glorious achieve-*
> *ment has been added to the list of those already acquired by our*
> *navy; but the pleasure and satisfaction with which I should give*
> *you the following account is greatly lessened by the death of the*
> *brave Captain Burrows.*[31]

Hull, who had seen Burrows off when he first took the *Enterprise* to sea, now hurried north to help bury him.

That Samuel Blyth had also fallen touched a nerve with the local populace. The town's residents decided that Blyth deserved the same respect he had shown James Lawrence at Halifax three months before; the people of Portland chose to defray the costs of both commanders' funerals and accord each equal honors.[32] The date for their interment was set for Thursday, September 9. In the meantime, Edward McCall was in the position of acting commander of both the *Enterprise* and her prize, the *Boxer*, and thus weighted with the responsibilities of explaining the actions of the former and arranging for the sale of the latter. He acquitted himself of the first responsibility with a professionalism and generosity of spirit that did him great credit. In his note to the secretary of the navy, McCall emphasized the role of his fellow officer, Thomas Tillinghast, and of the ship's company in general, in securing victory. He said nothing of his own role:

> *It would be doing injustice to the merit of Mr. Tillinghast, Second*
> *Lieut. were I not to mention the able assistance I received from*
> *him during the remainder of the engagement, by his strict atten-*
> *tion to his own division, and other departments. And the officers*

*and crew generally, I am happy to add their cool and determined
conduct have my warmest approbation.*[33]

The second responsibility with which Edward McCall was charged
was to secure prize money for the officers and crew of the *Enterprise*,
as well as to arrange for Blyth's personal effects to be delivered to his
family in England. Of these personal effects the most problematic was
the bill of exchange stuffed in Blyth's breeches pocket. This, along
with other items on his person at the time of his death, had been stowed
in his seaman's chest to be delivered to his widow. Ashore, Charles
Tappan and his associates realized this simple piece of paper could
compromise them in the extreme if disclosed to the public. The American textile importers who had purchased protection for their shipment
from Blyth in New Brunswick had been involved in dealings that were
questionable at best, treasonous at worst. And the bill of exchange
found on Blyth's body proved it.

Two days after the *Boxer*'s arrival in Portland, Tappan "employed
Esquire K. to take 500 specie dollars on board the captured ship and
exchange them for the paper."[34] Lieutenant McCall was now in the
awkward position of either abetting, however indirectly, possibly treasonous business dealings or bringing the matter to light. Those five
hundred dollars, however, could mean a great deal to Samuel Blyth's
widow, Delia. For their part, Tappan and his associates justified their
transaction by claiming that the textiles they were importing were
needed to clothe U.S. forces fighting along the Great Lakes. Whether
McCall found this explanation sufficiently compelling enough, or
whether the thought of five hundred hard silver dollars in Blyth's
widow's palm convinced him, he chose to accept "Esquire K.'s" offer.
The matter remained a secret until Tappan's disclosure of these events
sixty years later, as he neared his ninetieth year.

The prize money McCall was responsible for securing for his fellow officers and the crew of the *Enterprise* was itself not necessarily a

straightforward matter. U.S. Navy bylaws concerning the taking of prizes made it clear that the rating* of an enemy prize could make a significant difference in shares for a victorious crew:

> . . . *the proceeds of all ships and vessels, and the goods taken on board them, which shall be adjudged good prize, shall, when of equal or superior force to the vessel or vessels making the capture, be the sole property of the captors; and when of inferior force, shall be divided equally between the United States [government] and the officers and men making the capture.*[35]

Thus, the key for any victorious vessel was having its opponent rated of "equal or superior force."[36] Much to McCall's pleasure, this was done on September 27 before a federal court sitting at Wiscasset, Maine.

The decision may have been encouraged by the position taken by the *Constitution*'s former commander, Isaac Hull, whose letter of September 10 to his counterpart William Bainbridge stated that he had "no doubt that she [the *Boxer*] had one hundred men aboard," and further that "she is in every respect completely fitted; and her accommodations exceed anything I have seen in her class."[37] His description of both the *Boxer*'s attributes and the damage inflicted on her by the *Enterprise* was based on his personal inspection of the prize after arriving in Portland. The greater glory to be garnered by his dead friend and the greater share of prize money to be remitted to his grieving heirs may have played some part in Hull's estimate of the *Boxer*. In the end, Burrows's heirs "received eleven hundred and fifteen dollars prize money. The seamen's shares were fifty-five dollars."[38]

Life aboard the *Enterprise* carried on. Lieutenant McCall signed for a long list of items from the same chandlery Blakely had transacted

---

*Determining the relative strength of a vessel based on the number of guns it carried and the total amount of metal its guns could throw.

navy business with back in July of that same summer. Over a period of sixteen days, he ordered everything from marlin spikes to needles, beeswax to handsaws, nails to quills for writing. Of note were the three joiner's chests that he also purchased for the *Enterprise*. These were expensive items, containing the ship's carpenters' tools of the trade. It certainly is not out of the question to surmise that these chests were replacements for chests destroyed by the *Boxer*'s broadsides.[39]

The joint funeral of William Burrows and Samuel Blyth on September 9, 1813, stands as a testament to the resonance that the battle had for the people of Portland. There was something about the deaths of these two young commanders that touched people deeply. Longfellow's poem of many decades later illustrated how even a six-year-old boy was somehow able to grasp the gravity and melancholy of the event:

> *I remember the sea-fight far away*
> *How it thundered o'er the tide!*
> *And the dead sea-captains as they lay*
> *In the graves o'erlooking the tranquil bay*
> *Where they in battle died.*
> *And the sound of that mournful song*
> *Goes through me with a thrill:*
> *"A boy's will is the wind's will,*
> *And the thoughts of youth are long, long thoughts."*

That there were those in Portland who saw the war in which Blyth and Burrows had fallen as a monstrous miscarriage of foreign policy, directed against a kindred people, mixed this mood of sorrow with disgust. As Henry Adams explained, "no incident in this quasi–civil war touched the sensibilities of the people more deeply."[40] Two noble souls gone, and for what? For "Mr. Madison's War"? A toast made by Henry Wadsworth Longfellow's father, Stephen, at a dinner held for all surviving officers four days after the funeral was a backhanded slap

PUBLIC DOMAIN

Longfellow, the lion in winter, bestowed a
degree of immortality on Blyth and Burrows.

at both the government and the unpopular war in which the two young
men had lost their lives:

> *The Nations of the Earth: May the time soon arrive when national*
> *policy shall be directed by wisdom and truth; and may a perma-*
> *nent peace soon be established upon the eternal principles of justice*
> *and good faith.*[41]

The general sentiment, however, was more in line with the description of the same dinner offered by one of the local newspapers:

> *Harmony and good fellowship was the order of the day, and party*
> *feelings and prejudices were absorbed in the general zeal to honor*
> *those who are the brightest ornaments of our country.*[42]

That this description was meant to apply equally to the fallen as well as to the living was indisputable. Burrows and Blyth were the "brightest ornaments" of their respective countries. As C. S. Forester later remarked, "It was a civilized gesture in a war that threatened to become uncivilized."[43]

Each of the bodies was placed in a mahogany casket and rowed in solemn procession to the foot of Portland's Union Wharf. There the caskets were met by a procession of officers and crew from both the conquering and conquered vessels, as well as by a long list of official dignitaries and politicians. Captain Isaac Hull served as one of the chief mourners for his young counterpart, Burrows. Winding its way up from the port, the somber procession stopped for a brief ceremony at the Second Parish Church, then out the eastern gate and up the grassy hill where Moody in his tower had spied the smoke from the battle with his glass. On to the Eastern burying ground, where two freshly dug graves lay side by side. Inside its casket, William Burrows's body was finally dressed in the uniform its owner had felt so unworthy to wear in life. Thunderous salutes echoed down the hill from volleys of muskets, and across the water from ships' guns. Church bells tolled and a young boy named Henry Longfellow had the moment imprinted onto his being forever.

CHAPTER 9

The Brotherhood

Two of the most remarkable aspects of the maritime war of 1812 were the extraordinarily high casualty rate among officers on both sides of the conflict, and the mass of recorded anecdotal evidence pointing toward an equally high incidence of magnanimous behavior on the part of these same officers toward their opposite numbers in the British or American navies. One cannot help but reach the conclusion that these men were a breed apart. Like the medieval knights of an earlier age, William Burrows and Samuel Blyth embodied not only a set of martial skills but a code for living, fighting, and dying.

To compare American and British naval officers of the Napoleonic era with knights from Europe in the Middle Ages might at first glance appear incongruous. The former served in an age of revolution and wars between nation-states in which firearms and artillery had expanded the range and force of weaponry exponentially; the latter served their feudal lords wrapped in chain mail or steel plates, fighting with steel swords, lances, and maces. Blyth, Burrows, and their brother officers fought at sea; medieval knights fought on dry land primarily, mounted on warhorses. However, these differences are to a large extent outweighed by the common ground each generation of warriors occupied. First, to serve as a U.S. Navy or Royal Navy officer, or to be knighted and carry one's lance into feudal combat, was to be part of a strict elite. Family connections, to be sure, played a part in securing a commission or squireship to enter the elite, particularly in Napoleonic-era Britain or medieval Europe. However, to gain promotion or lands, and simply to survive, aboard a man-of-war or on a medieval battlefield for any length of time one needed to possess certain specific skills. The training and character necessary to fight, survive, and prevail in the conditions naval officers of the War of 1812 or medieval knights found themselves in was not easy to attain or master. These elites, then, of which each were composed, were largely self-selecting and almost Darwinian in their ruthless winnowing of those unable to meet the exceedingly high standards established by the necessities of either sea or mounted/armored combat. What this did to those within these elites, in terms of their relationship with the great majority that lay outside their brutal and exclusive worlds, was to create a kinship among those inside these worlds. To a large extent, an American naval officer and a British naval officer, or an English knight and a French knight, had far more in common, for example, than either pair had with the general populations from whence they had come. The ferociousness of their combat in no way diminished this shared sense of mission, if not affinity. In fact, it was an extension of it.

For William Burrows and Samuel Blyth, the lives they had chosen came with the knowledge that each day could well be their last. Blyth recognized this in his last will and testament when he wrote of "the perils and dangers of the seas and other uncertainties of this transitory life."[1] In the War of 1812, it was far more likely than not that a naval officer would be either wounded or killed in battle. From June 1812 to March 1815 approximately twenty-seven engagements were fought between the American and British navies.[2] In 70 percent of these engagements officers on one or both sides became casualties.[3] In 59 percent of these engagements officers on one or both sides were either killed or mortally wounded and died soon thereafter.[4] Higher rank came with a certain degree of privilege, no doubt, but it also came with the expectation that one would put oneself in harm's way as a matter of course. The examples of both Decatur and Macdonough themselves firing the first shots in their engagements with the *Belvidera* and *Confiance*, respectively, demonstrate this hands-on yet dangerous style of leadership. A high-ranking officer on deck was a conspicuous target, exposed to broadsides from the front and enemy marksmen from above. They knew this and accepted it as part of the life they led. To have acted otherwise, to have sought cover under fire or to have delegated others to lead boardings of enemy vessels, would have exposed them to something more grievous—a diminution in respect from the men they led and criticism from their brother officers, whether compatriot or foe.

In large part it is this that explains why Burrows and Blyth acted as they did on that golden Sunday afternoon off Pemaquid Point in 1813, and throughout their careers for that matter. It also sheds light on how a young man like Burrows, with everything to live for, could claim to "die contented."[5] A civilian in that age or our own could be excused for finding this frame of mind perplexing. How could anyone be content with dying at the age of twenty-seven? Were Burrows and Blyth and their brother officers fanatics then? Would this be a fair description? No, it would not. That they may have possessed a certain fanatical commitment to their craft and to their code is nearly certain, but that is not the same as saying that they themselves were fanatics. A fanatic lacks reason and is more often than not fueled by rage. Samuel Blyth may have been a tiger in combat, but the accounts are almost universal in attributing to him a gentleness of character, a sweetness mixed with a gallant soul. In this war between what were essentially sister nations, the brotherhood of naval officers on both sides did not seek combat out of patriotic fury, but rather because it was their way of life and how they measured themselves (along with their skill as mariners) as men. It was the supreme test. Those who passed muster were quite like maritime superheroes. As the novelist Patrick O'Brian once explained:

> *When one is writing about the Royal Navy of the eighteenth and early nineteenth centuries it is difficult to avoid understatement; it is difficult to do full justice to one's subject; for so very often the improbable reality outruns fiction.*[6]

To inhabit this "improbable reality" was difficult and deadly, yet in its own unique way terribly life-affirming. Peacetime pursuits on land for those who survived the war and served out their commissions must have been dreadfully tame. And one must never forget the perils of going to sea, regardless of combat. Johnston Blakely, the *Enterprise*'s former commander and commander of the *Wasp*, which wreaked so much havoc on the *Reindeer* and British Channel shipping, cruised south with his indomitable vessel and crew in October 1814 and was never heard from again. As Henry Adams commented, "Somewhere under the waters of the Atlantic, ship and crew found an unknown grave."[7] That a ship like the *Wasp* could simply disappear is chilling. Davy Jones's locker could claim any mariner. Navy men were not exempted. This was understood.

Beyond the perils of the sea and of sea combat, another aspect separated the brotherhood from warriors in other eras—but tied them historically to their armored medieval predecessors: the code of chivalry. The conduct of medieval knights was expected to be brutal on the battlefield. Administering and sustaining terrific blows was the norm. These blows could hack off limbs, crush skulls, impale chests. It was gruesome. However, interjected over time into this martial culture was a set of evolving standards and mores. Christianity, no doubt, played a prominent role. Jesus of Nazareth's pacifist teachings were hard to reconcile with combat. By living one's life on a higher moral plane, and by exhibiting Christian behaviors in a decidedly unchristian environment, medieval knights attempted to transcend this dilemma. One important aspect of Jesus of Nazareth's worldview emphasized the central role mercy, generosity, and kindness could play in living the Christian life. Within the unwritten and evolving code of the knights the concept of showing gallantry toward one's defeated, yet worthy, opponents and their womenfolk became an expression of this desire. It demonstrated not only compassion but restraint.

As knights became more heavily armored and specialized, their martial elite status was married with a status based on acting as would become a "gentle man." That a knight's behavior in combat was the complete opposite of gentle (in fact, being gentle could make one vulnerable in the extreme in that environment) seems not to have proved to be an obstacle. Thus, killers looking to inflict a mortal wound could be transformed into brother knights sharing each other's good company, above the common lot. English rugby, which developed during the period in the first generation after the War of 1812, to a certain degree continues this ethos into the modern era. An elite sport much like American football without pads, helmets, or a forward pass, played by public school boys, rugby is violent and can be quite vicious. That said, "ruggers" take great pride in donning formal blazers and ties and convening with not only their comrades from "the pitch" but also the opposition for a pint or two after the match. Boys and men who have just tackled each other with determined ferocity—sometimes bordering on malice—trade jerseys, stories, and songs in a scene of bonhomme camaraderie. In its own peculiar way, the joint funeral for William Burrows and Samuel Blyth in Portland was an expression of these same sentiments. There was no ill will exhibited toward the British. The survivors took part in the ceremonies to honor the fallen. And the city went out of its way to be as gracious a host as they could be to both the living and the dead. As a toast made at the officers' dinner of September 13 demonstrated, the city's residents were very conscious of this role:

> *To The Inhabitants of Halifax—They honored our Lawrence—*
> *in deeds of magnanimity we will imitate, if we cannot excel.*[8]

Generous and chivalrous behavior between brother officers from opposite sides of the Atlantic in the War of 1812 was the rule and not the exception. Public displays of chivalrous behavior at a citywide level were uncommon; most chivalrous acts occurred privately, aboard ship on a more intimate level. Following the December 29, 1812, battle between the *Constitution* and the *Java* off the coast of Brazil, for instance, a surviving British officer remarked approvingly that "Our gallant enemy has treated us most generously."[9] The victor, Commodore Bainbridge, was presented with "a very handsome sword as a token for the kindness with which he had treated the prisoners."[10] This after an engagement that Henry Adams characterized as "slaughter."[11] Further testaments to the chivalrous conduct of enemy officers abound. The officers of the *Peacock* wrote of their opposite numbers aboard the victorious *Hornet*:

> *we ceased to consider ourselves prisoners; and every thing that*
> *friendship could dictate was adopted by you and the officers of the*
> Hornet *to remedy the inconvenience we would otherwise have*
> *experienced from the unavoidable loss of the whole of our property*
> *and clothes owing to the sudden sinking of the* Peacock.[12]

Apparently in this instance brother officers gave brother officers the shirts off their backs, literally. As at Halifax and Portland, the dead often received chivalrous treatment, as in the case of the *Lottery*'s captain:

Captain Southcomb, mortally wounded, was taken on board Byron's frigate, where he was treated with the greatest attention and most delicate courtesy, and when he died his body was sent ashore with every mark of respect due to so brave an officer. Captain Stewart [of the Constellation*] wrote Captain Byron a letter of acknowledgment for his great courtesy and kindness.*[13]

War heroes Perry and Macdonough were as attentive to their responsibilities as gentlemen after achieving victory as they were fearless in achieving it. Captain Barclay, the defeated commander at the Battle of Lake Erie, commented:

Captain Perry has behaved in the most humane and attentive manner, not only to myself and officers, but to all the wounded [and there were many].[14]

Captain Pring, one of the vanquished at Plattsburgh Bay, wrote of Macdonough:

I have much satisfaction in making you acquainted with the humane treatment the wounded have received from Commodore Macdonough; they were immediately removed to his own hospital . . . and furnished with every requisite. His generous and polite attention to myself, the officers, and men, will ever hereafter be gratefully remembered.[15]

Again, what is crucial not to lose sight of when reading these accounts is the fact that these men were only just removed from a state of attempting to butcher each other. Bloodlust must have been rampant, but it was checked once one side or the other struck its colors. The execution or ritual mutilation of the wounded and prisoners seems to have been entirely absent from the maritime war. The discipline and character necessary to pilot a ship and lead men in battle was given an opportunity to manifest itself in the restraint shown toward the defeated. These were exceptional men.

To be fair, other eras have produced men who lived, fought, and died according to a chivalrous code. The aces who fought in the skies over France during World War I come immediately to mind. The pilots in Manfred von Richthofen's "Flying Circus" or the Lafayette Escadrille, for instance, believed they were part of an elite that transcended the larger conflict that brought them into combat with each other. They had mastered the skills necessary to survive and triumph thousands of feet off the ground. However, one key element was absent that naval officers in the Age of Fighting Sail routinely experienced: physical proximity to one's foes, even intimacy. This intimacy is easier to comprehend when one considers that in many instances they literally had each other's blood all over them.

AND WHAT OF THE WAR, THEN? Did the causes of the War of 1812 motivate Burrows and Blyth and their fellow officers to fight to the death? The answer to this question is not as straightforward as it might appear at first glance. In one sense, of course, the war was a motivating factor. For Americans, in particular, the causes of the war were not an abstraction. Impressment had generated genuine bitterness in a seafaring class already disinclined to see Britain in a favorable light. However, there was somewhat of a division here between enlisted seamen and their officers, due to the fact that only the former were vulnerable to being impressed. For officers it was more a case of maintaining the dignity and sovereignty of the flag of the United States. Impressment was an affront to both. That navy men were extremely patriotic is without question. However, this was not a thinking man's patriotism. A naval officer would no more question his loyalty to his country than he would question whether the sky was up or the sea was wet. As Theodore Roosevelt observed:

> *Beyond almost any of his countrymen, he worshipped the "Grid-iron flag," and, having been brought up in the Navy, regarded its honor as his own.*"[16]

That the above quote in reference to U.S Navy officers could be used interchangeably to describe their counterparts in the Royal Navy merely underscores the point that they were all of a type in how they viewed the world and their place in it. King, country, flag—all served as vehicles for allowing members of the brotherhood to live their life according to their code. War provided opportunity for combat, valorous deeds, and advancement. Thus, the War of 1812 was a means, not an end in itself, for naval officers on both sides of the conflict. The flags and the war provided context, much as medieval coats of arms and quartered crests did for the knights of an earlier age. It was as if they were saying, "These symbols define me because I choose to have them define me, and here I make my stand." In this sense, then, the causes of the War of 1812 were not important motivating factors for members of the brotherhood. What Burrows and Blyth were fighting about was less important than the fact that they were fighting.

July 15, 2007

Two figures entered Portland's Eastern Cemetery at its Congress Street entrance. Dark bluish gray clouds rolled overhead, and in the quiet of the afternoon a groundskeeper seemed to appear out of the ether and asked the two figures what they were searching for. He directed them to three graves a bit farther along the grassy lane. Jagged, angry-looking streaks of lightning appeared out of the gloaming, and then a soft rain began to fall.

My former college adviser, Dr. Joyce Bibber, had agreed to meet with me and retrace Burrows's and Blyth's route through the city to their final resting place. Her reward was a rain-soaked head in the middle of a cemetery on Portland's Munjoy Hill. Snapping photographs of the three monuments that mark the spot of the two commanders' graves, and that of USN Midshipman Kervin Waters, who followed his commander in death a few years later from wounds he had sustained, I couldn't help but feel both disappointed and haunted. It is a shame to admit, but the monuments erected over the graves are in a generally poor state of upkeep. And, furthermore, they are not aesthetically impressive in any state. It is the act itself by the citizens of Portland, and the proximity of the opposing commanders' remains, that impresses the visitor. That afternoon convinced me that, like the mythical Achilles, these men deserved a degree of immortality not only for what they had done, but for what they had forgone. Neither ever became a father, let alone a grandfather, and only one was a husband. What did they leave behind? A pair of crumbling monuments in a neglected corner of a remote graveyard? Yes, and no. Time dims and miniaturizes the magnitude of an event. The "Tower moment" they had shared in one sense was a small affair, in a war most of their peers agreed afterward should never have been authorized and should never have been fought. But at the time, the battle touched a nerve. This is undeniable.

Burrows and McCall—in fact, the entire crew of the *Enterprise*—were lionized by the press in both Maine and Philadelphia. They were genuine war heroes in a country desperate for them after the devastating news of the capture of the *Chesapeake* a few weeks earlier. Congress acted swiftly to commend Burrows's and McCall's actions off Pemaquid Point and had medals struck to commemorate their victory. The sentiments expressed in the mottoes the medals carry strike a chord even today. To the fallen Burrows:

**VICTORIAM TIBI CLARAM,
PATRIAE MESTAM**
"A victory that brought fame to you,
but grief to your native land"

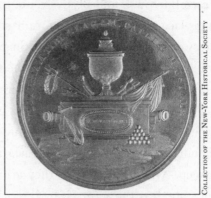

The medal struck in honor of Burrows.
No portrait of him was extant, so his
monument was shown instead.

For Burrows's steady second in command, Edward M. McCall:

SIC ITUR AD ASTRA
"This way to the stars"

The medal struck in honor of McCall

Curiously, the reverse side of both medals carried a message that was oddly out of place for William Burrows, considering the outcome:

VIVERE SAT VINCERE
"To live is sufficient victory"

Edward McCall would serve with distinction for the remainder of his naval career, but no glory would attach to his name as it had on September 5, 1813. He died just a few miles up the Delaware River from Philadelphia, in Bordentown, New Jersey, on July 31, 1853, a little over a month shy of the fortieth anniversary of his great hour. His country and the world had moved on in that time. The industrial revolution and the age of steam were transforming the American landscape, and the American navy as well. The set of skills necessary to pilot and fight a ship in the Age of Sail had become, if not obsolete, at least not entirely necessary, either. One could wonder if in his dying moments his thoughts drifted back to that golden September afternoon, and the overnight cruise along the silent Maine coast that followed, and the trying days when so many relied on him to make the right decisions. If he did, he could look back with satisfaction, knowing that he had recognized his great hour for what it was when it came and had risen to the occasion. How many men can say that?

There is no record of the five hundred specie dollars he had sent on to Samuel Blyth's widow in England. Delia herself granted an interview to the *Naval Chronicle*'s official biographer shortly afterward. That she made a deep impression on the biographer was clear, as he pleaded publicly for her to be allowed to remarry without risk of losing her late husband's pension, which was standard Royal Navy policy at the time:

> *The widow of Captain Blyth does not appear to be beyond twenty-five years of age: she has no children. However sincere her love for her brave and generous husband, time will infallibly reduce the poignancy of her feelings; and if she could meet with an offer of marriage from a man she could esteem well enough to marry, ought she to be restrained by the fear of losing a pension bestowed for the loss of a husband who fell in the flower of his days, gallantly fighting for his king and country.*[1]

One could be excused for perhaps reaching the conclusion that Blyth's biographer had fallen for Blyth's widow. In an endnote he shared a touching anecdote in which Delia produced the bow and arrows Blyth had brought back with him from French Guiana— talismans of victory and invincibility, after cheating death:

> *These arrows, and a bow, are in the possession of his widow; and the tear rose in her eye, and her lips quivered, as she shewed them to him who is now writing his memoir.*[2]

And what of Samuel Blyth? In Bermuda in early 1814 aboard HMS *Surprise*, the surviving officers of the *Boxer* sat before a court-martial to determine the extent to which they were responsible for one of His Majesty's ships falling into enemy hands. After a careful reading of Lieutenant David McCrery's letter relating the events of the afternoon of September 5, 1813, and examining McCrery himself and the other surviving officers and crew, it was determined they had done all that could have reasonably been expected of them. The most telling passage in the transcript made clear what the assembled judges believed had caused defeat:

> *. . . the capture of his Majesty's brig* Boxer, *by the United States vessel of war* Enterprise, *is to be attributed to a superiority of the enemy's force, principally in the number of men, as well as to a greater degree of skill in direction of her fire, and the destructive effects of her first broadside.*[3]

Essentially, the court found that the *Enterprise* was the superior vessel; and, as would so often have been the case in the War of 1812, that American gunnery was more accurate. What is missing in this verdict is the fact that the *Boxer* fired the battle's first broadside; therefore, as a result, one of two important conclusions may be drawn: The British crew were either poor gunners, or the American officers and crew were extraordinarily steady under fire, as the effect of the first British broadside seems not to have rattled them at all. Otherwise, how could the "destructive force of her (the *Enterprise's*) first broadside" have been the determining factor? To be fair, Blyth's crew handled their guns at a level commensurate with most Royal Navy crews in the War of 1812. Their performance was in no way exceptional—competent, but a little rusty. Conversely, the crew of the *Enterprise* was in no way exceptional in comparison to other U.S. Navy crews during the war as well—collectively they were the best trained and most highly skilled in the world at that time. The U.S. Navy made up for its small size with the quality of its officers, crews, and vessels. And again, Americans tended to hit what they aimed at.

Samuel Blyth was a hero, but some of his contemporaries were critical of his handling of the *Boxer*. However, the bold gesture he made of ordering his ensigns nailed in place before falling certainly lent itself to a romantic interpretation of the events as well. An interpretation befitting the type of life he had led in his thirty years. The editor of the then widely read *Naval Chronicle* penned a poem to honor Blyth as a preface to the publication's biography of him. Six lines in particular demonstrate that the British, too, appreciated his sacrifice, and that they recognized the citizens of Portland for what they had done:

> *His ensigns floating yet, in martial pride:*
> *Far from his native isle and widow'd bride . . .*
> *By generous foes the last sad rites were paid:*
> *In foreign earth the warrior's corse was laid . . .*
> *Whilst near his grave, in victory's arms laid low,*
> *Is seen the spot where rests his happier foe.*[*]

The vessel that Samuel Blyth commanded in battle spent the rest of its days as a merchantman flying the Stars and Stripes of his opponent. Under the jurisdiction of the United States marshal in Portland the *Boxer* was auctioned off to Thomas Merrill, while at the same time the ship's guns were auctioned off separately to a group of investors then outfitting a privateer for a cruise into the Indian Ocean. The privateer, named the *Hyder Ally*, successfully captured a number of British East Indiamen, but was never able to bring one of her prizes into port safely, thus giving rise to a myth that the *Boxer*'s ill luck had been transferred via her auctioned guns.[5] The *Boxer* itself was "still afloat as late as 1845."[6] She seemed to have had a rather more successful run in peacetime than in war.

The name *Boxer* was appropriated, as was the custom, by the victorious side in the engagement. Thus, to the present, the U.S. Navy holds rights to this ship's name among the navies of the world. Four *Boxer*s were built by the U.S. Navy and saw service in the Mediterranean and the Pacific, as well as in African coastal waters, the West Indies, and at the Naval Academy in Annapolis. The most recent of these *Boxer*s is a *Wasp*-class Multi-Purpose Assault Ship, built by Litton-Ingalls of Pascagoula, Mississippi, christened on August 28, 1993.[7] She has seen extensive action in the Persian Gulf region. The right of possession over the name *Boxer* for use by the U.S. Navy, however, has not stopped the Royal Navy from using the name again for its vessels six times. There is currently no Royal Navy vessel in service with that name. One final anecdote concerning the *Boxer* concerns its mahogany galley table. A newspaper report in 1954 claimed that a family in South Freeport, Maine, had inherited the table from an ancestor who had fought aboard the *Enterprise*, and who had somehow acquired it in the battle's aftermath.[8] The table had served variously as a kitchen and living room table, and had noticeable burn marks on one of its edges. One can only wonder if this family was aware that galley tables routinely doubled as operating tables in naval battles during the Napoleonic era.

THE NAME OF THE *BOXER*'s antagonist is one of the proudest in the U.S. Navy. The vessel that William Burrows only briefly commanded continued to play a role in asserting American sovereignty through the early 1820s—first guarding Charleston Harbor, then later cruising the pirate-infested waters of the Caribbean. In the end, she wrecked off Little Curaçao, but all hands were able to extricate themselves before she went down.[9] In 1968 a team of American and Dutch marines searched the waters off the island, trying to pinpoint the exact location of the wreck. Their goal was to salvage any items of note. The proximity of several other similar wrecks, as they eventually realized, made their stated endeavor nearly impossible to achieve.[10] That the attempt was even made some 140 years after it sank stands as a testament to the enduring hold the "lucky little *Enterprise*" has had on the affections of generations of seamen. In the words of Commander Edwin M. Jameson, "if battle stars had been in fashion during her lifetime the number to which she would have been entitled might well have covered her deckhouse."[11] Eight U.S. Navy vessels have since borne this proud name, none more famous than the World War II–era aircraft carrier that took part in most of the major sea battles in the Pacific. These included the turning-point Battle of Midway in June 1942. It was from her deck (and from that of her sister carrier, the *Yorktown*) that the decisive raid was launched against the cream of Japan's carrier fleet.[12] The most recent manifestation of the name was in the U.S. Navy's first nuclear-powered aircraft carrier, launched in 1960. This class of vessel has now become the ne plus ultra of the American navy, and a significant expansion has been undertaken at its base on Guam in order to accommodate these giants. The name also has been incorporated into popular culture in the form of the successful 1930 America's Cup defender, and, of course, as the fictional Captain James T. Kirk's spaceship boldly going "where no man has gone before. . . ."

Up on Portland's Munjoy Hill, William Burrows now lies clothed in the uniform he refused to wear in life. One could feel reasonably assured that he finally felt that he had earned the right to wear it. That he is an enigmatic figure there is no doubt. Unusually for a naval officer of that era, no portrait exists of him. This only adds to his mystique. The allusions to his Dr. Jekyll and Mr. Hyde–type personality intrigue, but do not satisfy, the curious. In Philadelphia there was extensive coverage of his battle with the *Boxer* and his heroic death, but today he is known to relatively few in that great city. Soon after news reached the public an advertisement was placed in a local paper making the following proposition:

1. *That a subscription be opened at the Mansion House, the High street Coffee House, and the Merchant's Coffee House, to raise a sufficient sum of money, for placing, in some public building in Philadelphia, a Marble Tablet, with proper inscriptions, commemorative of the gallant achievement of the late Lieut. W. Burrows, in the capture of the brig* Boxer, *by the United States' brig* Enterprise, *under his command.*

2. *That the application of the fund, be entrusted to the care of a Committee, to be appointed by the subscribers, at a general meeting.*[13]

What came of this is not known. To the northeast in Portland, Burrows's grave marker was originally neglected until Matthew L. Davis of New York, a confidant of the notorious Aaron Burr, came upon the grave during a visit to the city and, using his own resources, paid for the inscription in marble that today caps Burrows's tomb. The final lines read:

KNIGHTS OF THE SEA

Beside Burrows's marker rests that of his opponent. The marble slab erected by the *Boxer*'s surviving officers includes a line toward the bottom that any person might feel grateful to have said of them:

His friends long lament one of the best of men!

Loss: this sense can become overpowering in a setting such as Portland's Eastern burying ground. Did those three men buried in that hill die for something worthy? Is any death in war worthwhile, or are they all so many wasted souls? Perhaps these questions are unanswerable. However, what is abundantly clear is that the particular war in which these valiant knights of the sea lost their lives was a horrible and unnecessary miscarriage of leadership. If ever two countries blundered into war, it was the United States and Great Britain in 1812. And in this sense it is tragic. One can only hope that future leaders will exhibit more wisdom, flexibility, and nerve than did those in responsibility in Washington in the spring and summer of 1812. For the cost was high.

That said, in Samuel Blyth and William Burrows and the many other officers and seamen with whom they served, Britons and Americans can look back with pride on men who answered their countries' call to serve. These two attributes—a sense of a nation's history and a willingness to serve one's nation in time of crisis—are fundamental to the health of any functioning state. If these attributes become lost among the citizenry, the price can be as high as the very existence of the state itself.

July 15, 2007

When a land forgets its legends,
Sees but falsehoods in the past,
When a nation views its sires
In the light of fools and liars
'Tis a sign of its decline,
And its glories cannot last.
Branches that but blight their roots
Yield no sap for lasting fruits.[14]

Appendix A

COURT-MARTIAL OF *BOXER*'S SURVIVING OFFICERS

The following record of the court-martial appointed by the British commander in chief on the American station is taken from *The Naval Chronicle for 1814*, volume 32, page 472:

> At a Court Martial assembled and held on board H.M.S. *Surprise* at Bermuda, on the 6th, and, by adjournment, on the 7th and 8th days of January, 1814,
>
> ### Present
>
> The Hon. Henry Hotham, Captain of the Fleet, and Second Officer in the command of his Majesty's Ships and Vessels at Bermuda, President.
>
> ### Captains
>
> Robert Dudley Oliver   Andero Fitzherbert Evans
> Robert Lloyd   Richard Byron
> Sir Thomas John Cochrane, Knt.
>
> Being all the captains present, except Hugh Pigo, Esq., captain of H.M.S. *Orpheus*, who, from ill health, was unable to attend.

Appendix A

The Court, pursuant to an order from the Right Hon. Sir John Borlase Warren, Bart. K. B. Admiral of the blue, and commander-in-chief of his Majesty's ships and vessels employed, and to be employed, on the American and West Indian station, etc. etc. to the Hon. Henry Hotham, captain of the fleet, and second officer in command of his Majesty's ships and vessels at Bermuda, dated the 4th day of January, 1814, having been duly sworn (The President having received a letter from the commander-in-chief, setting forth that his Majesty's service required Captain Oliver should put to sea immediately, in the *Valiant*, the Court dispensed with his attendance), proceeded to inquire into all the particulars attending the capture of his Majesty's brig *Boxer* by the enemy, and to try Lieutenant David M'Crery, her surviving officers and company, for the same; and having heard Lieutenant M'Crery's official letter and narrative of the action, and strictly examined the said Lieutenant, and the surviving officers and company, produced to the Court, and carefully investigated all the particulars attending the capture of his Majesty's brig *Boxer*, by the United States vessel of war *Enterprise*; and having very maturely and deliberately weighed and considered the whole and every part thereof, the Court is of opinion, that the capture of his Majesty's brig *Boxer*, by the United States vessel of war *Enterprise*, is to be attributed to a superiority of the enemy's force, principally in the number of men, as well as to a greater degree of skill in the direction of her fire, and the destructive effects of her first broadside.

The Court is also of the opinion, that the surviving officers and company (with the exception hereinafter made) appear to have done their utmost to capture the enemy's vessel, to defend his Majesty's brig *Boxer*, and to have conducted themselves with the courage and determination, not to surrender while any prospect of success remained, and the Court will therefore adjudge Lieutenant M'Crery, the surviving officers and company, to be acquitted, with the exception of Mr. Hugh James, quartermaster, doing duty as master's mate; John Dodd, James Jackson, and Wm. Slattery, seamen; who have not appeared before the Court, and have been stated to have deserted their quarters during the action, and through cowardice, negligence, or disaffection, to have withdrawn themselves from their duty in the engagement; and the said Lieutenant David M'Crery, the surviving officers and company, are hereby acquitted accordingly, with the exception of the said Mr. Hugh James; John Dodd, James Jackson, and Wm. Slattery, seamen.

Signed by the Court, and by
J. Irving, Officiating Judge Advocate.

Appendix B

Court-martial of William Harper
(*Selected Excerpts*)

Proceedings of a General Court-martial, held on board the United-States Brigantine *Enterprize*, in the Harbour of Portsmouth New Hampshire, on Tuesday the twenty-eight day of December current, by virtue of the following orders.

Navy Yard, Portsmouth New Hampshire
December 24th: 1813.

Orders

A General Court-martial to consist of seven members, will assemble on board the United States Brigt, *Enterprize*, in the Harbour of Portsmouth-on Tuesday the twenty eight day of December current, at eleven o'clock in the forenoon-for the trial of Sailing-master William Harper on a charge exhibited against him Lieutenant Edward R McCall, both of the United States Navy-

President-Captain Isaac Hull of the United States Navy-commanding at Portsmouth New Hampshire.

Captain John Smith

Appendix B

Captain John Orde Creighton
Lieut. Commandt. James Renshaw
Lieut. John H. Elton
Lieut. Otho Norris
Lieut. Henry B. Rapp &
George W. Prescott Esquire, Judge Advocate
appointed by the President of said Court.-

Signed:—Isaac Hull

DECEMBER 28TH: 1813

The Court being duly sworn, in the presence of the Prisoner proceeded to the trial of Sailing-master William Harper of the United States Navy, who being previously asked if he had any objections to the members named in the order, & replying in the negative—was arraigned him by Lieutenant Edward R. McCall of the United States Navy.

CHARGE—COWARDICE.—

Specification 1st:

For leaving his station on board the United States Brig *Enterprize*, in the early part of the engagement between the said Brig and the British Brig *Boxer* on the fifth day of September, Eighteen Hundred & Thirteen—and endeavoring to screen himself from the shot of the enemy by getting behind the fore-mast, and under the heel of the bowsprit whilst the enemy lay on the quarter of the *Enterprize*—by doing which the said Harper set an example to the crew, that might have led to her surrender—and to the disgrace of the American character.—

Appendix B

Specification 2nd.

For having advised me to haul down the colors of the United States Brig *Enterprize* during the time of the engagement aforesaid—and when the firing of the enemy was much diminished and when that of the *Enterprize* could have been continued with unabated effect.

Signed—E. R. McCall

To which the Prisoner pleaded NOT GUILTY.

(Tillinghast's testimony)

Lieutenant Thomas G. Tillinghast of the United States Navy—a witness for the prosecution, being duly sworn, says—He was an officer on board the United States Brig *Enterprize* during the engagement aforesaid—was a Lieutenant and stationed on the Quarter-Deck—that the prisoner was not on the Quarter-deck, during the action—after the Captain fell—that when the *Boxer* was in a raking position—near thirty minutes after the action commenced—he heard the Prisoner call out—the *Boxer* is going to rake us—which alarmed some of the marines and brace men who immediately got in the wake of the mast—he then ordered to man the starboard guns, and let fall the foresail—when he saw the Prisoner go forward, but could not see for what purpose—that his orders were obeyed, and the Prisoner, afterward told him he went forward, at the time, to execute them.

Question by the Court—Did you at any time during the action observe the Prisoner endeavor to screen himself,—by getting behind the Foremast—or under the heel of the Bowsprit?
Answer—No—his situation at the gangway was an exposed one.

Appendix B

Question by the Court—Did you hear or see the prisoner, at any time during the action ask Lieutenant McCall to haul down the Colors of the *Enterprize*?

Answer—No.

Question by the Court—Did you, during the action, discover any symptoms of cowardice in the Prisoner?

Answer—None, unless it shall be inferred from his exclaiming—"The *Boxer* is going to rake us."

Question by the Court—Did the Prisoner whilst at the gangway appear to be attending to his duty, and to the orders given him?

Answer—I can't tell—I was otherwise engaged—I asked the Prisoner if it would not be better to take a raking position—he replied "we shall soon be in one"—which was the only time I spoke to him—he then appeared to be very cool and collected—this was about thirty five minutes after the commencement of the action—and the enemy was then on the weather quarter.

Question by the Court—Did you see the Prisoner go forward after you had this conversation with him?

Answer—No.

Question by the Court—Where was the Prisoner when the enemy struck?

Answer—I can't positively say—but think he was in the larboard gangway.

Question by the Prisoner—Was there a debate among the officers of the *Enterprize* previously to the engagement between that Brig and his Britannic Majesties Brig *Boxer*, on the expediency of engaging, and the probability of conquering?

Answer—I knew of no debate.

Question by the Prisoner—Was I very earnest in urging an attack?

Answer—You appeared to be very anxious.

Question by the Prisoner—Did I discover symptoms of consternation when I said the enemy were going to rake us—or at any time during the action that you observed?

Answer—I did not observe any.

Question by the Prisoner—Did you hear Lieutenant McCall declare after the engagement—that I behaved as well as any man could have done during the action?

Answer—No.

Question by the Prisoner—Have you heard Lieutenant McCall declare that he did not know anything concerning the grounds of the complaint against me?

Answer—I did not—I never heard any complaint of your conduct till about twenty four hours after the action—when the *Enterprise* had got into Port—you had charge of the *Boxer* till she anchored.

Question by the Prisoner—Who first discovered that the *Boxer* had surrendered?

Answer—I believe I did.

Question by the Prisoner—Who hailed her—and ordered her officer to haul down the Colors?

Answer—I think it was myself—though I may mistake.

Question by the Prisoner—Did you consult with me concerning the expediency of letting fall the foresail, before you ordered it?

Answer—No.

Question by the Prisoner—Was I capable, and punctual in the discharge of the duties of my office before this action took place?

Answer—Yes.

(Aulick's testimony)

John H. Aulick, a witness for the prosecution—being duly sworn—says he was on board Brig *Enterprise* during the action with the *Boxer*—acting masters-mate—stationed on the Forecastle—he saw the Prisoner about ten or fifteen minutes after the action commenced on the Fore Castle—at a time when the *Boxer* was passing under the stern of the *Enterprise*—heard him call out two or three times—"She is going to rake us," when he saw him get directly before the Foremast where he remained two or three minutes from this the Prisoner went aft and stayed some time. Soon after he came forward as far as the Galley—and with his trumpet called out to cheer the men.

Appendix B

Question by the Court—Was it your impression that the Prisoner got before the Foremast to screen himself from the shot of the enemy?

Answer—It was.

Question by the Court—Did you see the Prisoner under the heel of the Bowsprit, at any time during the action?

Answer—I did not.

Question by the Court—Could he have been there without your seeing him?

Answer—He could.

Question by the Court—Did you see or hear the Prisoner at any time during the action advise Lieut. McCall to haul down the Colors?

Answer—I did not.

Question by the Court—At what time was it you saw him use the trumpet—was it at the time the Foresail was let fall?

Answer—I do not recollect whether it was at that time, or not.

Question by the Court—Did you see the Prisoner assist in letting fall the Foresail?

Answer—I did not.

Question by the Court—Was it possible for a man to screen himself under the heel of the Bowsprit without laying down?

Answer—I believe I could.

Question by the Court—Could Lieut. McCall, & the Prisoner have been in conversation—without your perceiving them?

Answer—They might.

Question by the Court—Did you observe whether the calling out of the Prisoner "they are going to rake us" had an effect upon the crew inducing them to leave their quarters?

Answer—I did not observe any such effect.

Question by the Prisoner—What was your opinion after the action of my fidelity in the discharge of the duties of my office during the action?

Answer—It was that you had not behaved yourself as became an Officer—by reason of your having left the Quarter Deck and coming forward where there was no apparent duty for you to do.

Question by the Prisoner—What conversation did you hold with me, on board the *Boxer* after the action, relative to it?

Answer—I do not recollect.

Question by the Prisoner—Did I appear terrified when I said the enemy was going to rake us?

Answer—'Twas my impression you was.

Question by the Prisoner—What was the state of the wind during the action?

Answer—It was light.

Question by the Prisoner—Was not the Flying-Gib set & hauled down several times during the engagement?

Answer—It was two or three times.

(Robinson's testimony)

Joseph Robinson a witness for the prosecution, being duly sworn, says, he was Carpenter on board the *Enterprise* at the time of the engagement with the *Boxer,* and stationed at the Pumps—about thirty minutes after the action commenced, he was standing on the main hatch, and saw the Prisoner come round on the larboard-side—betwixt the forward gun from the gangway, & the next—and call to Lieutenant McCall, who was forward, & say to him the Captain is killed—the braces are all shot away, and had not we better haul down the colors—that he, the witness observed to the Prisoner, recollect Sir, Captain Burroughs said the colors should not be hauled down for nothing, that he saw no more of the Prisoner till after the enemies main-topmast went—and then he was very active.

Question by the Court—Did you hear the Prisoner cheer the crew at any time during the action?

Answer—No.

Question by the Court—Did you observe the prisoner at any time during the action attempt to screen himself by getting behind the foremast—or under the heel of the Bowsprit?

Answer—No.

Question by the Court—Was there any officer or officers as near or nearer than you was to the Prisoner at the time of the conversation you state as having taken place between the Prisoner & Lieutenant McCall?

Answer—I did not observe any.

Question by the Court—When the Prisoner asked Lieut. McCall if he had not better haul the Colors down—was he on the side nearest the enemy?

Answer—He came from the starboard to the larboard side on which was the enemy.

Question by the Court—What was the situation of the *Enterprise* at the time you heard the Prisoner ask Lt. McCall to haul down the Colors?

Answer—The Captain was wounded—the braces much cut away—and one boy killed.

Question by the Prisoner—Where did Lieut. McCall stand at the time when you say you heard me advise him to haul down the colors?

Answer—Forward—on the larboard side.

Question by the Prisoner—Where did you stand at that time?

Answer—On the after-main-hatch.

Question by the Prisoner—Where was Lieut. Tillinghast then?

Answer—Abaft on the Quarter-Deck.

Question by the Prisoner—Was the main-topsail laid to the mast at the time when you say you heard me advise Lieut. McCall to strike the Colors?

Answer—I can't say.

Question by the Prisoner—Was not Lieut. Tillinghast nearer to me than Lieut. McCall was at the time of the conversation you have stated?

Answer—I did not observe.

Question by the Prisoner—Was not the main-topsail hove aback before a gun was fired from either vessel?

Answer—I do not recollect that it was.

Appendix B

(McCall's testimony)

Lieutenant E. R. McCall, a witness for the prosecution, being sworn, says he was first Lieutenant on board the Brig *Enterprise* at the time of her engagement with the British Brig *Boxer*—stationed forward, in command of the first Division— that on the evening of the 5th of September last about fifteen minutes after the action commenced he saw the Prisoner forward—whenever he heard the report of a gun the prisoner would get behind the foremast and on the side of the Bowsprit opposite the enemy—and stoop down to avoid the balls—that he picked up shot that fell about the foremast and put them in his pocket, which conduct tended to discourage the men. At one time, the *Boxer* had the *Enterprise* in a raking position—when the Prisoner observed, in the presence of the men "by God we shall all be killed." Shortly after the Prisoner was standing on the combings of the ward-room hatch—when he, the witness, asked him if there was anything he could advise to have done, that would secure the victory, he answered "by God we shall all be killed," at which time the fire of the *Enterprise* was kept up as warmly as it was at the commencement of the action, and that of the enemy considerably diminished—the Carpenter standing by at this time, hearing the observations of the prisoner, tapped me on the shoulder & said, Mr. McCall let the Colors fly as long as there shall be six men alive—they will all stand by you—on which, he the witness went forward, and saw no more of the Prisoner during the action.

Question by the Court—At the time you saw the Prisoner picking up the balls forward of the foremast did he appear to be alarmed?
Answer—I thought he did.
Question by the Court—Did you reprimand him at the time for his conduct forward, or order him to go aft?
Answer—I told him to go aft & look out, & keep the vessel in a favorable position.

Appendix B

Question by the Court—Did you order the prisoner to take charge of the *Boxer* after her surrender?

Answer—I did—after the prisoners were removed.

Question by the Court—Where was Lieut. Tillinghast at the time you had this conversation with the Prisoner?

Answer—He was on the Quarter-deck—between the two after guns—if I do not mistake.

Question by the Court—Did you, at any time during the action, hear the Prisoner cheering the men?

Answer—No.

Question by the Court—What did you see in the men that led you to believe that the Prisoner's conduct, in getting behind the Fore-mast, had a bad effect on them?

Answer—I saw none at all—they all behaved extremely well.

Question by the Prisoner—How long did I remain forward by the Fore-mast and bowsprit?

Answer—I can't exactly say—but saw you there several times.

Question by the Prisoner—How near was you to me?

Answer—So near, that in passing from one side of the fore-castle of the other I brushed you.

Question by the Prisoner—What officers were there then on the Fore-castle?

Answer—Midshipman Aulick—and Ball—the Boatswain.

Question by the Prisoner—Did you not come to me twice as far aft as the main-hatch, and exclaim, "Mr. Harper, what in God's name shall we do—had we not better haul down the colors?"

Answer—No.

Question by the Prisoner—Do you say that you did not speak to me but once relative to the colors?

Answer—I did not speak to you at all about the colors, only in reply, said they should not be hauled down, they should fly.

Question by the Prisoner—Did I not say to you—if you think proper I will put the helm up, run down a small distance, and reeve new-braces—and then engage anew?

Answer—Not to my knowledge.

Question by the Prisoner—Did you at any time during the action, give any order, other than in one instance, to call out "boarders away"?

Answer—Yes, I did several.

Question by the Prisoner—Did you reply to the enquiries of any gentleman or gentlemen concerning my conduct in the action, that I had behaved well—or very well—or as well as any man?

Answer—I believe I did—with a view to prevent the circulation of a contrary report—that it might not get to your family.

Question by the Prisoner—Did you not make such reply to some person or persons before the *Enterprise* arrived at Portland and before you had gone to that Town?

Answer—No—not to any one before the *Enterprise* arrived.

(Drinkwater's testimony)

The evidence on the part of the prosecution being closed Samuel Drinkwater—a witness for the Prisoner, being duly sworn says—he was Pilot on board the *Enterprise* at the time of the action between that vessel and the *Boxer*—that three or four minutes before the action commenced, Capt. Burrows ordered him below—frequently, in the course of the action, he heard the Prisoner's voice giving directions concerning the management of the vessel—about twenty minutes after the action commenced he came on deck and stood on the gratings of the fore-hatch—and soon after, saw the Prisoner stepping aft, hastily, on the larboard-side, on which was the enemy—that he remained there a few minutes and went below again—that he saw the Prisoner no more during the engagement.

Question by the Prisoner—Did you hear me cheer the men at any time during the action?

Answer—I do not know that I did.

Question by the Prisoner—Was you below when Snow Jones went below wounded?

Answer—I was.

Question by the Prisoner—How long after the action commenced was it?

Answer—Fifteen or twenty minutes.

Question by the Prisoner—In what condition was it?

Answer—He was helped down by someone, and appeared to be in much distress.

Question by the Prisoner—Did you observe my conduct before the action commenced whether I was earnest, or unwilling to engage?

Answer—I did—you appeared as anxious to engage as any officer on board—and spoke as encouraging.

Question by the Prisoner—Did you hear any complaint of my conduct during the action, from Lieut. McCall, after it in going to Portland?

Answer—No—I did not.

Question by the Prisoner—Did the crew of the *Enterprise* appear much opposed to me—before, and after, the action?

Answer—Yes—I have heard the crew, generally, say, they disliked you—that you was cross and crabbed.

Question by the Prisoner—What did you hear expressed as the wish of many of the crew of the *Enterprise*, should she be engaged—as to my fate?

Answer—I have heard many of them say they hoped, if ever they got into action—you would get killed.

Question by the Prisoner—Did I know the British-vessel, when she came in view—did I inform Captain Burrows that it was the *Boxer* and state what was her force?

Answer—Yes—to the officers generally—Captain Burrows was present.

Samuel Drinkwater was again called, and questioned as follows:

Question by the Prisoner—What did I say to the men when we were about to engage the *Boxer*?

Answer—Just before the action commenced, I heard you say to the men "now boys we have a job to do, and we must stick to them."

Question by the Prisoner—What did I at that time say about capturing the *Boxer*?

Answer—I heard you say, you knew that Brig. That it was the *Boxer*, and that if the Captain would engage her she would be taken in fifteen or twenty minutes.

Question by the Prisoner—What did you hear me say, in a conversation off pumpkin-Rock?

Answer—When in conversation with Captain Burrows, off pumpkin-Rock, about fifteen minutes before the commencement of the action—on the subject of passing round it—you said—what in hell are we going round pumpkin-Rock for—we are going to fight that Brig.

SENTENCE

The court, after the most attentive consideration of the evidence adduced, is of opinion, that the Prisoner, Sailing-master William Harper, is NOT GUILTY of the charge exhibited against him—and do therefore acquit him, in which opinion the Court is unanimous.

Isaac Hull, President
John Smith
J. Blankeley
Jon. H. Elton
J.P. Oellers
Geo. W. Prescott
Judge Advocate.—

THE COURT ADJOURNED *SINE DIE*.—

Isaac Hull
Geo. W. Prescott
Judge Advocate.

Selected Bibliography

Books

Adams, Henry. *The War of 1812.* Washington, D.C.: The Infantry Journal, 1944.

Anderson, Laurie Halse. *Fever 1793.* New York: Aladdin Paperbacks, 2000.

Anderson, Mary Powers. "'It is My Duty to Support My Officers . . .': William Ward Burrows, First Commandant of the Marine Corps," *The Wards and Bakers of the Deep South,* 5th ed. (June 1995).

Anderson, Mary Powers. "The Thoughts of Youth are Long, Long Thoughts: William Burrows, Lt., USN," *The Wards and Bakers of the Deep South,* 6th ed. (September 1995).

Bailey, Isaac. *American Naval Biography.* Providence, RI: H. Mann & Co., 1815.

Bell, Whitfield J. *Patriot-Improvers: Biographical Sketches of Members of the American Philosophical Society,* vol. 1. Philadelphia: American Philosophical Society, 1997.

———. *Patriot-Improvers: Biographical Sketches of Members of the American Philosophical Society,* vol. 3. Philadelphia: American Philosophical Society (forthcoming).

Borneman, Walter R. *1812: The War That Forged a Nation.* New York: HarperCollins, 2004.

Bowen, A. *The Naval Monument: Containing Official and Other Accounts of All the Battles Fought Between the Navies of the United States and Great Britain During the Late War.* Boston: Phillips, Sampson & Co., 1836.

Selected Bibliography

Breck, Edward. *Burrows, William (Oct. 6, 1785–Sept. 5, 1813).* Washington, D.C.: Department of the Navy Operational Archives Branch, n.d.

Carnes, Mark C., and John A. Garraty. *American National Biography,* vol. 4. New York: Oxford University Press, 1999.

Chapelle, Howard L. *The History of the American Sailing Navy.* New York: Bonanza Books, 1949.

———. *The History of American Sailing Ships.* New York: Bonanza Books, 1935.

Cordingly, David. *The Billy Ruffian: The* Bellerophon *and the Downfall of* Napoleon. New York: Bloomsbury USA, 2003.

Cournoyer, Jill, and Susan Gold. *The History of Union Wharf.* Saco, ME: Custom Communications, 1998.

Ellis, Joseph J. *American Sphinx.* New York: Alfred A. Knopf, 1997.

Foner, Eric. *Tom Paine and Revolutionary America.* New York: Oxford University Press, 1976.

Forester, C. S. *Beat to Quarters.* New York: Little, Brown & Co., 1938.

———. *The Age of Fighting Sail: The Story of the Naval War of 1812.* Garden City, NY: Doubleday & Company, 1956.

———. *Hornblower and the Hotspur.* New York: Little, Brown & Co., 1962.

———. *Young Hornblower.* New York: Little, Brown & Co., 1960.

Garraty, John A. *Encyclopedia of American Biography.* New York: Harper & Row Publishers, 1974.

Gibson, R. Hamond. *Who Built the Enterprise?* Unpublished manuscript, n.d.

Goold, William. *Portland in the Past: With Historical Notes on Old Falmouth.* Portland, ME: B. Thurston & Company, 1886.

Great Books: The Art of War. Produced and directed by N. Diane Smith. The Learning Channel, 1994.

Guttridge, Leonard F. *Our Country, Right or Wrong: The Life of Stephen Decatur, the U.S. Navy's Most Illustrious Commander.* New York: Forge Books, 2006.

Hall, Rosa Baylor. *Revolutionary War Patriots and Soldiers.* Shepherdstown, WV: Rosa Baylor Hall, 2003.

Hanna, Joshua. *The Pemaquid Peninsula of Maine: A Study of Economic and Community Development 1815–1915.* Unpublished manuscript, 1994.

Haskell, P., S. Quail, R. Riley, and J. Webb. *The Spirit of Portsmouth: A History.* Chichester, West Sussex: Phillimore, 1989.

Hickey, Donald R. *The War of 1812: A Forgotten Conflict.* Urbana and Chicago: University of Illinois Press, 1989.

Selected Bibliography

Hitsman, J. Mackay. *The Incredible War of 1812: A Military History.* Toronto: University of Toronto Press, 1965.

Howarth, David, and Stephen Howarth. *Lord Nelson: The Immortal Memory.* New York: Viking, 1989.

Isaacson, Walter. *Benjamin Franklin: An American Life.* New York: Simon & Schuster, 2003.

James, William. *James' Naval History.* Robert O'Byrne, ed. London: W. H. Allen & Co., 1888.

Jameson, Edwin M. *The Saga of the U.S. Schooner* ENTERPRIZE. Unpublished manuscript, n.d.

Johnson, Allen. *Dictionary of American Biography*, vol. 1. New York: Charles Scribner's Sons, 1958.

Johnson, Paul. *A History of the American People.* New York: HarperCollins, 1997.

Johnston, John. *A History of Bristol and Bremen.* Albany: Joel Mussell, 1873.

Longfellow, Henry Wadsworth. *The Poems of Henry Wadsworth Longfellow.* New York: Modern Library, n.d.

McCullough, David. *John Adams.* New York: Simon & Schuster, 2001.

McInnis, Edgar. *Canada: A Political and Social History*, rev. ed. New York: Holt, Rinehart, and Winston, 1963.

Mee, Charles. *Playing God: Seven Fateful Moments When Great Men Met to Change the World.* New York: Simon & Schuster, 1993.

Milano, Kenneth W. *Remembering Kensington & Fishtown: Philadelphia's Riverward Neighborhoods.* Charleston: The History Press, 2008.

Moulton, John K. *Captain Moody and His Observatory.* Falmouth, ME: Mount Joy Publishing, 2000.

Nash, Gary B. *First City: Philadelphia and the Forging of Historical Memory.* Philadelphia: University of Pennsylvania Press, 2002.

The Naval Chronicle for 1814: Containing a General and Biographical History of the Royal Navy, vol. XXXII. London: Joyce Gold, 1814.

Newman, Simon P. *Embodied History: The Lives of the Poor in Early Philadelphia.* Philadelphia: University of Pennsylvania Press, 2003.

Norton, Lemuel. *Autobiography of Lemuel Norton.* Portland, ME: Brown Thurston, 1862.

O'Brian, Patrick. *Master and Commander.* Glasgow: William Collins & Son, 1970.

————. *Men-of-War: Life in Nelson's Navy* (first American ed.). New York: W. W. Norton & Company, 1995.

Selected Bibliography

————. *The Nutmeg of Consolation.* New York: W. W. Norton & Company, 1991.

————. *The Wine-Dark Sea.* New York: W. W. Norton & Company, 1993.

Page, Joseph A. *The Brazilians.* Reading, MA: Addison-Wesley Publishing Company, 1995.

Pastore, Christopher. *Temple to the Wind: The Story of America's Greatest Naval Architect and His Masterpiece,* Reliance. Guilford, CT: The Lyons Press, 2005.

Picking, Sherwood. *Sea Fight off Monhegan.* Portland, ME: Machigonne Press, 1941.

Potter, E. B. *The Naval Academy Illustrated History of the United States Navy.* New York: Thomas Y. Crowell Company, 1971.

Pratt, Fletcher. *The Compact History of the United States Navy.* New York: Hawthorn Books, 1962.

————. *Preble's Boys: Commodore Preble and the Birth of American Sea Power.* New York: William Sloane Associates, 1950.

Remer, Rich. *Old Kensington.* Philadelphia: The Historical Society of Pennsylvania, n.d.

Roberts, Kenneth. *Trending into Maine.* New York: Doubleday & Co., 1934.

Roosevelt, Theodore. *The Naval War of 1812.* New York: G. P. Putnam's Sons, 1882; Kessinger Publishing reprint, 2004.

Seaman, L. C. B. *From Vienna to Versailles.* London: Routledge, 1955.

Thompson, Peter. *Rum Punch & Revolution: Taverngoing & Public Life in Eighteenth-Century Philadelphia.* Philadelphia: University of Pennsylvania Press, 1999.

Weber, Joseph. "The Sea Battle Between the *Enterprise* and *Boxer*," *Discover Maine 2003–2004.*

Weigley, Russell F., et al. *Philadelphia: A 300-Year History.* New York: W. W. Norton & Company, 1982.

DOCUMENTS

1790 United States Census, William Burrowes, Philadelphia County.

"An Act for the Gradual Abolition of Slavery in Pennsylvania," March 1, 1780.

Burrows-Thompson Family Bible (Rosa Baylor Hall; copy of original held by United States Marine Corps).

Chandler's record book, missing its first (identifying) page, circa 1813, Portland, ME (held in a private collection).

Selected Bibliography

Dockyard Officers card index, Samuel Blyth—Sheerness, Master Attendant 1 April 1791–23 December 1794 Died (National Maritime Museum, Greenwich, UK).

Last Will & Testament of Samuel Blyth (Public Records Office: The National Archives, Kew, UK).

Lieutenant John Gallagher letter to Secretary of the Navy Smith Thompson, August 1, 1823 (Chesapeake Bay Maritime Museum, St. Michaels, MD).

Lieutenant William Burrows letter to Commodore John Rodgers, June 23, 1810 (Gratz Collection: The Historical Society of Pennsylvania).

Master Commandant Thomas Robinson Jr. letter to Secretary of the Navy, April 23, 1805 (Chesapeake Bay Maritime Museum, St. Michaels, MD).

President James Madison letter to Secretary of the Navy William Jones, September 16, 1813 (William Jones Papers: The Historical Society of Pennsylvania).

"Report of Search for Wreck of *Enterprise* submitted by Commander Amphibious Squadron Ten United States Atlantic Fleet," December 24, 1968 (Chesapeake Bay Maritime Museum, St. Michaels, MD).

Secretary of the Navy William Jones letter to Lieutenant William Burrows, August 6, 1813 (Operational Archives Branch, Department of the Navy, Washington Navy Yard, D.C.).

United States Constitution, Article III, Section 3.

PERIODICALS

Analectic Magazine, November 1813

Dayton Daily News, August 29, 2004

Eastern Argus, September 9, 1813

Eastern Argus, September 23, 1813

Eastern Argus, September 30, 1813

Eastern Argus, October 7, 1813

Gentleman's Magazine, July to December 1813

Portland Evening Express, September 23, 1954

Portland Gazette, September 13, 1813

Portland Gazette, September 27, 1813

Portland Gazette, October 4, 1813

Poulson's American Daily Advertiser, September 11, 1813

Selected Bibliography

Poulson's American Daily Advertiser, September 13, 1813

Poulson's American Daily Advertiser, September 15, 1813

Poulson's American Daily Advertiser, September 16, 1813

Seaside Oracle, June 12, 1875

Transcript, January 3, 1894

Washington Post, July 4, 1993

Zion's Advocate, August 6, 1834

INTERVIEWS

Ken Milano, Kensington Historical Project

Commander Richard M. Detwiler, USN Reserve (ret.)

David Sweetman, Old Wirralians Rugby Club, Birkenhead, England (ret.)

Patrick Runyon, USN (ret.), member, Swift Boat Sailors Association

Seaman Christina Nichols, USN, guide USS *Constitution*, Charlestown
Naval Yard

Senator Doug White, Ohio State Senate–Manchester (ret.), member,
Vietnam Veterans of America

INTERNET SITES

Clerk, United States House of Representatives: clerk.house.gov/evs/2002/
roll455.xml

David Glasgow Farragut, National Park Service: www.nps.gov/archive/
vick/visctr/sitebltn/farragut.htm

Pennsylvania State Archives: www.docheritage.state.pa.us/documents/
slaveryabolition.asp

The Churchill Center: www.winstonchurchill.org/i4a/pages/index.cfm?
pageid=112

United States Senate: www.senate.gov/legislative/LIS/roll_call_lists/
roll_call_vote_cfm.cfm?congress=107&session=2&vote=00237

USS *Boxer* LHD-4: www.boxer.navy.mil/site%20pages/history.aspx

Endnotes

CHAPTER 1

1   *The Complete Works of William Shakespeare: The Alexander Text* (London and Glasgow: HarperCollins, 1985), p. 454.

2   P. Haskell, S. Quail, R. Riley, and J. Webb, *The Spirit of Portsmouth: A History* (Chichester, West Sussex: Phillimore, 1989), p. 27.

3   Barry Stapleton and James H. Thomas, eds., *The Portsmouth Region* (Gloucester, UK: Alan Sutton Publishing, 1989), p. 52.

4   Edward VI, 1552, in Margaret Hoad, ed., "Portsmouth—As others have seen it: 1540–1790," in P. Haskell, S. Quail, R. Riley, and J. Webb, *The Spirit of Portsmouth: A History* (Chichester, West Sussex: Phillimore, 1989), p. 57.

5   C. S. Forester, *Young Hornblower* (New York: Little, Brown & Co., 1960), p. 671.

6   Stapleton and Thomas, eds., *The Portsmouth Region*, p. 15.

7   Haskell, Quail, Riley, and Webb, *The Spirit of Portsmouth*, p. 2.

8   Stapleton and Thomas, eds., *The Portsmouth Region*, p. 70.

9   Haskell, Quail, Riley, and Webb, *The Spirit of Portsmouth*, p. 80.

10 Stapleton and Thomas, eds., *The Portsmouth Region*, p. 70.

11 Patrick O'Brian, *Men-of-War: Life in Nelson's Navy* (first American ed.) (New York: W. W. Norton & Co., 1974), p. 91.

12 Ibid., p. 54.

13 *The Naval Chronicle for 1814: Containing a General and Biographical History of the Royal Navy*, vol. XXXII (London: Joyce Gold, 1814), p. 441.

14 C. S. Forester, *The Age of Fighting Sail: The Story of the Naval War of 1812* (Garden City, NY: Doubleday & Company, 1956), pp. 37–38.

15 O'Brian, *Men-of-War*, p. 19.

16 Stapleton and Thomas, eds., *The Portsmouth Region*, p. 169.

17 Ibid., p. 78.

18 Ibid.

19 Dr. George Pinckard, 1795, in Margaret Hoad, ed., "Portsmouth—As others have seen it: 1540–1790," in P. Haskell, S. Quail, R. Riley, and J. Webb, *The Spirit of Portsmouth: A History* (Chichester, West Sussex: Phillimore, 1989), p. 27.

20 Ibid., pp. 148–49.

21 Ibid., p. 149.

22 Jane Austen, *Mansfield Park* (New York: Everyman's Library, 1992), p. 380.

23 Ibid., p. 389.

24 G. Measom in "Official South Western Railway Guide" (n.d.), in P. Haskell, S. Quail, R. Riley, and J. Webb, *The Spirit of Portsmouth: A History* (Chichester, West Sussex: Phillimore, 1989), p. 51.

25 Austen, *Mansfield Park*, p. 249.

26 *The Naval Chronicle for 1814*, vol. XXXII, p. 445.

27 Ibid.

28 Austen, *Mansfield Park*, p. 409.

29 Haskell, Quail, Riley, and Webb, *The Spirit of Portsmouth*, p. 151.

30 *Hampshire Telegraph*, July 3, 1809, in P. Haskell, S. Quail, R. Riley, and J. Webb, *The Spirit of Portsmouth: A History* (Chichester, West Sussex: Phillimore, 1989), p. 151.

31 Haskell, Quail, Riley, and Webb, *The Spirit of Portsmouth*, p. 151.

32 *The Naval Chronicle for 1814*, vol. XXXII, p. 441.

33 Ibid.

34 Ibid., p. 442.

35 Ibid., p. 441.

36 David Howarth and Stephen Howarth, *Lord Nelson: The Immortal Memory* (New York: Viking, 1989), p. 9.

37 O'Brian, *Men-of-War*, p. 37.

38 Ibid., pp. 38–39.

39 *The Naval Chronicle for 1814*, vol. XXXII, p. 443.

Endnotes

CHAPTER 2

1 William Penn, 1681, in Gary B. Nash, *First City: Philadelphia and the Forging of Historical Memory* (Philadelphia: University of Pennsylvania Press, 2002), p. 26.

2 Rosa Baylor Hall, *Revolutionary War Patriots and Soldiers* (Shepherdstown, WV: Rosa Baylor Hall, 2003), p. 131.

3 Washington Irving, "Biographical Notice of the Late Lieutenant Burrows," in *Analectic Magazine*, November 1813.

4 Johann David Schoepf, journal, *Travels in the Confederation, 1783–84*, in Eric Foner, *Tom Paine and Revolutionary America* (New York: Oxford University Press, 1976), p. 187.

5 United States Census, 1790, "William Burrowes, Philadelphia County."

6 "An Act for the Gradual Abolition of Slavery in Pennsylvania," March 1, 1780.

7 Pennsylvania State Archives; available at www.docheritage.state.pa.us/documents/slaveryabolition.asp.

8 Russell F. Weigley, et al., *Philadelphia: A 300-Year History* (New York: W. W. Norton & Company, 1982), p. 5.

9 Ibid.

10 Ibid., p. 208.

11 Lord Adam Gordon, 1765, in Gary B. Nash, *First City: Philadelphia and the Forging of Historical Memory* (Philadelphia: University of Pennsylvania Press, 2002), p. 45.

12 Whitfield J. Bell Jr., *Patriot-Improvers: Biographical Sketches of the American Philosophical Society*, vol. 1 (Philadelphia: American Philosophical Society, 1997), p. 47.

13 John A. Garraty, *Encyclopedia of American Biography* (New York: Harper & Row Publishers, 1974), p. 114.

14 E. H. Thomson, "Thomas Bond, 1713–1784: First Professor of Clinical Medicine in the American Colonies," *Journal of Medical Education* (September 1958), in Rosa Baylor Hall, *Revolutionary War Patriots and Soldiers* (Shepherdstown, WV: Rosa Baylor Hall, 2003), p. 63.

15 John Adams letter to Abigail Adams, July 17, 1775, in Whitfield J. Bell Jr., *Patriot-Improvers: Biographical Sketches of the American Philosophical Society*, vol. 3 (Philadelphia: American Philosophical Society, forthcoming).

16   Mary Powers Anderson, "'It is My Duty to Support My Officers . . .': William Ward Burrows, First Commandant of the Marine Corps," *The Wards and Bakers of the Deep South*, 5th ed. (June 1995).

17   Weigley, et al., *Philadelphia: A 300-Year History*, p. 172.

18   Ibid., p. 211.

19   Ibid., p. 177.

20   Ibid.

21   Ibid., p. 178.

22   Ibid., p. 179.

23   Ibid., p. 208.

24   Peter Thompson, *Rum Punch & Revolution: Taverngoing & Public Life in Eighteenth-Century Philadelphia* (Philadelphia: University of Pennsylvania Press, 1999), p. 185.

25   Ibid., p. 80.

26   Weigley, et al., *Philadelphia: A 300-Year History*, p. 202.

27   Nash, *First City*, p. 150.

28   Laurie Halse Anderson, *Fever 1793* (New York: Aladdin Paperbacks, 2000), p. 246.

29   Weigley, et al., *Philadelphia: A 300-Year History*, p. 181.

30   Ibid., p. 180.

31   Anderson, *Fever 1793*, p. 244.

32   Weigley, et al., *Philadelphia: A 300-Year History*, p. 186.

33   Thomas Jefferson letter to James Madison, 1793, in Russell F. Weigley, et al., *Philadelphia: A 300-Year History* (New York: W. W. Norton & Company, 1982), p. 182.

34   Weigley, et al., *Philadelphia: A 300-Year History*, p. 186.

35   Dr. Benjamin Rush letter to Dr. James Hutchinson, August 24, 1793, in Russell F. Weigley, et al., *Philadelphia: A 300-Year History* (New York: W. W. Norton & Company, 1982), p. 184.

36   Charles Brockden Brown, *Arthur Mervyn; or Memoirs of the Year 1793*, in Laurie Halse Anderson, *Fever 1793* (New York: Aladdin Paperbacks, 2000), p. 105.

37   Anderson, *Fever 1793*, p. 244.

38   Kenneth W. Milano, *Remembering Kensington & Fishtown: Philadelphia's Riverward Neighborhoods* (Charleston: The History Press, 2008), p. 109.

39   Ken Milano

Endnotes

40 Nash, *First City*, p. 60.

41 Weigley, et al., *Philadelphia: A 300-Year History*, p. 191.

42 Ibid.

43 Ibid.

44 Nash, *First City*, p. 136.

45 Ibid., p. 138.

46 Isaac Bailey, *American Naval Biography* (Providence, RI: H. Mann & Co., 1815), p. 232.

47 Ibid.

48 Nash, *First City*, p. 68.

49 Bailey, *American Naval Biography*, p. 231.

50 Irving, "Biographical Notice of the Late Lieutenant Burrows."

51 Anderson, "'It is My Duty to Support My Officers . . .': William Ward Burrows, First Commandant of the Marine Corps."

52 Lew Feldman, "First Commandant of the U.S. Marine Corp," *Leatherneck* (April 1928), in Rosa Baylor Hall, *Revolutionary War Patriots and Soldiers* (Shepherdstown, WV: Rosa Baylor Hall, 2003), p. 131.

53 Irving, "Biographical Notice of the Late Lieutenant Burrows."

54 Anderson, "'It is My Duty to Support My Officers . . .': William Ward Burrows, First Commandant of the Marine Corps."

55 Fletcher Pratt, *Preble's Boys: Commodore Preble and the Birth of American Sea Power* (New York: William Sloane Associates, 1950), p. 241.

56 Anderson, "'It is My Duty to Support My Officers . . .': William Ward Burrows, First Commandant of the Marine Corps."

57 Irving, "Biographical Notice of the Late Lieutenant Burrows."

CHAPTER 3

1 O'Brian, *Men-of-War*, p. 18.

2 *The Naval Chronicle for 1814*, vol. XXXII, p. 442.

3 Ibid.

4 David Cordingly, *The Billy Ruffian: The* Bellerophon *and the Downfall of Napoleon* (New York: Bloomsbury USA, 2003), p. 18.

5 *The Naval Chronicle for 1814*, vol. XXXII, p. 441.

6 O'Brian, *Men-of-War*, p. 13.

7 Forester, *The Age of Fighting Sail*, p. 129.

8   O'Brian, *Men-of-War*, p. 59.

9   Ibid., p. 54.

10 Ibid.

11 Ibid., p. 60.

12 Cordingly, *The Billy Ruffian*, pp. 109, 112.

13 *The Naval Chronicle for 1814*, vol. XXXII, p. 443.

14 Ibid.

15 O'Brian, *Men-of-War*, p. 79.

16 *The Naval Chronicle for 1814*, vol. XXXII, p. 444.

17 Ibid.

18 Prince William Henry, in David Howarth and Stephen Howarth, *Lord Nelson: The Immortal Memory* (New York: Viking, 1989), p. 31.

19 O'Brian, *Men-of-War*, p. 85.

20 *The Naval Chronicle for 1814*, vol. XXXII, p. 446.

21 Sherwood Picking, *Sea Fight off Monhegan* (Portland, ME: Machigonne Press, 1941), p. 90.

22 *The Naval Chronicle for 1814*, vol. XXXII, p. 447.

23 Lieutenant Samuel Blyth letter, n.d., in *The Naval Chronicle for 1814: Containing a General and Biographical History of the Royal Navy*, vol. XXXII (London: Joyce Gold, 1814), p. 447.

24 Ibid.

25 *The Naval Chronicle for 1814*, vol. XXXII, p. 449.

26 Lieutenant Rival letter to Senator Fabre (de l'Aude), Count of the Empire, Paris, February 18, 1809, in *The Naval Chronicle for 1814: Containing a General and Biographical History of the Royal Navy*, vol. XXXII (London: Joyce Gold, 1814), p. 448.

27 Joseph A. Page, *The Brazilians* (Reading, MA: Addison-Wesley Publishing Company, 1995), pp. 49–50.

28 Ibid., p. 50.

29 Ibid., p. 49.

30 *The Naval Chronicle for 1810*, in *Portland Gazette*, October 4, 1813.

31 O'Brian, *Men-of-War*, p. 62.

32 Patrick O'Brian, *The Wine-Dark Sea* (New York: W. W. Norton & Co., 1993), p. 66.

33 *The Naval Chronicle for 1814*, vol. XXXII, p. 451.

34 Ibid.

35 Ibid., p. 452.

36 Ibid.

37 Ibid., p. 453.

38 William James, *James' Naval History*, Robert O'Byrne, ed. (London: W. H. Allen & Co., 1888), p. 443.

39 Ibid., p. 444.

40 Lieutenant Samuel Blyth letter to Delia Blyth, August 15, 1811, in *The Naval Chronicle for 1814: Containing a General and Biographical History of the Royal Navy*, vol. XXXII (London: Joyce Gold, 1814), pp. 456–57.

41 Forester, *The Age of Fighting Sail*, p. 189.

42 Ibid., p. 190.

43 *The Naval Chronicle for 1814*, vol. XXXII, p. 459.

44 Picking, *Sea Fight off Monhegan*, p. 113.

45 Ibid.

46 Lord Melville letter to Commander Samuel Blyth, August 15, 1812, in *The Naval Chronicle for 1814: Containing a General and Biographical History of the Royal Navy*, vol. XXXII (London: Joyce Gold, 1814), p. 448.

47 Picking, *Sea Fight off Monhegan*, p. 91.

CHAPTER 4

1 Howard I. Chapelle, *The History of American Sailing Ships* (New York: Bonanza Books, 1935), p. 101.

2 Edwin M. Jameson, *The Saga of the U.S. Schooner* ENTERPRIZE (unpublished manuscript, n.d.), p. 4.

3 Ibid., pp. 3–4.

4 Picking, *Sea Fight off Monhegan*, p. 96.

5 Fletcher Pratt, *The Compact History of the United States Navy* (New York: Hawthorn Books, 1962), p. 60.

6 Mary Powers Anderson, "The Thoughts of Youth are Long, Long Thoughts: William Burrows, Lt., USN," *The Wards and Bakers of the Deep South*, 6th ed. (September 1995).

7 Ibid.

8 Simon P. Newman, *Embodied History: The Lives of the Poor in Early Philadelphia* (Philadelphia: University of Pennsylvania Press, 2003), p. 105.

9 Ibid., p. 110.

10 Theodore Roosevelt, *The Naval War of 1812* (New York: G. P. Putnam's Sons, 1882; Kessinger Publishing reprint, 2004), p. 24.

11 Richard M. Detwiler, USN Reserve (ret.).

12 Howarth and Howarth, *Lord Nelson*, p. 9.

13 Newman, *Embodied History*, p. 12.

14 Patrick O'Brian, *The Nutmeg of Consolation* (New York: W. W. Norton & Co., 1991), p. 9.

15 Pratt, *The Compact History of the United States Navy*, p. 63.

16 Jameson, *The Saga of the U.S. Schooner* ENTERPRIZE, p. 15.

17 Pratt, *The Compact History of the United States Navy*, p. 65.

18 Bailey, *American Naval Biography*, p. 233.

19 Irving, "Biographical Notice of the Late Lieutenant Burrows."

20 Paul Johnson, *A History of the American People* (New York: HarperCollins, 1997), p. 262.

21 Mary Powers Anderson, "The Thoughts of Youth are Long, Long Thoughts: William Burrows, Lt., USN."

22 Pratt, *Preble's Boys*, p. 244.

23 Jameson, *The Saga of the U.S. Schooner* ENTERPRIZE, p. 25.

24 Ibid., p. 28.

25 Picking, *Sea Fight off Monhegan*, p. 97.

26 Jameson, *The Saga of the U.S. Schooner* ENTERPRIZE, p. 30.

27 Pratt, *The Compact History of the United States Navy*, p. 65.

28 Jameson, *The Saga of the U.S. Schooner* ENTERPRIZE, p. 31.

29 Pratt, *Preble's Boys*, p. 244.

30 Irving, "Biographical Notice of the Late Lieutenant Burrows."

31 Picking, *Sea Fight off Monhegan*, p. 98.

32 E. B. Potter, *The Naval Academy Illustrated History of the United States Navy* (New York: Thomas Y. Crowell Company, 1971), p. 35.

33 Bailey, *American Naval Biography*, p. 235.

34 Irving, "Biographical Notice of the Late Lieutenant Burrows."

35 Secretary of the Navy Robert Smith letter to Marine Corps Commandant William Ward Burrows, March 1804, in Mary Powers Anderson, "'It is My Duty to Support My Officers . . .': William Ward Burrows, First Commandant of the Marine Corps," *The Wards and Bakers of the Deep South*, 5th ed. (June 1995).

36 Pratt, *Preble's Boys*, p. 245.

37 Newman, *Embodied History*, p. 72.

38 Ibid., p. 105.

39 Pratt, *Preble's Boys*, p. 245.

40 Bailey, *American Naval Biography*, p. 236.

41 Irving, "Biographical Notice of the Late Lieutenant Burrows."

42 William Burrows letter to Commodore John Rodgers, June 23, 1810.

43 Irving, "Biographical Notice of the Late Lieutenant Burrows."

44 Ibid.

45 Chapelle, *The American Sailing Navy*, p. 145.

46 Master Commandant Thomas Robinson Jr. letter to Secretary of the Navy, April 23, 1805.

47 Picking, *Sea Fight off Monhegan*, p. 99.

48 Chapelle, *The History of American Sailing Ships*, p. 102.

49 Picking, *Sea Fight off Monhegan*, p. 99.

50 Pratt, *Preble's Boys*, p. 247.

51 Picking, *Sea Fight off Monhegan*, p. 6.

52 Bailey, *American Naval Biography*, p. 239.

CHAPTER 5

1   Walter R. Borneman, *1812: The War That Forged a Nation* (New York: HarperCollins, 2004), p. 57.

2   L. C. B. Seaman, *From Vienna to Versailles* (London: Routledge, 1955), p. 32.

3   Thomas Jefferson, in Peter Thompson, *Rum Punch & Revolution: Taverngoing & Public Life in Eighteenth-Century Philadelphia* (Philadelphia: University of Pennsylvania Press, 1999), p. 166.

4   Lemuel Norton, *Autobiography of Lemuel Norton* (Portland, ME: Brown Thurston, 1862), pp. 38–39.

5   Roosevelt, *The Naval War of 1812*, p. 13.

6   C. S. Forester, *Beat to Quarters* (New York: Little, Brown & Company, 1938), p. 181.

7   Donald R. Hickey, *The War of 1812: A Forgotten Conflict* (Urbana and Chicago: University of Illinois Press, 1989), p. 46.

8   United States Senate; available at www.senate.gov/legislative/LIS/roll_call_lists/roll_call_vote_cfm.cfm?congress=107&session=2&vote=00237; and Clerk, United States House of Representatives; available at clerk.house.gov/evs/2002/roll455.xml.

9   Report of the Hartford Convention, in Donald R. Hickey, *The War of 1812: A Forgotten Conflict* (Urbana and Chicago: University of Illinois Press, 1989), p. 277.

10 J. Mackay Hitsman, *The Incredible War of 1812: A Military History* (Toronto: University of Toronto Press, 1965), p. 80.

11 Malcolm Gladwell, "The Revolting Truth: Now It Can Be Told! A Canadian Exposes Our July 4 Charade," *Washington Post*, July 4, 1993.

12 Hitsman, *The Incredible War of 1812*, p. 50.

13 Ibid., p. 103.

14 *Morning Post*, January 18, 1814, and *Times of London*, May 24, 1814, in Henry Adams, *The War of 1812* (Washington, D.C.: The Infantry Journal, 1944), p. 325.

15 Joseph H. Nicholson letter to Secretary of the Navy William Jones, May 20, 1814, in Donald R. Hickey, *The War of 1812: A Forgotten Conflict* (Urbana and Chicago: University of Illinois Press, 1989), p. 182.

16 Henry Adams, *The War of 1812* (Washington, D.C.: The Infantry Journal, 1944), p. 205.

17 Henry Goulburn, British Peace Commission 1814, in Donald R. Hickey, *The War of 1812: A Forgotten Conflict* (Urbana and Chicago: University of Illinois Press, 1989), pp. 294–95.

18 Roosevelt, *The Naval War of 1812*, p. 22.

19 Adams, *The War of 1812*, p. 248.

CHAPTER 6

1 Roosevelt, *The Naval War of 1812*, p. 151.

2 Hitsman, *The Incredible War of 1812*, pp. 44–45.

3 Roosevelt, *The Naval War of 1812*, p. 25.

4 Ibid., p. 29.

5 Hitsman, *The Incredible War of 1812*, p. 45.

6 Norton, *Autobiography of Lemuel Norton*, p. 53.

7 Adams, *The War of 1812*, p. 45.

8 Roosevelt, *The Naval War of 1812*, p. 61.

9   Leonard F. Guttridge, *Our Country, Right or Wrong: The Life of Stephen Decatur, the U.S. Navy's Most Illustrious Commander* (New York: Forge Books, 2006), p. 200.

10 Adams, *The War of 1812*, p. 46.

11 Hickey, *The War of 1812*, p. 98.

12 Adams, *The War of 1812*, p. 144.

13 Ibid.

14 Roosevelt, *The Naval War of 1812*, p. 92.

15 Hitsman, *The Incredible War of 1812*, p. 171.

16 Ibid., p. 170.

17 Hickey, *The War of 1812*, p. 132.

18 Ibid., p. 133.

19 "Great Naval Events," *Eastern Argus*, October 7, 1813.

20 Hitsman, *The Incredible War of 1812*, p. 174.

21 Roosevelt, *The Naval War of 1812*, p. 83.

22 David Glasgow Farragut, National Park Service; available at www.nps.gov/archive/vick/visctr/sitebltn/farragut.htm.

23 David Farragut, in Loyall Farragut, *The Life of David Glasgow Farragut* (New York: D. Appleton and Co., 1879), in *The Naval War of 1812* (New York: G. P. Putnam's Sons, 1882; Kessinger Publishing reprint, 2004), p. 92.

24 Adams, *The War of 1812*, p. 225.

25 Ibid., p. 226.

26 Michael Scott, in Henry Adams, *The War of 1812* (Washington, D.C.: The Infantry Journal, 1944), p. 155.

27 Ibid.

CHAPTER 7

1   Hickey, *The War of 1812*, p. 52.

2   *Augusta Chronicle*, in John E. Talmedge, "Georgia's Federalist Press and the War of 1812," *Journal of Southern History* (November 1953), in Donald R. Hickey, *The War of 1812: A Forgotten Conflict* (Urbana and Chicago: University of Illinois Press, 1989), p. 55.

3   *Washington National Intelligencer*, June 27, 1812, in Donald R. Hickey, *The War of 1812: A Forgotten Conflict* (Urbana and Chicago: University of Illinois Press, 1989), p. 55.

Endnotes

4   Address of Massachusetts House, June 26, 1812, in *Niles Register,* August 29, 1812, in Donald R. Hickey, *The War of 1812: A Forgotten Conflict* (Urbana and Chicago: University of Illinois Press, 1989), p. 53.

5   Eugene B. Sledge, *With the Old Breed: At Peleliu and Okinawa* (New York: Presidio Press, 1981), p. 315.

6   Thomas Bond Sr. to American Philosophical Society, May 21, 1782, in Rosa Baylor Hall, *Revolutionary War Patriots and Soldiers* (Shepherdstown, WV: Rosa Baylor Hall, 2003), p. 63.

7   George Prevost letter to Isaac Brock, July 10, 1812, in J. Mackay Hitsman, *The Incredible War of 1812: A Military History* (Toronto: University of Toronto Press, 1965), p. 63.

8   Ibid.

9   John Sherbrooke proclamation, July 3, 1812, in J. Mackay Hitsman, *The Incredible War of 1812: A Military History* (Toronto: University of Toronto Press, 1965), p. 54.

10   George Prevost letter to Lord Bathhurst, August 27, 1814, in Henry Adams, *The War of 1812* (Washington, D.C.: The Infantry Journal, 1944), p. 77.

11   Hickey, *The War of 1812*, p. 117.

12   "More Supplying the Enemy," *Eastern Argus*, September 9, 1813.

13   Stephen Decatur letter to Secretary of the Navy William Jones, December 20, 1813, in Henry Adams, *The War of 1812* (Washington, D.C.: The Infantry Journal, 1944), p. 137.

14   Journal of Henry Edward Napier, May 29, 1814, in Donald R. Hickey, *The War of 1812: A Forgotten Conflict* (Urbana and Chicago: University of Illinois Press, 1989), p. 216.

15   Samuel Taggart, speech reprinted in *Alexandria Gazette*, June 24, 1812, in Donald R. Hickey, *The War of 1812: A Forgotten Conflict* (Urbana and Chicago: University of Illinois Press, 1989), pp. 73–74.

16   General William Westmoreland, U.S. Army (ret.), in *Great Books: The Art of War*, produced and written by N. Diane Smith, The Learning Channel, 1994.

17   Hitsman, *The Incredible War of 1812*, p. 279.

18   Johnson, *A History of the American People*, p. 265.

19   *Baltimore Federal Republican*, June 1, 1812, in Donald R. Hickey, *The War of 1812: A Forgotten Conflict* (Urbana and Chicago: University of Illinois Press, 1989), p. 57.

20   Hickey, *The War of 1812*, p. 65.

21 David Osgood, "A Solemn Protest Against the Late Declaration of War 1812," in Donald R. Hickey, *The War of 1812: A Forgotten Conflict* (Urbana and Chicago: University of Illinois Press, 1989), p. 257.

22 Hickey, *The War of 1812*, p. 308.

23 Patrick Runyon, USN (ret.), Swift Boat Sailors Association.

24 Doug White, Ohio State Senate–Manchester (ret.), Vietnam Veterans of America.

25 United States Constitution, Article III, Section 3.

26 Hitsman, *The Incredible War of 1812*, p. 248.

27 Adams, *The War of 1812*, p. 202.

28 William Elliot, 1814, in John Johnston, *A History of the Towns of Bristol and Bremen* (Albany: Joel Munsell, 1873), pp. 412–13.

29 John Johnston, *A History of the Towns of Bristol and Bremen* (Albany: Joel Munsell, 1873), p. 413.

CHAPTER 8

1 Thomas Shaw, in Sherwood Picking, *Sea Fight off Monhegan* (Portland, ME: Machigonne Press, 1941), p. 27.

2 Captain Samuel Drinkwater obituary, *Zion's Advocate*, August 6, 1834.

3 Chandler's record book, missing its first (identifying) page, circa 1813, Portland; entry for July 1–8, 1813.

4 Charles Tappan, in *Seaside Oracle*, June 12, 1875.

5 Johnston, *A History of the Towns of Bristol and Bremen*, p. 407.

6 Roosevelt, *The Naval War of 1812*, p. 105.

7 Colonel Ulmer letter to Samuel Blyth, July 2, 1813, in Sherwood Picking, *Sea Fight off Monhegan* (Portland, ME: Machigonne Press, 1941), p. 91.

8 Tappan, in *Seaside Oracle*, June 12, 1875.

9 Roosevelt, *The War of 1812*, p. 104.

10 Adams, *The War of 1812*, p. 138.

11 Roosevelt, *The Naval War of 1812*, p. 104.

12 Forester, *The Age of Fighting Sail*, p. 125.

13 O'Brian, *Men-of-War*, p. 33.

14 Roosevelt, *The Naval War of 1812*, p. 104.

15 Adams, *The War of 1812*, p. 138.

16 C. S. Forester, *Hornblower and the Hotspur* (New York: Little, Brown & Co., 1962), p. 389.

17 Picking, *Sea Fight off Monhegan*, pp. 39–40.

18 Mark C. Carnes and John A. Garraty, *American National Biography*, vol. 4 (New York: Oxford University Press, 1999), p. 58.

19 O'Brian, *Men-of-War*, pp. 30–32.

20 William G. Merrill, "The Affair of the *Enterprise* and *Boxer*," *Transcript*, January 3, 1894.

21 Ibid.

22 Ship's Carpenter Joseph Robinson U.S. brig *Enterprise* testimony given in court-martial of Sailing Master William Harper, December 30, 1813, in Sherwood Picking, *Sea Fight off Monhegan* (Portland, Maine: Machigonne Press, 1941), p. 133.

23 "Another Brilliant Naval Victory," *Eastern Argus*, September 9, 1813.

24 John K Moulton, *Captain Moody and His Observatory* (Falmouth, ME: Mount Joy Publishing, 2000), p. 58.

25 William Goold, *Portland in the Past: With Historical Notes of Old Falmouth* (Portland, ME: B. Thurston & Company, 1886), p. 488.

26 Picking, *Sea Fight off Monhegan*, p. 55.

27 Edward R. McCall letter to Captain Isaac Hull, September 7, 1813, in Sherwood Picking, *Sea Fight off Monhegan* (Portland, ME: Machigonne Press, 1941), p. 63.

28 Goold, *Portland in the Past: With Historical Notes of Old Falmouth*, p. 488.

29 *The War*, August 26, 1814, in John Johnston, *A History of the Towns of Bristol and Bremen* (Albany: Joel Munsell, 1873), p. 408.

30 Moulton, *Captain Moody and His Observatory*, p. 58.

31 Samuel Storer letter to Captain Isaac Hull, USN, September 6, 1813, in Sherwood Picking, *Sea Fight off Monhegan* (Portland, ME: Machigonne Press, 1941), p. 59.

32 Picking, *Sea Fight off Monhegan*, p. 64.

33 Edward McCall letter to Secretary of the Navy William Jones, September 7, 1813, *Eastern Argus*, September 23, 1813.

34 Tappan, in *Seaside Oracle*, June 12, 1875.

35 "An ACT for the better government of the navy of the United States," sec. 5, April 23, 1800, in Sherwood Picking, *Sea Fight off Monhegan* (Portland, ME: Machigonne Press, 1941), p. 177.

36 Ibid.

37 Isaac Hull letter to Commodore William Bainbridge, USN, September 10, 1813, *Eastern Argus*, September 30, 1813.

38 Goold, *Portland in the Past: With Historical Notes of Old Falmouth*, p. 490.

39 Chandler's record book, missing its first (identifying) page, entry for September 12–28, 1813.

40 Adams, *The War of 1812*, p. 138.

41 Stephen Longfellow, *Eastern Argus*, September 23, 1813.

42 "Naval Dinner," *Portland Gazette*, September 20, 1813.

43 Forester, *The Age of Fighting Sail*, p. 193.

CHAPTER 9

1 Samuel Blyth, Last Will and Testament of Samuel Blyth, Commander HMS *Boxer*, December 28, 1812.

2 Figures compiled by the author from Theodore Roosevelt, *The Naval War of 1812* (New York: G. P. Putnam's Sons, 1882).

3 Ibid.

4 Ibid.

5 "Another Brilliant Naval Victory," *Eastern Argus*, September 9, 1813.

6 O'Brian, *Master and Commander*, author's note.

7 Adams, *The War of 1812*, p. 245.

8 "Naval Dinner," *Portland Gazette*, September 20, 1813.

9 Lieutenant Chads, RN, in Theodore Roosevelt, *The Naval War of 1812* (New York: G. P. Putnam's Sons, 1882), p. 68.

10 Roosevelt, *The Naval War of 1812*, p. 68.

11 Adams, *The War of 1812*, p. 46.

12 Surviving officers of HMS *Peacock* letter published in New York, in Theodore Roosevelt, *The Naval War of 1812* (New York: G. P. Putnam's Sons, 1882), p. 85.

13 Roosevelt, *The Naval War of 1812*, p. 86.

14 Captain Barclay, RN, letter, in Theodore Roosevelt, *The Naval War of 1812* (New York: G. P. Putnam's Sons, 1882), p. 127.

15 Captain Pring, RN, letter, in Theodore Roosevelt, *The Naval War of 1812* (New York: G. P. Putnam's Sons, 1882), p. 182.

16 Roosevelt, *The Naval War of 1812*, p. 23.

Endnotes

EPILOGUE

1   *The Naval Chronicle for 1814*, vol. XXXII, p. 472.

2   Ibid., p. 447.

3   Record of court-martial convened aboard HMS *Surprise*, at Bermuda, January 6, 7, 8, 1814, in *The Naval Chronicle for 1814: Containing a General and Biographical History of the Royal Navy*, vol. XXXII, pp. 472–73.

4   *The Naval Chronicle for 1814*, vol. XXXII, p. 441.

5   Kenneth Roberts, *Trending into Maine* (New York: Doubleday & Co., 1934), pp. 224–25.

6   Picking, *Sea Fight off Monhegan*, p. 78.

7   USS *Boxer* LHD-4; available at www.boxer.navy.mil/site%20pages/history.aspx.

8   "British Brig Galley Table Now Holds Violets," *Portland Evening Express*, September 23, 1954.

9   Lieutenant John Gallagher letter to Secretary of the Navy Smith Thompson, August 1, 1823.

10 "Report of Search for Wreck of *Enterprise*, Commander Amphibious Squadron Ten United States Atlantic Fleet," December 24, 1968, C, E3-4.

11 Jameson, *The Saga of the U.S. Schooner* ENTERPRIZE, Introduction.

12 Potter, *The Naval Academy Illustrated History of the United States Navy*, pp. 200–201.

13 "Lieutenant William Burrows," *Poulson's American Daily Advertiser*, September 16, 1813.

14 Anonymous, in Frank Shay, *A Sailor's Treasury*, in Edward M. Jameson, *The Saga of the U.S. Schooner* ENTERPRIZE (unpublished manuscript, n.d.).

Index

Index

Index

Index

Index

Index

Index

Index

David Hanna teaches history at Stuyvesant High School in New York City. He lives with his family in Morris County, New Jersey.